LOS QUE MANDAN

(THOSE WHO RULE)

JOSE LUIS DE IMAZ

TRANSLATED AND WITH AN INTRODUCTION BY

CARLOS A. ASTIZ

WITH MARY F. McCARTHY

STATE UNIVERSITY OF NEW YORK PRESS

ALBANY

Originally published in 1964 as *Los Que Mandan*
© 1964 by Editorial Universitaria de Buenos Aires

Published by State University of New York Press
Thurlow Terrace, Albany, New York 12201

Translation © 1970 by The Research Foundation
of State University of New York. All rights reserved

First paperbound printing 1970

International Standard Book Number 0–87395–073–9
Library of Congress Catalog Card Number 69–12100

Printed by the Riverside Press, Inc., Cambridge, Massachusetts

CONTENTS

FOREWORD

THIS STUDY constitutes an attempt to identify and analyze the leadership groups in Argentine society. At the time the first Spanish edition of this study was published, in 1964, there was really nothing available that could have served as a general base or even as a starting point; the few relevant materials, most of them unpublished, are mentioned throughout the text.

The scope of this book has been limited to the domestic situation of Argentina; therefore, it fails to take into account the influence of external factors on Argentine politics. Furthermore, this case study may or may not be relevant to other countries' realities, either in Latin America or elsewhere; it is hoped that other studies will provide comparable data for the rest of the region and that then, and only then, meaningful comparisons will be made.

The first and last chapters of the English version were not included in the Spanish edition. Footnotes have been added by the translator and, when this is the case, they are identified with his initials.

Many persons contributed to the preparation of the original Spanish version, and others made this English translation possible. Some of the students of the Department of Sociology of the University of Buenos Aires searched files and explored documents; they are identified throughout the text. Professor Gino Germani, then Director of the Institute of Sociology of that University, other members of the faculty, scholars who met under the auspices of the Economic and Social Development Institute, officers of the Argentine armed forces, and members of the business community are entitled to the deepest appreciation for their willingness to discuss the original manuscript and make useful suggestions. Finally, the research support of the Center for Inter-American Studies, State University of New York at Albany, which made this English version possible, is hereby gratefully acknowledged.

INTRODUCTION

Historical Outline of the Political Evolution of Argentina

WHAT IS TODAY the Argentine Republic declared its independence from the Spanish crown on July 9, 1816, formally announcing what had *de facto* been developing since May 25, 1810. In the meantime, the Creole political elite centered in the city of Buenos Aires had equipped armies, arranged alliances with provincial *caudillos*, and developed a security perimeter which was constantly enlarged until the Spanish forces withdrew from the southern part of South America. The Buenos Aires elite was not equally successful in giving Argentina a stable, legitimate, and broadly effective political structure. Firm and widely accepted political institutions materialized only in 1853, with the approval of that year's Federal Constitution, and culminated in 1880, when the city of Buenos Aires officially became a federal district and the capital of the nation.

Regardless of the constitutional modifications, the traditional upper class that was centered in the city of Buenos Aires constantly increased its control of Argentine politics. This political power in turn served to award to its members a large share of the socioeconomic rewards that the country could offer. The distribution of landholdings, in Buenos Aires province and elsewhere, bears witness to the exercise of that power.[1] Nevertheless, the Argentine traditional upper class does not seem to have been as narrow-minded as most of its counterparts elsewhere in Latin America. While it reserved a large share of benefits for itself, the traditional upper class made it possible during the last decades of the nineteenth century for others to acquire land (although not necessarily of similar quality to that reserved for itself) and to improve their social and economic condition within the philosophical framework of last century's liberalism. What is perhaps more important, the traditional upper class facilitated and often encouraged the inflow of European immigrants, who moved into Argentina in large numbers from approximately 1870.[2] Regardless of the motivations

1

which led the nation's rulers to this policy, the fact is that many of these immigrants settled in the urban areas, particularly in Buenos Aires, where they constituted the backbone of a large and relatively independent urban middle class, and later on of an urban lower class as well. The middle class thus formed became the first political competitor of the traditional rulers at the beginning of this century.

The growing demands of a large number of Europeans located in urban areas, occasionally intensified by economic crises such as the one which occurred in 1890, challenged the legitimacy and, to a certain extent, the stability of the Argentine political system. Faced with the possibility of revolution from below, the traditional upper class, after some hesitation, followed the dictates of President Roque Sáenz Peña and enacted an effective electoral reform law (known as the Sáenz Peña Act) in 1912. In effectively subscribing to the one-man, one-vote principle, the traditional upper class realized that it was surrendering political power to its newly arrived competitors. Be that as it may, the law was enacted and enforced, and in the first presidential election under it (1916) the middle class Radical Party won, as indicated in Table I; the middle class retained control of the executive branch in the two succeeding presidential elections (1922 and 1928), but it was unable or unwilling to make the political system more responsive to the demands of its backers, as well as of the growing urban lower class and the small farmers. The resulting discontent and the economic crises caused by the world depression in 1930 gave those members of the traditional upper class who were unhappy with the Radicals a golden opportunity. It did not go to waste: In 1930 the Argentine military establishment, which had remained ostensibly outside the political arena, overthrew the administration led, for the second time, by the old *caudillo* of the Radical Party, Hipólito Irigoyen. They thereby began a period of governments of questionable representativeness which closed most interest-articulation channels to large portions of the middle class and to the urban lower class. This period lasted thirteen years. In 1943 the Argentine military again decided to take over the government, although the objectives of those leading the coup turned out to be quite different from the first military intervention.

The series of military regimes that governed Argentina from 1943 to 1946 (there were a number of internal changes during the period) showed various tendencies; it is possible to identify fascist, chauvinistic, and reformist elements which operated in shifting coalitions. But the end result of the confused process was the constant ascent of

2

TABLE I

Selected Argentine Presidential Election,
Results, in Percentages 1916–1937

Party	1916	1931	1937
Radical Party (including splinter groups)	49.35	6.80*	41.05
Socialist Party	8.88	0.35*	2.50
Conservative Parties	26.09	60.31	53.77

	1946–51	
Party	1946	1951
Peronist	52.40	62.49
Radical	43.56†	31.81
Socialist	——	0.72
Conservative Parties	1.53	2.33

	1958–63	
Party	1958	1963
Peoples Radical	28.80	25.15
Intransigent Radical	44.79	16.40
Socialist	2.91	0.10
Neo-Peronist	1.33‡	1.38‡

* The main Radical organization abstained.
† Includes total votes for anti-Perón coalition (which included Radicals and Socialists) as well as splinter Radicals.
‡ Peronist organizations were in fact prevented from participating.
SOURCE: Prepared from data published in Darío Cantón, *Materiales para el estudio de la sociología política en la Argentina*, Vol. I (Buenos Aires: Editorial del Instituto Torcuato Di Tella, 1968).

Colonel Juan D. Perón, who finally became the official candidate and triumphed in the 1946 election. At that time he faced the combined opposition of most political parties. Perón did not have the support of any of the old parties (although he was backed by a number of former Radicals) and was forced hastily to organize his *Movimiento Justicialista*; this electoral machine[3] received the bulk of its support from organized labor, which Perón had cultivated and strengthened during the 1943–46 period. What is particularly important here is that the urban lower class (or at least a significant portion of it) was given the first opportunity to formally participate as an entity in the selection of

TABLE II

Argentine Presidents Since 1862, and Mode of Accession to Office

Name	Period	Mode of accession to office
Bartolomé Mitre	1862–68	military victory
Domingo F. Sarmiento	1868–74	election
Nicolás Avellaneda	1874–80	election
Julio A. Roca	1880–86	election
Miguel Juárez Celman	1886–90	election
Carlos Pellegrini (v.p.)	1890–92	president resigned
Luis Sáenz Peña	1892–95	election
José E. Uriburu (v.p.)	1895–98	president resigned
Julio A. Roca	1898–1904	election
Manuel Quintana	1904–06	election
José Figueroa Alcorta (v.p.)	1906–10	president died
Roque Sáenz Peña	1910–14	election
Victorino de la Plaza (v.p.)	1914–16	president died
Hipólito Irigoyen	1916–22	election
Marcelo T. de Alvear	1922–28	election
Hipólito Irigoyen	1928–30	election
José F. Uriburu	1930–32	military revolt
Agustín P. Justo	1932–38	election
Roberto M. Ortíz	1938–40	election
Ramón S. Castillo (v.p.)	1940–43	president delegated authority
Arturo J. Rawson	1943	military revolt
Pedro Pablo Ramírez	1943–44	coup d'état
Edelmiro J. Farrell	1944–46	coup d'état
Juan D. Perón	1946–55	election
Eduardo Lonardi	1955	military revolt
Eugenio P. Aramburu	1955–58	coup d'état
Arturo Frondizi	1958–62	election
José M. Guido	1962–63	coup d'état
Arturo Illia	1963–66	election
Juan Carlos Onganía	1966–	military revolt

the Argentine government. The opportunity was not missed, and the Argentine labor movement became a power factor in the country's politics, and a number of its leaders actually joined the administration and were influential in Congress.[4]

Although the Perón regime retained the allegiance of the bulk of the labor movement, it alienated some of its middle class supporters and, particularly, a portion of the Army and Air Force and most of the Navy. Finally, the Catholic Church, which had backed Perón in the 1940s and had facilitated his ascent to power, turned against him to

4

the point where some churches were burned and priests jailed or expelled from the country. After some failures, the opposition overthrew Perón in September, 1955, through a military coup d'état. The regime was replaced by a military government, which outlawed Peronism and in its three years in power managed to alienate many of its original supporters.

This introductory section cannot do justice to the Perón administration and its military aftermath; in fact, an adequate study of the regime is still lacking.[5] However, it would not be too controversial to indicate that the regime opened the doors of the political system to organized labor, mostly based in the rural areas. While it is true that Perón and his political machine occasionally decided who the leaders of certain unions should be, and that no one could be a leader without Perón's approval, regardless of the process actually followed, the interests of unionized labor were heard, and the size of the unions grew significantly. Whether the procedure to select labor spokesmen was democratic or not (and very often it was not), the net results were pleasing to the majority of the rank and file; one of the most important consequences of this newly acquired political voice was the gain in the share of the national income going to salary and wage earners, as opposed to profits, capital gains, and other earnings. It should be noted that, until the year 1946 salaries and wages received approximately 46 percent of Argentina's net domestic income; in 1952 their share reached a high mark of almost 57 percent. It was a meaningful transfer of purchasing power, which remained above 52 percent until 1958, when it dropped to less than 46 percent.[6] What is probably as important, the Perón regime was able and willing to maintain a situation of near full employment, a situation that has not continued after his overthrow. While there have been ups and downs since 1955, it is quite clear that, on the whole, there has been significant unemployment which, as it happens throughout the world, has been borne mostly by the lower sectors of society.[7]

The regimes which followed Perón have been of two general varieties. The Frondizi and Illia administrations gained power through elections from which the Peronists were formally excluded. Although both administrations were closely supervised, and finally overthrown, by the military, they made attempts in the direction of balancing the interests of organized labor and other Peronist supporters against those of the other interest groups opposed to them. The military regimes in power during the periods 1955–58 and (although a civilian was nomin-

5

ally president) 1962–63 were more clearly anti-Peronist and tried, with varying degrees of success, to downgrade the political power of those groups known to be Perón supporters. But throughout the period the general direction has been the same: socio-economic rewards were redistributed in favor of the upper and upper middle classes and against the lower and lower middle classes.[8]

The military regime which replaced President Illia in 1966, after a coup d'état forced him out of office, has continued the general trend shown by the previous military regimes. It is apparent, however, that the two factions represented in the Onganía administration (nationalists and liberals) have tried to use the labor movement and other Peronist followers to broaden their popular support and, simultaneously, have acted to prevent the other side from succeeding in doing it. In this political game, the nationalists have been shown to be in a better position to develop such an alliance, although the liberals have been quite effective in blocking their competitors' efforts. These and other cleavages within the ruling military establishment have prevented, at least to a certain extent, the Onganía regime from becoming an Argentine neo-developmental elite, a role which the military clearly assigned to itself on the occasion of Illia's overthrow. Regardless of its actual achievements, however, the Onganía regime has presented itself as Argentina's developmental elite and has given itself a mandate which will tend to maintain the military establishment in direct control of the government for a long, although as yet undetermined, period.

Argentine Political Parties

A HISTORY OF THE political parties which have existed and exist (regardless of the formal prohibition enacted by the Onganía regime) would go beyond the limited aims of these introductory remarks.[9] Suffice it to say that at least 37 parties participated in the 1934 congressional elections and 39 did so in the 1958 presidential contest. Needless to say, many of the parties participating in the first example had disappeared by the time of the 1958 electoral contest. In other words, Argentina is a case of a multiparty system, although many of the parties have no hope of exercising any real influence, at least at the national level.

6

It is apparent, however, that throughout this century, two parties have played a very important role. First it was the middle class, urban-based, Radical Party; it pressured the traditional upper class into re-forming the electoral system through the Sáenz Peña Act and it won the presidency when the mechanism went into effect, in the 1916 election. The party remained in power until the military entered politics and revolted in 1930, then refused to participate in the 1931 election, came in second in 1937, provided the bulk of the votes and the candidates for the coalition known as Acción Democrática (which lost to Perón), came in second in 1951, won the 1958 contest (the party had split, with the Intransigent Radicals electing Arturo Frondizi), and again in 1963 (this time the other branch, the People's Radicals, elected Arturo Illia). It is apparent that, when honest elections have been held, the Radical party and its splinter groups and branches have been shown to possess a majority of the electoral support, except in 1946 and 1951, when the Peronists enjoyed majority support.

The other party with sizable popular support, essentially of urban lower class and lower middle class origin, is the Peronist Party. Although originally an electoral machine organized in order to provide Juan D. Perón with a popular base, the Peronist Party, now divided, seems to have acquired a permanency which transcends that of its leader. Inasmuch as all indications are that Argentina will become more urban and more industrialized in the future, it can be assumed that the urban lower and lower middle class will continue to grow, probably faster than the total population; since the Peronist Party seems to articulate their interests, its clientele will tend to increase unless another party or leader enters in real competition with the Peronists; at the time of this writing (1969) such a competitor does not seem to have appeared on the Argentine political horizon.

Both the Radical and the Peronist parties have split a number of times (the former more so, since it has been in existence for more than seventy years). These divisions have, generally speaking, been due to personality disagreements or diverse tactical preferences, rather than to profound ideological struggles. The best example is the division of the Radical Party into its Intransigent and People's factions, which have been running separate candidates in national elections since 1958. While certain ideological differences have evolved, it is possible to trace personal disagreements between Arturo Frondizi (Intransigent leader) and Ricardo Balbin (People's leader) as one of the key causes

7

of the division. Similar disagreements have appeared among the Peronists, although Perón's influence seems to have been successful in slowing down divisive tendencies.

The role played by the other parties has been minimal in recent times. The conservatives were able to mount victorious coalitions only when there were administrations willing to use pressure and fraud in their favor (as in 1931 and 1937). Since that time, they have done very poorly. The ideological parties, essentially the Socialists and Communists, have never been very important, except in a few districts. In view of the fact that the military regime led by Juan C. Onganía has decreed a moratorium on partisan activities, the future of the Argentine party system seems unpredictable. However, it is difficult to foresee free political interaction in Argentina without a Radical and a Peronist party, regardless of the formal names they adopt.

Institutional Features of the Argentine Polity

It may be considered purposeless to discuss the institutional features of Argentina when one is aware of the fact that, since 1930, a significant number of its governments acceded to office in violation of such features. However, a brief review probably has some value, because a nation's institutions, when they have existed for a relatively long period of time, when they have brought about prosperity (whether there was direct relationship between prosperity and the institution lacks significance for the majority of the population), have a way of influencing the political actions even of those who acceded to power in violation of the formal rules of the game. The institutions which fit the above description acquire a degree of legitimacy which makes their violation unpopular. Violators are thus forced to provide twisted interpretations in order to justify their actions and claims.

The Constitution of 1853 remained, with a few amendments, as the formal institutional framework until 1949, when Perón had it replaced by another document which made it possible for him to constitutionally seek reelection.[10] The Peronist constitution lasted only as long as its spiritual creator was in power. The military government which replaced him returned the country to the 1853 document which, with one more amendment, is said to be in effect today. It can be, and is, hotly debated whether the Argentine Constitution has ever been fully in force. This is not the place to tackle such a challenging subject.

8

The fact seems to be that the Constitution of 1853 has provided the ideal of what Argentine political institutions ought to be. Even such obvious violators of the institutional system as those who brought General Onganía to power claim to subscribe to the 1853 document and proclaim it to be at least partially in operation.[11]

The Argentine constitutional system was heavily influenced by the American Constitution and by texts such as de Tocqueville's *Democracy in America* and Hamilton's *Federalist Papers*. One writer emphasizes that,

> The Constitution of the United States, we repeat, was present at the time when the Argentine project was drafted, and the committee on constitutional matters stated that the Argentines, "as Christians and democrats, and wishing to emulate the example of rapid growth and of civil and political freedom of the federals of the North" should not fail to show their hospitality; and Juan María Gutiérrez declared that the Constitution, eminently federal, was patterned after that of the United States, "the only federation existing in this world which warrants imitation." . . . In approximately sixty articles and in numerous sections the presence of the American model can be perceived. . . .[12]

There were, however, significant differences, both in theory and in practice, from the much-admired model. Although the country formally accepted the federal system, the central government was specifically given the power of *intervención*. Regardless of the background, objectives, and limitations of the constitutional provision in question (Art. 6),[13] the fact remains that the central government has used it to appoint federal officials who superseded provincial authorities and that this power has been used mostly against provinces whose authorities were in disagreement with the national government. Obviously, the mere existence of such a power has made provincial administrations extremely cautious in their political relationships with the central government. While federal interventors were supposed to remain in control of provinces for brief periods, this has not always been the case. Furthermore, while they were in control, the interventors often took steps which insured the election of friendlier provincial governments which succeeded them. The power of *intervención*, plus the economic resources controlled by the federal government have converted Argentina into a pseudo-federal nation. The Onganía regime has, for the time being at least, dispensed with the formalistic aspects of the federal system adopted by the 1853 Constitution by deciding

9

that the executive branch could not only remove, but also appoint the provincial authorities. Thus, under the Onganía regime, Argentina has become a unitary nation *de jure*.[14]

Another significant difference between the American and Argentine constitutional documents is the recognition, in the latter, of the preeminent position enjoyed by the Catholic Church. According to the Argentine Constitution, the federal government is responsible for supporting Catholicism, and the president must be a Catholic. These and other constitutional provisions only confirm the fact that the Church has continued to be an important element in Argentine politics and is quite capable of articulating its interests. Unquestionably, the Church's interests were powerfully expressed at the constitutional convention.

A third important difference is the greater power given the Argentine executive branch, both at the national and provincial levels. This theoretical recognition of the preference for a strong chief executive has been reinforced by political custom. The result has been the widespread belief that, in Argentine politics, things get done by the executive branch, if they get done at all. The predominance of the executive branch and the other provisions mentioned above have made it possible for some *de facto* regimes to develop sophistic arguments showing that they were not exceeding the provisions of the constitution.

Argentine constitutional development has intensified and given permanency to those political characteristics found in Argentina in the second half of the nineteenth century. Internal redistributions of political power, to the extent that they have taken place, have often occurred in conflict with basic constitutional provisions and their original interpretations. This is not to say, however, that the Argentine Constitution did not have some features which made minor changes possible; had this not been the case, it would not have lasted as long as it did. But these minor changes have been essentially adjustments to the broad status quo. When more profound modifications were attempted, they had to be accompanied by legal moves of doubtful constitutionality.

Carlos A. Astiz

Notes

1. The best study of land allocations in Argentina is that of Jacinto Oddone, *La burguesía terrateniente argentina*, third edition (Buenos Aires: Ediciones Libera, 1967).

2. Evidence can be found in the by-now-classic work by Gino Germani, *Política y sociedad en una época de transición. De la sociedad tradicional a la sociedad de masas* (Buenos Aires: Editorial Paidos, 1962), particularly chapter seven.

3. On the distinction between political parties and electoral machines see Carlos A. Astiz, *Pressure Groups and Power Elites in Peruvian Politics* (Ithaca, N.Y.: Cornell University Press, 1969), chapter six. It should be indicated that the *Movimiento justicialista* was an electoral machine; during his first term in office Perón dissolved it and created the Peronist Party, which has shown a significant degree of permanency.

4. Evidence of the participation of labor leaders in the Argentine Congress during the Perón administration can be found in the excellent study by Darío Cantón, *El parlamento argentino en épocas de cambio: 1890, 1916 y 1946* (Buenos Aires: Editorial del Instituto, 1966), *passim.*

5. A recent attempt has been Carlos S. Fayt (ed.), *La naturaleza del peronismo* (Buenos Aires: Viracocha Editores-Distribuidores, 1967).

6. Aldo Ferrer, *La economía argentina; Las etapas de su desarrollo y problemas actuales* (Mexico City: Fondo de Cultura Económica, 1963), 200.

7. For recent data on unemployment see *La Nación* (Buenos Aires) June 7, 1969, p. 7. The unemployment rate of between 5 and 6 percent which has been recorded since 1964 (it was 8.8 percent in July, 1963) should be considered conservative, and it does not take into account the problem of underemployment, so prevalent throughout Latin America.

8. This is clearly demonstrated in Aldo Ferrer and others, *Los planes de estabilización en la Argentina* (Buenos Aires: Paidos, 1969). As indicated on pp. 89 and 104, real wages in industry grew from 1955 to 1958 and decreased from 1958 to 1963. The wage freezes put into practice by the Onganía regime coupled with a constant, although decreasing, rate of inflation have intensified the economic losses of the lower and lower middle classes.

9. One of the best historical outlines of the Argentine party system is Carlos R. Melo, *Los partidos políticos argentinos*, third edition (Córdoba: Universidad Nacional de Córdoba, 1964). Also see Alfredo Galletti, *La realidad argentina en el siglo XX; La política y los partidos* (Mexico City: Fondo de Cultura Económica, 1961).

10. The 1853 constitution provides in Art. 77 that the president and vice-president may not be reelected until a full term (six years) has elapsed.

11. See the Acta de la Revolución Argentina, Articles 3 and 7. It should be pointed out that the military officers who installed the Onganía regime qualified their commitment to the Constitution by indicating that its provisions would be respected as long as they did not oppose the ends outlined in the above-mentioned Acta. On this topic see Instituto de Ciencia Política, Universidad del Salvador, *La "revolución argentina"; análisis y perspectiva* (Buenos Aires: Ediciones Depalma, 1966), *passim.*

12. Diego Abad de Santillán, *Historia institucional argentina* (Buenos Aires: Editora Tipográfica Argentina, 1966), p. 491.

11

13. For a comprehensive discussion of this subject, see Juan A. González Calderón, *Curso de derecho constitucional*, fourth edition (Buenos Aires: Editorial Guillermo Kraft, 1963), chapter 6.

14. *Estatuto de la revolución argentina*, Art. 9. It is interesting to note that the use of *intervención* has become so common to Argentines that even relatively well-informed ones are unable to understand the conflicts which have recently developed in the United States between the federal government and some state administrations over issues such as school integration. They feel that, if the United States federal government were sincere in its efforts, it would replace the authorities of unreceptive states with individuals who would enforce federal policies.

1. PRESIDENTS, GOVERNORS, MEMBERS OF THE NATIONAL CABINET

In 1936, eight of the twelve persons who made up the National Cabinet, the president of the Chamber of Deputies, and the governor of the province of Buenos Aires, were members of an exclusive club, the *Círculo de Armas*. In 1941, four of those in the same offices were members of that institution. With rare exceptions, no members of the *Círculo de Armas* have been in the national cabinet since then.[1]

In 1936, eight of the twelve members of the National Cabinet belonged to the traditional families. In 1941, five out of twelve were members of another exclusive organization, the Jockey Club, and that percentage diminished gradually in succeeding cabinets. It was lowest during the Perón era, but rose again in the group that surrounded President Frondizi (Ministers Cárcano, Acevedo, Mugica, and others).

In 1936, only the secretary of war and two governors of important provinces were sons of immigrants. One of these two governors, the governor of Córdoba, belonged to an opposition party. In 1941 the minister of the interior and the two military ministers were sons of immigrants. The majority of the members of the government in 1951 were first-generation Argentines, sons of immigrants; half of them were Spanish (all of them descendants of *Gallegos*, all of them born in Buenos Aires) and the other half, Italian.

Argentines, though conscious of the changes that have taken place in the personnel of the successive ruling teams, have not always been aware that these political phenomena were related to structural changes in the society. Although the changes in the names, in the groups, and in the sectors that have taken turns in power have been evident, the recruitment techniques, the channels for advancement and the processes of selection used to fill the highest offices were not always so evident.

Basically, there are two fundamental mechanisms for the achievement of political power in Argentina: by the active search of a power

13

base or by co-optation by the "inner circle." Co-optation occurs when a group in power attracts, calls, and incorporates other individuals to perform responsible functions, generally in the lower echelons, but opening up opportunities for advancement to them.

The search for formal political power can be pursued through popular elections, through the force of arms, or through the co-optation of technicians, specialists, or representatives of power sectors. One remaining procedure is that of "authoritarian appointment," which generally takes place through the arbitrary decision of a leader or of his coterie and tends to subordinate the new appointee to the leader's will. These forms of selection of the higher echelons are the principal ones used in Argentina.

The analysis in this chapter will deal with how these forms of selection have been applied by the different Argentine regimes; it will also consider whether the advancement channels have operated as established. The analysis covers the period between 1936 and 1961, and insofar as possible, the two following years as well. The study has been limited to "formal public leaders," or to all those persons who, whatever their merits, may have held the highest political positions: presidents, members of the cabinet, presiding officers of the Chamber of Deputies, and governors of three key provinces of Buenos Aires, Santa Fe, and Córdoba. The analysis is based on statistical samples, selected at five-year intervals, made up of all those who from 1936 on have held high institutional positions.

The ruling group in 1936 was that of the *Concordancia* under the presidency of General Agustín P. Justo. Five years later, in 1941, the country was ruled by the most thoroughly conservative group that has been in office since the passing of the Sáenz Peña Electoral Act.[2]

In 1946, with the success of Perón, a new group of men had just come to power. In 1951 Eva Perón was still alive, Peronism was at its apogee, and its leaders would at last make up the basic team of the Peronist movement.

In 1956 a second group emerged from the revolution that had overthrown Perón the previous year. This group was to entrench itself and, in one way or another, become identified with the revolution of 1955. In 1961 the country was ruled by President Frondizi, whose governing team included two clearly differentiated factions: one that followed the party line and the other that represented some of the other power factors in existence at the time.

14

These governing teams, grouped at five-year intervals, make up the samples. The analysis has been based on two questions: Where did the various teams who have ruled the country in the last quarter of a century come from? And what were the mechanisms applied to the selection of the governing personnel? During this twenty-five year period, three ruling teams have followed each other in office in Argentina.

The first team is the one that ruled until 1943. It was a restricted group in which birth, personal relationships, family position, and club affiliations operated as selective criteria because, basically, those in positions of the highest level, except in the case of the ministers of the armed forces, were chosen by ascriptive criteria.

The group that ruled between 1936 and 1943 reduced co-optation to a minimum because almost all of the ruling team came from within the ranks of the upper class. There was little co-optation; one simply belonged in government by right of ascription. In any case, positions were usually filled by a limited number of peers. On occasion, the group applied the criterion of "recognition." In other words, positions that were of little interest to peer members were filled through the "recognition" of certain personal qualities or virtues.

The first qualities recognized for reaching the highest official positions were business ability or legal capacity. Miguel J. Culaciati, minister of the interior in the 1941 cabinet, would be the classic example of this type of appointment. The group had recognized in him qualities that could overcome the differences of birth, background, and family position.

The other recognized ability was electoral success. Manuel Fresco in 1936 was governor of the province of Buenos Aires, but his position as ruler, since it was only recognized, had to be constantly proved through reelection. Electoral success provided only a relative charisma, and those outside the group knew that electoral failure involved the loss of recognition. The sample used does not include Antonio Barceló, senator for the province of Buenos Aires, but we cannot overlook him. Barceló's career was the classic example of this type of recognition, which had to be renewed at each election.[3]

On the other hand, members of the basic group maintained their ascriptive status regardless of success or failure in their political roles. If a man who had been recognized succeeded, he was raised to the highest allowed position, but he could not go beyond that, and only

15

"born" members could be candidates for the presidency of the country. To be president it was not enough to be a great politician; it was also necessary to belong to the highest social stratum.

It was truly a complete ruling class, one of the few cohesive, functional ones the country has had. The cohesive social group operated at the top levels of government; those who had achieved recognition because of their ability were in charge of specific activities; those who had achieved recognition through electoral success had carte blanche at the intermediate levels. The whole machine was supported by two pillars: electoral fraud and the apolitical attitude of the armed forces.

Cohesion was furnished by the inner group, and thus there was no need to resort to a community of interests. Members of the group had identical visions of the country, their attitudes toward economic order were quite similar, and their views on foreign countries were the same: they admired the French in cultural affairs, the British in the economic field, and the Germans in military matters.

They even coincided as to profession: 69 percent of the 1936 sample and 92 percent of the 1941 sample were lawyers. Three ministers in 1936 and six in 1941 were professors of the School of Law in Buenos Aires. The differences among them were rather of a personal nature, and only one external factor—imminent war or war already under way —could disrupt the close cohesion of the class governing Argentina.

The team that replaced this inner group until 1955 reversed the terms of selection for high political office. In 1943, the previous ruling class having been replaced, the criteria for legitimation (such as the "political formula" already mentioned), the sources of leadership, and the recruitment criteria were modified.

The new political group that established itself after the electoral success of the Peronists did not recognize the previous ascriptive values, and the standard of loyalties it inaugurated had nothing in common with previous criteria. At first they were not a single cohesive group. On the contrary, those who eventually would be the Peronist rulers came from several different groups. In 1946 four channels for advancement can be discerned, one of which was completely new.

The Peronist leaders of 1946 constituted a very broad, open, and extensive group of newcomers, the product of wider recruitment than had ever been known before. In 1946 the criterion for advancement was exclusively personal success. But such success had to have been demonstrated previously in one of the four basic divisions on which

16

Peronism was to be structured: the plutocracy, activity in labor unions and social policy, the party, and the armed forces.

1. The plutocracy as a channel for advancement was only relatively new, for individuals with this background had already participated in previous regimes. The novelty lay in that this plutocracy was based on industry, not on exporting or importing. This group was made up of first-generation Argentines, sons of Spaniards.[4] They all had had previous experience in organizations representing management. Two of them had been officers of the Argentine Industrial Union, an exponent of the nation's industrialist interests, although according to the political climate prevalent from 1946 on, they seemed marginal with reference to it and to the social sector from which they came.

2. To attain political power after only a labor union career was something unheard of in Argentina. No labor leaders had ever performed political functions. In 1946 the secretary of the Confederation of Commercial Employees, also a former member for several terms of the secretariat of the General Confederation of Labor (GCL), was appointed minister of the interior. A former attorney for the railway union was named minister of foreign affairs, and in Santa Fe Province the new governor had a long history of activity in labor circles and in the regional offices of the GCL. Aside from these extreme cases, in 1946 labor unionists filled only some middle-level posts and part of the legislative seats representing the Federal District and the province of Buenos Aires.

3. In the previous team ward politics had been used to grant recognition to some technical experts. This time it also raised to the first ranks some party figures, although in this instance the losers in previous electoral battles were so raised. These leaders, these "party committeemen," all came from the ranks of the Radicals. Quijano, Auschter, Bavio, etc., within the sample were former Radicals who had left their party and permanently joined the Peronists. But within the ranks of the Radicals they had not been in the top echelons; on the contrary, they had acted on a secondary level in terms of importance. Their political success was due not so much to personal merit as to their foresight in joining a new movement that accepted them and to which they contributed their mastery of traditional techniques and methods for political proselytizing.

4. The fourth sector was made up of recently retired officers of the armed forces. Recruitment from this sector was not new. In fact, Pres-

17

ident Justo, the leader of the previous governing team, had also been a military man. The novelty in this case resulted from the number of senior officers involved in political affairs and especially from the fact that the officers who obtained the two highest positions, the president of the Republic and the governor of Buenos Aires Province, had not reached the top rank in their military careers.

This new political class differed from the preceding one in several ways. In 1946 the new group was not unified since its members came from dissimilar backgrounds. There was no ascription nor recognition by co-optation. The new political class was made up of different individuals who had advanced by different channels. There were no common values in 1946, and no system of loyalties existed other than those of military men and labor unionists toward their respective institutions.

The recruitment base was too broad to support a political regime. The system of loyalties was too diffuse, and those loyalties "manufactured" around the movement were impersonal, fluid, and unstable, such as those based on a faction that had seceded from the Radical Party and on a Labor Party that was only a union superstructure in the Greater Buenos Aires metropolitan area. On this very broad recruitment base a strict regime of personal loyalties was built.

Little by little, as the role of the leaders was clarified, individual responsibility diminished. As the absolutist and charismatic nature of the leadership became more pronounced, the political group became more bureaucratic. As power became more centralized in the hands of the governing couple, the role of others tended to be reduced to that of channels for the transmission of orders.

The four recruitment channels tended to disappear and were merged into a single one. Toward 1950, and around 1951, the governing group was set apart and began to discriminate clearly between "we" and "they." The group had developed its own standards, norms, and values. What was formerly the result of personal merit had now been replaced by bureaucratic careers. Impersonality was the rule everywhere, and it became a value that was taken into account for promotion.

Selection of the ruling personnel began to be made on the basis of norms developed exclusively by the regime. Co-optation was the rule, but it was now a bureaucratic process and was conducted always within the bureaucratic structure. Thus, outstanding personal success in the end became a liability rather than an advantage.

In 1951 the basic team of ministers was made up of sons of immi-

18

grants, especially of Spaniards, and among these the most numerous were the *Gallegos*.[5] The other leaders of immigrant stock were sons of Italians. The rest of the ministers came from the traditional families, but, except for two who were from Buenos Aires and as such were fully marginal,[6] they belonged to Creole families from the interior. The ministers of the armed forces,[7] the vice-president, and the minister of public health were among the latter.

Two ministers had had previous experience in labor unions, one among the already mentioned commercial employees, and the other as a glass worker. The minister of public works, a military man, was the son of Italian farmers, as was the secretary to the president, also a military man. The governor of Buenos Aires, another military man, was the son of a railroad employee. If to this we add that for the first time in the history of the country a Jew occupied the office of secretary with ministerial rank, we will have an idea of how social mobility had worked up to that time in Argentina. Conditions were created that, at an opportune political juncture, permitted a very significant percentage of the rulers to emerge from the lower social strata.

Thus, the members of the governing group came from diverse backgrounds, but were unified by an institutionalized system of absolute loyalties. There were no values except those endogenous to the regime, and the group holding power co-opted others, though always on the basis of open and proved loyalty. Working only at the secondary levels of power and relegated to the task of transmitting orders, this group of individuals was not actually a "ruling group." Its cohesion did not arise from loyalty to abstract principles or to norms established by the group itself, but rather from absolute loyalty to a common point of reference: the president of the Republic and his wife.

In many cases the leaders of other social sectors did not agree with the values of the political rulers. However, the latter held the actual power and imposed it in such a way that gradually the leadership teams of the other sectors were modified. Finally, the criteria for making up the cadres were institutionalized not only on the political, but on the cultural and economic levels as well, through a process of exclusion. This "pseudo ruling class," however, was not able to survive the leader on whom it depended.

The characteristics of the new political class become defined in 1956 after the fall of Perón. In 1956, 42 percent of the highest institutionalized positions were occupied by military men and 24 percent, by entrepreneurs. This combination of military men and entrepreneurs lasted

19

throughout the whole revolutionary period until Arturo Frondizi came to power in 1958.

Theoretically, the fact that half the posts were held by men subject to military discipline should have made for cohesion, but such was not the case, partly because the armed forces, with their purges, reinstatements, internal conflicts, and so forth, went through an acute process of disorientation, and partly because the content of the ideology that might have unified them was somewhat diffuse. In its positive aspects this ideology did not rise above the level of the slogan—democracy and liberty—but it was expressed more in negative terms, being characterized by disavowal of all that might be a reminder of the previous political regime.

The "inner group," being very weak, lacked cohesion and a system of specific values, and it was only on occasion that it closed ranks and recovered its strength. But such unity was a reaction to their opponents positive action; that is, the Peronists might have some partial and isolated successes by winning some labor union election, holding demonstrations, or threatening to hold them, and the like. Such isolated Peronist intervention operated as a catalyst, giving rise to a temporary strengthening of the holders of power.

Until 1958, the advancement channels for the new elite were two: the armed forces and the ruling groups in industry, or rather, as to the latter, participation in great economic corporations. This source of political leaders from industry was a novelty: the political leaders before 1943 were legal advisors of foreign enterprises; the Peronist industrialists of 1946, rather than true entrepreneurs in the contemporary sense, were *patrones* in the old sense, or "captains of industry." In contrast, the 1956 leaders held posts simultaneously on the boards of various great corporations. Thus, for the first time, corporation executives appeared within the ruling teams. This development was congruent with structural changes that had occurred and with those that were coming about in the makeup of the managerial class.

As a general rule, in 1956 these public leaders were second-generation Argentines. The military ministers, those for the Navy and Air Force who were the sons of Germans; the president of the Republic, who was the son of Basque immigrants; and the minister of education, who came from an Italian family, were the exceptions.

The percentage of members of the traditional families in the cabinet was more or less the same as in the previous period. An estimate would indicate that both during the Perón period and during the regime that followed his overthrow the percentage fluctuated between 10 and 15 percent. The difference lay in the fact that under Peronism those ministers were marginal to their own class, while in the latter period they truly represented it, at least with respect to the type of political conduct adopted in each case by their class.

In 1958 there was a change. President Frondizi came to power as the result of an electoral choice between two acceptable candidates. Despite this, his team, from the point of view which interests us now, was not so different from the previous one as might be supposed.

In the 1961 sample, entrepreneurs occupied 36 percent of the cabinet posts, the number of apolitical technicians, all engineers, remained the same (16 percent, a similar percentage to that of 1956), and the role of the military changed. Military men disappeared as public leaders; in the cabinet they retained only the military ministries and the intelligence service, although they became "informal leaders" as guarantors of the institutional continuity of the diffuse ideology, in its positive and negative aspects, of which they became the depositaries.

In the 1961 team, however, an important change took place: the reappearance of "party politicians," that is, those who have made politics a professional career, and also the institutionalization of the party machine as the channel for qualifying advancement. This had not been true in Argentina since the fall of the Conservative Party. The "party politicians" who represented 23 percent of the highest posts in 1936, who were 38 percent of the 1941 team, and who had practically disappeared during Peronism, again gained 36 percent of the posts in 1961.

Thus in the governing team which took over in 1958, there was a mixture of disparate origins, careers, and loyalties. These were not only narrow personal loyalties to the president of the Republic, but also institutional loyalties, such as those held in the military ministries towards the armed forces.

None of the entrepreneurs within the 1958 governing team was able to assume representation of a whole new and rising social sector because it lacked cohesion. In some cases, such as in the 1961 cabinet, ministers with entrepreneurial backgrounds came from two different management organizations, sometimes opposed to each other. Also, the whole entrepreneurial group in charge of economic policy was expressly or implicitly disavowed by both management organizations.[8]

Thus this 1961 governing team, as a group, might have been only a

21

"group by classification," the members of which came together only by a general coincidence in time to exercise power in the highest offices. Only those political ministers and the secretaries personally identified with the president of the Republic and his alter ego, Rogelio Frigerio, could be considered united by a solid web of internal loyalties. Only they constituted an "inner group," while the rest of the governing team did not belong. The officials did not, therefore, become a coherent ruling group united around common objectives and a common system of values. Rather, they were divided into three different groups converging and competing on common ground.

In the 1961 sample, we find that 11 of the 23 rulers were first-generation Argentines, sons of immigrants. Only one could properly be considered a typical self-made man: the minister of industry and mining, who had been born in Spain. An immigrant, after a long career as a maté producer, he rose to the leadership of the trade organization for the industry. Seven of the 23 rulers came from the traditional upper class, or at least from the traditional families. In 1961, the percentage was higher than that found in the previous teams.

Outside the sample and after 1961, a whole new governing team appears, the one that rose to power in October, 1963, as a result of the Presidential elections in July of that year. There is little doubt that the channel for recruitment of this group was the People's Radical Party, which won the elections. All the members of the governing team, with the customary exception of the military ministers, were party men. But an explanation is in order with respect to those responsible for the national economy: though they were party men, they were not professional politicians.

The president of the Republic, the vice-president, the ministers of foreign affairs, labor, defense, and the governors of the provinces of Buenos Aires and of Córdoba had all previously been national legislators representing their party. The minister of the interior had been a government minister in his native province, and the one for justice and public education had also been a national minister previously. The others, who had no previous experience in public office, had been candidates for elective posts.

The party, therefore, had reappeared as the great instrument for selection, with a significance and scope greater than in any other period we have analyzed. The previous careers of the men in the government, with the exception already mentioned of those responsible for

22

the national economy, had been political. To evaluate this fact and to measure its implications in the governing of the nation let the reader consult the proper chapter on the *cursus honorum* of the professional politicians.

Three Generations

If Argentine presidents have been relatively young, compared to European chiefs of state and prime ministers, their staffs have not always been young. Table 1.1 divides the governing teams included in the sample into two age groups; as may be seen there, in two periods those over 50 years of age constitute a sizable majority, and in one period the opposite is true.

TABLE 1.1

Governing Teams According to Age Group

Governing teams	1936	1941	1946	1951	1956	1961
Over 50	7	12	6	11	15	15
Under 50	5	2	13	15	11	8
Team Total	12	14	19	26	26	23

The older group predominated during the conservative regimes, and we find the greatest predominance in 1941. The "biological" fact is in accordance with the predominant political attitude, and it occurs again. In 1961, when conservative groups reappear in the Frondizi cabinet, the prevalence of those over 50 years old acquires a certain significance. During the Perón regime these figures are reversed, very definitely so in 1946 when a new governing group came to power. It was the first time that a chief of state had surrounded himself with such a young group, at least in relation to the political teams of other years.

There is nothing particularly significant about age 50 in itself; it has been arbitrarily adopted only to classify groups. It would be more useful to reassemble the data in order to reveal how two extreme age groups are represented in government. The results can be seen in table 1.2.

TABLE 1.2

Governing Teams by Years and Extreme Age Groups

Governing Teams	1936	1941	1946	1951	1956	1961
Over 60	2	6	2	2	6	4
Under 40	1	–	7	6	2	1
Team Total	12	14	19	26	26	23

The previous hypothesis is thus confirmed. During the conservative regime of 1941, almost half the governing team was over 60 years old. Later, in 1956 and in 1961, some ministers older than 60 accompanied the chief of state, but the percentages do not reach those occurring in 1941, as table 1.3 shows.

TABLE 1.3

Government Teams by Years and Extreme Age Groups in Percentages

Governing Teams	1936	1941	1946	1951	1956	1961
Over 60	16	43	10	8	23	17
Under 40	8	–	36	23	8	4

It is evident that the average age for becoming a minister is around 50. Only in the conservative period would there be a significant percentage over 60, and only during the Perón period did the number of young ministers have quantitative significance.

In general, a trend toward younger ministers cannot be established. The youngest minister the country has had was President Frondizi's first minister of foreign affairs who was appointed when he was 29 years old. Under Perón two secretaries with ministerial rank were 33 when appointed. One might expect to find a recent trend toward rejuvenation and the promotion of young talent to ministerial rank. But the appointment of ministers made by the Illia government, which took office in October, 1963, refutes this assumption.

Taking into account dates of birth, it is evident that the principal leaders in the conservative period were born prior to 1880. Only three were born later, as table 1.4 indicates.

Looking at dates of birth of the Peronist teams, two groups may be identified: the military and the civilians and politicians. With only one exception, that of General Pistarini, all the military men who sur-

24

rounded Perón were former comrades of the same graduating class at the Military Academy. Among civilians only Vice-President Quijano was not born in the twentieth century.

TABLE 1.4

Date of Birth of Conservative Elites

Julio A. Roca	1873	R. Patrón Costas	1878
Ramón S. Castillo	1873	Roberto M. Ortiz	1886
Agustín P. Justo	1878	Manuel Fresco	1888
Carlos Saavedra Lamas	1878	M. A. Cárcano	1889

TABLE 1.5

General Pistarini	1882	Hortensio Quijano	1884
Adm. Teissaire	1891	J. A. Bramuglia	1903
General Sosa Molina	1893	A. Borlenghi	1906
General Perón	1895	N. Gómez Morales	1908
General Lucero	1897	R. Guardo	1909
General Mercante	1898		

These civilians and politicians came to public office as relatively young men in 1946. The presidents, governors, and cabinet members of 1956 and 1961 were born, with only one exception, in the first decade of this century:

TABLE 1.6

Dr. Noblía	1901	Dr. Frondizi	1908
Lt. General Ossorio Arana	1902	Dr. Alende	1909
Lt. General Aramburu	1903	Dr. Vítolo	1910
Dr. MacKay	1905	Eng. Alsogaray	1913
Adm. Rojas	1906		

Grouping all these dates of birth together, it is apparent that the conservative governing teams were born when national organization was becoming stronger, when the doors were being opened to mass immigration, and when a liberal generation governed, all prior to the crisis of 1890.[9] This governing group of the conservative period was surprised in full early maturity by the great political change brought about by the Sáenz Peña Act. The youngest of all was 30 years old, and the oldest 44, an age bracket propitious to the assimilation of experi-

25

ences. In 1943, when the revolution which deposed them occurred, the group was about to organize the most flagrant electoral fraud that would have violated the law which they, or their peers, had passed. The revolution found them "elderly," since the youngest was 59 and the oldest 73.

Perón and the military men who surrounded him constitute the second of the generations that have governed within the period here analyzed. They were all born before the end of the nineteenth century and, at the time of the 1930 revolution, were between 31 and 45 years old. The youngest was then a first lieutenant. At the time of the revolution of 1943, in which they would be the most prominent participants, the youngest was 44 and a lieutenant colonel. The oldest, a general, was 58.

Almost all the political leaders who have had top roles from 1946 to the present time have been born between the beginning of this century and the enactment of the Sáenz Peña Act, whether they were Peronist civilians and politicians, military men who took part in the government of the revolution which overthrew the Perón regime, civilians who accompanied them in that government, or leaders of the Intransigent Radical Party or of the People's Radical Party who took office in October, 1963. The only exception was Vice-President Perette. But all of them as a whole constitute the third governing generation that has arisen in a quarter of a century.

Almost all sons of immigrants, this third governing generation was born during a period in which the newly arrived groups were beginning to settle during the height of the *belle époque,* around the one hundredth anniversary of the country's birth. It was a time when no one seemed to have doubts regarding the nation's unlimited progress, when immigrant fathers swelled with pride at the mere thought of the "great Argentina" that their children would enjoy.

The differences in birth dates do not necessarily imply ideological differences. Between the first and the second generation, the ideological difference is indeed striking. Between the second and third, it is not, especially since in the latter case there is little ideological cohesion among the politicians. But differences may be found if the time intervals between the birth of each of the typical or most representative examples of each governing team are considered.

Between the dates of birth of Agustín Justo and Robustiano Patrón Costas and of Perón, seventeen years elapsed; between this former president and Álvaro Alsogaray, three times minister, eighteen. The future will tell to what extent each one of these men personified an era. But the equal intervals of time will interest those who have set themselves the task of elaborating a theory on the generations in history. Without adopting this theory, a fact which supports it is recorded.

Constants and Variables During a Quarter of a Century

During a quarter of a century a generation passes, but, regardless of the physical disappearance of an individual, the interests or professional groups he represented remain. In this case, these interests and professional groups appear as constants. Let us see what professional groups might seem to be constants in the personnel of government. In table 1.7, drawn up on the basis of the occupations of the rulers, all military ministers have been excluded in order to avoid distortions.

TABLE 1.7
Governing Teams, by Occupational Group (Percentages)

Occupational Groups	1936	1941	1946	1951	1956	1961
Military men	8	8	20	19	42	4
Lawyers	69	92	30	23	20	52
Entrepreneurs	16	8	10	—	24	32
Professional Politicians	23	38	20	15	—	36

In these public posts the military became dominant only in 1956. This was the only governing team among those studied here which came directly out of a military revolution. As they had the responsibility for leadership, the figure confirms it. In the others, except in the Peronist period, the numbers of the military men are small. Here we included in the analysis only the "visible leaders"; the military influence will be discussed in Chapter 3. That military men have occupied relatively few high institutionalized posts does not mean they were without power; the history of the country in the last few years shows the power of the military has been greater than these figures indicate. A different approach is needed to assess the military's influence and will be attempted later.

On the other hand, the percentage of lawyers is very significant. There is an absolute predominance of lawyers during the conservative period, and they hold half the posts during the Frondizi government.

27

The predominance of lawyers in 1936 and 1941, as will be seen later, is related to the limited development of the country in those years. In new countries, recently emerged into independent life, teachers and specialized professors predominate in the governing teams. They are the local "intelligentsia," as is true of the *instituteurs* in all the former French possessions in Africa, that now are independent states. However, in the countries with a traditional Latin American social structure, lawyers predominate, and their proportion increases in the more traditional and stationary societies. In highly developed countries, specialized technocrats (engineers, professional economists, graduates in political science and administration) predominate in the governing teams.

The membership of the entrepreneurial groups varies in the different periods being analyzed. Until 1943 the few entrepreneurs who participated were attorneys—thus they are included under the preceding heading in table 1.7—representing the large corporations that controlled the international trade in basic products (such as meat and grains). In the 1946 team there were entrepreneurs, merchants, and industrialists who actually owned their enterprises; there were also personal *patrones*, or captains of industry, and other archetypes of little-evolved forms of capitalism, in tune with the managerial situation of the era. They sought to use political power as a means of consolidating their enterprises. The entrepreneurs who took part in government in 1956 and 1961 worked for multiple corporations and were true corporate executives, not easily identified as the owners. They were managers or advisers of many corporations of the modern type.

Obviously, in this analysis of occupations, the percentages should not be added together. It may be that some officials may have to be included in more than one category. This is true of the professional politicians. Without prejudice to what will be said about them in Chapter 2, "professional politicians" are those who live for politics—although not always from politics—follow a *cursus honorum* within the party groups, and occupy elective posts representing their party.

Professional politicians by definition are the ones belonging to the conservative period. Even if they were lawyers, and even though their families were supported by income from landed property, they were professional politicians because these men were wholly devoted to political activities and in an almost uninterrupted manner occupied public office for a very long period. The revolution of 1943 cut all their careers short.

28

Simply as examples, we reproduce the public offices occupied period by period, by two of the most characteristic figures in the conservative old ruling class.

Personal data on Robustiano Patrón Costas:
Born in Salta Province in 1878
Lawyer in Buenos Aires in 1901
1902–04: Minister of the Treasury in the Province of Salta
1910–12: Minister of Government in Salta
1913–16: Governor of Salta
1916–25: National Senator for Salta
1926–29: Senator in the provincial legislature
1932–38: National Senator for Salta
1938–43: National Senator for Salta
He was President *Pro Tempore* of the Senate from 1932 to 1943. He was going to be a candidate for President of the Republic when the revolution of 1943 took place.

Personal data on Dr. Julio A. Roca:
Born in Córdoba in 1873
Lawyer in Buenos Aires in 1894
1904–16: National Deputy for Córdoba
1916–22: Governor for Córdoba
1928–30: National Deputy for Córdoba
1932–38: Vice President of the Republic
1938   : Ambassador to Brazil
1940   : Minister for Foreign Affairs until his death in 1942.

Similar careers cannot be found in later periods. During the Perón regime there were very few professional politicians. Some with a Radical Party background joined the Peronist movement, but they did not carry great weight once the regime became consolidated. During the regime there were administrators, men identified with the regime, rather than professional politicians in the strict sense of the term.

Once Perón was ousted, the consultative council was composed of professional politicians or party men, but they did not occupy ministerial offices. With the triumph of the Intransigent Radical Party in 1958, the party men reappeared in the key offices. But none of them could boast of a career similar to those shown above. At most, those politicians might claim a background of one or two legislative terms. They were younger than the former conservative politicans, they had had to face much greater competition, and the Peronist hiatus had interrupted their careers.

Aside from these tendencies, one of the most curious facts is the presence of nontechnical professionals at the head of very specialized

29

administrative departments. Of six ministers of education included in the samples, five are lawyers and the remaining one is a physician. There is no educator. The six ministers of foreign affairs are lawyers, which to a certain extent is understandable in a country which does not recognize a specific university degree in political science and diplomacy.[10]

The professional activity of the various ministers of agriculture is also strange. Of the six included in the samples, three are lawyers; one, a businessman and rancher; another, a physician, but also devoted to farming; and only one, an agricultural engineer. Until the appointment of Carlos Alberto Emery (an engineer) as minister of agriculture, all those who had been at the head of the ministry were lawyers. Emery was succeeded by a notary public. Not until 1963, during José M. Guido's presidency, was a specifically trained professional appointed minister of agriculture. In the Arturo Illia governing team that took over in October of 1963, the new minister also had an university degree in accordance with his office.

Until 1946 all the ministers of the treasury had been lawyers. That year the first certified public accountant was appointed, and from that time on, in general, professional graduates in economic sciences were to be at the head of the corresponding portfolios. Until the appointment of General Pistarini, who was a military engineer, the previous ministers of public works had been lawyers. From Pistarini on, the ministers and their immediate subordinates would be engineers.

The appointment of nontechnical professionals operates as an indicator of two facts: a) the relatively slight development of a specific professional corps at the head of specific offices, professional specialization of the ministers beginning with Peronism; and b) the predominant influence of the schools of law on the formation of the ruling teams, and especially, according to the sample, the School of Law of the University of Buenos Aires. The latter's influence was due not only to the professionals it produced, but also because in each period its faculty lounge became a source of ministers. In fact, in each governing team there has been at least one who had been a member of that School's faculty. In accordance with the data shown by the sample there were 3 professors in the 1936 team; 6 in that of 1941; 1 in each of the Peronist cabinets; 3 in the 1956 team; and only 1 in 1961.

Aside from lawyers, only physicians and engineers have a certain significance, as a professional group, in the composition of the ruling teams.

30

TABLE 1.8

Percentage of Physicians and Engineers in Each Governing Team

Professional Groups	1936	1941	1946	1951	1956	1961
Physicians	16	–	5	15	10	16
Engineers	–	–	–	11	15	16

Engineers as a professional group began to have significance only when the Perón regime fell. The engineers' professional organization (known as *Centro de Ingenieros*) was taken over by the government, and so the technicians who occupied ministerial posts under Peronism did so as indivduals, without in any way assuming representation of their professional group.

The difference between these two professions is shown by their different roles in politics. The engineers have always acted as technicians. The physicians, except where one may have been in charge of the Ministry of Public Health, have basically acted as politicians, especially at the provincial level. The fact is understandable in the provinces. The physicians in traditional and rural areas constitute a part of the intelligentsia. Moreover, they have, as lawyers do not, contact vis-à-vis their patients which is at the same time professional and political.

Taking the list of the governors of the three provinces included in the analysis (Buenos Aires, Santa Fe, and Córdoba), we find that during a quarter of a century there have been 12 elected governors and 6 *interventores*[11] representing the national government. Separating these 18 provincial chief executives according to profession, and bearing in mind that many of the *interventores* were military men, we find:

4 physicians
6 military men
4 lawyers
2 businessmen
1 engineer
1 labor union official

But we wish to pause a moment over the physicians. While quantitatively they number the same as lawyers and less than the military men, they become politically perhaps the most significant. In fact, Governor Sabattini of Córdoba, Governors Fresco and Alende of Buenos Aires, and Sylvestre Begnis, governor of Sante Fe, are or have been physicians by profession. And all of them have at the same time been true professional politicians.

31

Notes

1. They were Julio A. Roca, Carlos Saavedra Lamas, Roberto M. Ortíz, Basilio Pertiné, Eleazar Videla, Miguel Angel Cárcano, Manuel Alvarado, and Martín Noel.

2. The Sáenz Peña Electoral Act was presented to (and pushed through) the Argentine Congress by President Roque Sáenz Peña, a member of the traditional upper class, in 1912. It provided, among other things, for secret ballot and many voting guarantees; it made it an obligation for most male citizens over 18 years of age to report to the polls on election day, thus increasing participation. This act, which has been ignored by most political scientists, constitutes a clear and sincere attempt at partial revolution from above. C.A.A.

3. See the study by Norberto Folino, *Barceló, Ruggierito y el populismo oligárquico*. (Buenos Aires: Falbo Librero Editor, 1966.)

4. Such as Miguel Miranda, the son of Asturians, Lagomarsino, and Picazo Elordy.

5. Cereijo, Méndez San Martín, Ares, Gómez Morales, Barro, and Freire.

6. The two were Jesús H. Paz and Belisario Gache Pirán.

7. Army Generals Sosa Molina and Lucero and Air Force General Ojeda.

8. The management organizations were the already mentioned Argentine Industrial Union and the General Economic Confederation; both are discussed in Chapter 7. C.A.A.

9. The so-called "Crisis of 1890" refers to the socio-political agitation which took place that year, intensified by an economic depression and by the demands of the growing urban middle class. The newly created Civic Union Party organized a revolt against President Miguel Juárez Celman which, although unsuccessful, forced his resignation and replacement by Vice-President Carlos Pellegrini, who carried out some political reforms. C.A.A.

10. It is only recently that Argentine universities (mostly private) have begun offering degrees in political science and international relations, and even today training in those fields does not guarantee adequate employment. In fact, the appearance of these disciplines in Argentine institutions of higher learning has caused defensive reactions on the part of more traditionalist scholars. C.A.A.

11. The *interventor* is a representative of the federal government, chosen by the president, who takes over one or more branches of a provincial government for a certain period of time, thus legally overthrowing the previous officials. If the *interventor* was given jurisdiction over the executive and/or the legislative branch, elections follow his term. In this way, the federal government can constitutionally replace provincial administrations. C.A.A.

32

2. THE POLITICAL TEAMS AND THEIR INTERESTS

OUR ANALYSIS of the social origins of the political and administrative rulers of Argentina will allow us to make three generalizations about them.

1. The majority comes from the middle sectors. Being professionals, but sons of nonprofessionals, they are examples of upward social mobility. The more important the role played by the party as a mechanism for selection, the greater the representation of the middle sectors in the composition of the governing elite. This holds true for all the governors, presidents, and ministers who have had party careers in the ranks of the People's Radical Party, the Intransigent Radical Party, and the Peronists. Many of the entrepreneurs who reached public office came from the middle sectors, although others, such as Miguel Miranda and Eugenio Blanco, started at the bottom and worked their way up to the top. The military men who occupied public posts also came from the same background. The predominance of the middle sectors in the composition of Argentine ruling elites seems to be the norm throughout the quarter of a century.

2. The largest minority is made up of members of the traditional upper class. The presence of persons with social prestige in the cabinets is a constant, though the percentages and the degree of representation vary. The members of the upper class were in the majority as long as the political forces which articulated their points of view successfully used electoral fraud as a means of achieving power. After that, they were significant only during the Frondizi government.

During the Perón regime, the percentages of members of the traditional upper class in government were low and, besides being marginal to the highest prestige group, their presence in the cabinet was limited to the performance of specific functions. Although the traditional upper class lost direct control of political power after 1943, it always retained some vestiges of power to the extent that it adapted itself to

33

the exercise of these functions. In this sense, what has been shown in the case of Argentina fits the classic patterns described by Pareto and especially by Mosca in his analyses of the vestigial powers of the "former governing classes."[1]

3. Considered marginal, leaders of "popular" or "labor" background reached the highest political positions only during the Peronist period. This ascendence was not always the result of personal success, but rather of the ideology of the moment and of the sectors that supported the government. In the few documented cases these prestige-seeking individuals took advantage of the positions they had achieved to assure their own rapid promotion. In these cases economic ascent was followed by a change in status mentality, or their perception of their new status, but this new personal attitude did not necessarily imply a betrayal of their original background. They continued to belong and to act within the Peronist movement, which was identified with the working class. Nevertheless, those leaders coming from the popular sectors seldom returned to their previous environment once their economic expectations had been satisfied.

These studies of the background of the politico-administrative leaders are useful for evaluating the broadness of political recruitment and the openness of Argentine society. In all these cases of social mobility, status mentalities are created, which make the original class barriers more flexible and easier to cross. In the case of the entrepreneurs this is quite evident, since the upward mobility very often occurs in one generation, but where it appears most genuine is among the military. The reader is referred to Chapter 4, where the manner in which the process of military socialization erases class differences is discussed. In the final analysis, it is the military rank that counts, and status is determined exclusively by the rank attained.

Next, it is interesting to ascertain what those politico-administrative rulers represent once the teams have been made homogeneous by the holding of cabinet positions and whether beyond each individual a continuity of interests or ideologies may in fact exist.

The modern functional approach to comparative political systems is concerned with discovering what functions are constant, that is, which are found in all political systems, whether contemporary states or primitive polities. Working together with sociologists and modern specialists in political science, anthropologists have gathered revealing data for interpretation in great world centers. Through this patient

34

labor it has been possible to identify four functions that in one way or another are present in all political systems, whether their institutional structure is simple or complex, whether they have all the outward signs of development or an extreme degree of immaturity. Of the four functions found, only two are significant for the present purpose.[2]

In all political societies various groups in one way or another attempt to articulate their interests, their ideologies, and their world views. The more modern, the freer, the more pluralistic the society, the more varied the aspects and the more complex the number of interests, ideologies, and world views to be articulated. Articulation is one of the permanent functions of every political system. This function is performed by groups which may be of any type: communities, primary groups, associational interest groups, voluntary associations, and in the case of Argentina, political parties and interest groups also.

The second permanent function goes a step further: it aggregates these interests, ideologies, and world views, in one way or another, into the existing political system. The performance of this function of aggregation, or incorporation, may also be made through groups, communities, or associational interests, and in this case political parties and interest groups.

Of course, not every articulated interest is eventually aggregated, even though the aggregration function is one of the constants. But whether some interests are aggregated and others are not depends upon a series of variables, such as the degree of liberty, the viability of the interest or ideology articulated, the possibility that the interests articulated and those to be aggregated may be mutually exclusive or, on the contrary, that they may be compatible, and so forth.

That those interests being articulated may not become aggregated does not, therefore, invalidate the function. In subsequent chapters it will be shown how some interests, values, ideologies, and world views are articulated in Argentina. Some are wholly aggregated into the system; others, partly; still others, not at all. Whether they are aggregated or not will vary in each case.

One way of ascertaining which interests will be well articulated and aggregated is to analyze who and what the formal leaders of the politico-administrative elite represent. Sometimes a whole group, or part of a group, or at least a governmental leader aggregates this interest or, in other words, serves as guarantor that this interest will be aggregated. In other cases, the interest is not aggregated through a governmental leader of the first rank (such as those included in the samples), but rather through an individual at a secondary level, as, for example, through a cabinet undersecretary.

In all these cases open aggregation of interests and ideologies into the political system would occur. If the analysis led only to this conclusion everything would be simple and easy to determine. Such simplicity, however, is not found in reality, for a considerable part of the interests and ideologies that are adequately articulated become aggregated without the intervention of a governmental leader who publicly espouses them. This would be non-public aggregation.

In any case, analyzing governmental leaders as has been done heretofore gives us a clue to how interest aggregation occurs. The simpler and less complex the social structure, the less diversified it is, the easier it will seem at first glance to identify the aggregated interests.

Some of these interests are very clearly represented by members of the first governmental team analyzed. Not all the members of the team were large landowners; on the contrary, only 4 out of a sample of 36 were. But among these 4 we find the vice-president of the Republic, a very important landowner in the provinces of Córdoba and Buenos Aires; the president of the Senate, who was one of the most important landowners in the province of Salta; the minister of agriculture, a high-level rancher from Córdoba; and in 1941 the minister of agriculture, who was a large landowner in the province of Corrientes.

The identity of interests during the period under discussion (expressed at the political level) is established by pointing out that the minister of the interior[3] in 1941 was a well-known attorney who had represented a number of grain-exporting firms, a man who had sponsored the Rosario City Grain Exchange, and a recognized spokesman for the interests of the large European import-export firms.

It is not necessary to investigate further the teams of that period because the results of an analysis of this type simply confirm what is obvious. Agriculture and related businesses were the primary economic activities of that period, and the interests of these groups were expressed through the formal holders of political power.

By continuing to use the technique of evaluating interests that were articulated and fully and openly aggregated within the 1946 Peronist governing group, it is found, first, that Peronist political ideology was shared by all the members of the team. This ideological agreement had not been characteristic of previous ruling groups because, though they had started with a common ideological denominator, neverthe-

36

less there were conservative wings, such as those which supported President Ramón Castillo and Minister Enrique Ruiz Guiñazú, and liberal wings, such as the one led by Agustín Justo.

In ideology, both the Peronist governing team of 1946 and the 1951 team presented a solid bloc. There was only one ideology in power in both periods. The difference was that the ideology in 1946 was not clearly defined, but in 1951 an ideological body of doctrine and a value system existed, as did a profusion of party signs, slogans, and symbols. This ideology had the monopoly of political representation, with a growing tendency to subsume any other group, interest, or ideology in Argentina.

Thus the procedures for expressing interests changed during the Perón period. Interests were not articulated or aggregated by one individual, but instead had to pass through a political screening by Perón's immediate subordinates. Simultaneously, new interests were created from the top. In brief, some interests were the same as before and some were new, but the articulators were indeed all new.

In the 1946 team interests which a few years before had not been adequately articulated appear aggregated for the first time (such as those of the labor unions, as discussed in Chapter 11). The interests of some entrepreneurs were also aggregated, but they acted as individuals, not as spokesmen for entrepreneurial interests. The entrepreneurs, through their representative organization, had publicly placed themselves in opposition to the Peronist movement. Those relatively few entrepreneurs who joined the governing Peronist team, therefore, although they were former officials of the Industrial Union, could not represent the entrepreneurs. Eventually, because of the credit facilities granted for expansion, many industrialists shifted from nearly total opposition to a significant degree of adjustment to Peronism.

Using functional analysis, we can easily single out from among the members of the governing team those who undertook the representation of the aggregated interests. The private secretary to the president, Perón's brother-in-law, embodied in himself a conglomorate of new interests—that is, the same old interests, but held by new people—which were articulated under the protection of the Presidency.

This situation might seem to be an example of the primacy of the political realm. It was necessary to have political power in order to be able to subsume the other relatively autonomous national sectors and to integrate with the latter, in apparent confrontation, a collection of newly articulated interests. The example, however, is not really valid:

37

primacy of the political realm exists only if political power is in authoritarian hands. In a weak political regime there is no primacy of the political, only primacy of group interests.

On the other hand, the interests of the great landholders do not appear to be articulated through the formal leaders. In 1951 the minister of agriculture was an agricultural engineer who had had an administrative career in that ministry. Thus we must look elsewhere for an explanation of how landholding interests are articulated. The fact is that the great landholders went through the Perón era unscathed. While the laws freezing rents hurt many, during the Perón regime there was little more than talk about the expropriation of any land, with the exception of the case of the Bemberg group, and that episode had other causes.[4] The clue to this lies in the fact that from 1936 to date all the ministers of agriculture have been members of the Argentine Rural Society, with but very few exceptions: Frondizi's first minister of agriculture and the minister appointed when Alsogaray was brought into the cabinet, as well as the minister named by the Illia regime. The two ministers of agriculture for 1946 and 1951, respectively, belonged to the Rural Society. They were followed by a notary public from the city of Pergamino who was not a member of the Society, but was made a member.

It has been said that the functional system of analysis could provide a clue but, if it were to be followed exclusively, sight of the main objective may be lost. In fact, the large corporations engaged in international trade—represented in the 1941 leadership—came to play a diminished role under the Perón regime. The foundations of IAPI[5] were laid in 1946, and it got under way as the state foreign trade organization. Its functions were the same in 1951, but a new group of private firms gradually took over many of the functions that had been in the hands of the large foreign capital firms before 1946. This fact was brought out by the governmental investigating commissions that went into action after the fall of the Perón regime.

It seems apparent that by continuing with the functional method it would have been impossible to show that these new interests had spokesmen in the Peronist governing teams. The fact becomes apparent, however, when one looks at the concessions and grants awarded to these new interests because they were part of the economic environment built by the Peronist powerholders for their own benefit. These interests were agricultural, exporting, and industrial, and they were

38

closely connected with foreign capital invested in the country. This economic empire-building was carried out after the consolidation of political power, through the facilities afforded by authoritarian control and after excluding competitors.

After the fall of the Perón regime, the interests that had been excluded during that period reappeared according to their natural "weight" and in whatever guises they had been able to survive. From that time on the representation of interests was continued to such an extent that it becomes one of the constants in the membership of the cabinets. There were many corporation lawyers and entrepreneurs with varied economic interests in the 1956 cabinet.

But politicians are not always spokesmen for certain interests, nor do these interests always succeed in imposing their men. Politicians have economic power in their favor and the prestige of connections which helps them, especially at critical moments when parties do not function as selective machinery and necessitate that the teams be made up of nonparty men who have achieved prestige by other means.

By what means, other than economic, can aspiring politicians achieve prestige? Since most are lawyers, it can be achieved by acting as counsellors to corporations. The minority who are technicians can establish industries. What happens in these cases—or at least in many, though not in all—is that once in power they articulate new interests for exclusively personal advantage.

In the 1961 sample there were both party men who monopolized political functions, and a minister of economics with wide corporate experience and with acknowledged prestige among the businessmen who upheld the free competitive economy principle; a minister of public works who was chairman of the board of one of the most important heavy industry corporations financed by Argentine capital; a minister of agriculture who was a rancher and a large landholder; a minister of industry who was an executive and former president of an organization representing management; a minister of commerce who was presiding officer of a grain exporting company; and a minister of communications who had just left a position as an important official of an international communications corporation.

In the team that accompanied Minister of Economics Álvaro Alsogaray twice, once when Frondizi was president and the other after Frondizi fell, and who had ministerial or equivalent rank, one had wide official participation on the boards of local corporations and one was

39

counsel for a very important North American chemical firm. All had experience in mixed capital corporations with only partial national financing.

Between May 1, 1958, and October 12, 1963, eight different ministers held the economics portfolio.[6] Regardless of the change in ministers, in practice their conduct of economic affairs remained substantially the same. Continuing the economic policy initiated at the end of 1955, they followed more or less flexibly the liberal economic orthodoxy and the philosophy of free enterprise. In this respect, anecdotes which may serve to identify the administration of any of them do not matter. What does matter for our purposes is that the well-articulated interests of the free enterprisers, encouraged by the economic attitude of the governing sectors, were sure to be aggregated.

The aggregation of those interests at the political level was in relation to their real "weight," given the stage of economic growth and the then fashionable ideology that Argentina was an insufficiently capitalized country—a pre-capitalist country—and it was necessary to start capitalizing. No others were in a better position to become agents for this process than those who articulated the interests of industry. Capitalization had to take place domestically, and extra capital had to be attracted from the financial markets of the world because of insufficient domestic savings and capital formation. No others were in a better position to sponsor and guarantee the continuity of that policy. Nothing is more convenient than to call, from the seat of political power, upon free-enterprise industrialists and liberal economists, "big names" during the necessary period of capitalization, to share leadership posts.

Thus the curious coincidences that link those who occupied the economic ministries during Frondizi's presidency act as "indicators" of ideological continuity and transcend the unavoidable distrust reflected in the daily press.[7] Even though it may be argued that this stage was essential, that political power was not taken over by powerful economic interests, that the political group in fact co-opted the above mentioned economists, the fact remains that their overwhelming presence was felt at the political level, to the detriment of others. Facts speak for themselves and only on the basis of fact can judgments be made. In this case, the fact is that these powerful interests and the economic ideologies derived from them appeared to be overrepresented, although this might be just a stage in a continuing development process.

40

This type of functional analysis in no sense has critical connotations. Functions should be carried out by those who have a direct involvement in them; it is to be expected that economic functions should be carried out by economic leaders, who are the ones who articulate and aggregate them. Of course, aggregation may be carried out by the leaders themselves or by technocrats, or by a combination of both.

In a country such as Argentina, the problem does not lie in having great corporation men take part in performing economic functions of the government. Argentina is a pre-capitalist country, and the presence of corporation men at the political level may have a significance beyond their performance of a function. What matters is how they do so, that is, up to what point entrepreneurs and economists-industrialists may efficiently carry on this function. Furthermore, it is important to know whether the service they render also benefits the whole community, and whether their behavior is modern, in tune with the requirements of world economy, and is guided by a minimum knowledge of current economic science.

In some countries, businessmen do function in this way. In affluent societies—the United States, the French Fifth Republic, Federal Germany—this identification of the entrepreneurs with political power and a more or less flexible liberal economic philosophy seems to be functionally useful for the whole community, but in others it does not. There is no general rule; each case must be judged individually. Sociological analysis is always highly empirical and, in this case as in others, it must begin by setting aside all dogmas, whether it is the liberal dogma that advocates the unity of the "political team" and the "economic team" or the Marxist dogma that denounces this unity in capitalist societies.

Since sociological analysis is highly empirical, it must necessarily start with the data supplied by reality. In Argentina analysis of this possibility of identification with or exclusion by the various governing political teams permits four generalizations:

a) At each historical juncture (1936–1961) well-articulated interests have been aggregated into the political system, even though this may have been done on a purely personal and direct basis. Whether at the top or at the intermediate administrative levels, one or more direct spokesman for those interests has always had a place on the governing team. This is the rule; an exception may occur when a single party is in power.

b) The make-up of all politico-administrative elites may reflect

41

some of the structural changes that occur, but this is not necessarily so. Given the lack of synchronization of political and social changes, and in view of the coexistence of elements which are not contemporary, reflection at the governing political level of a change in the social structure may be delayed.

c) If the political ruling team aggregates the change, it institutionalizes the same. If it is incapable of reflecting it and the change is very deep or radical, this incapacity will sooner or later bring about the fall of the whole team. This was what happened in 1945 to the groups who wanted to hold on to power, but disregarded the changes taking place in Argentine society.

d) When a great structural change takes place, if a political team adopts and aggregates it, succeeding teams have to do likewise. Insofar as they fail to do so, they may give rise to grave legitimacy crises. This is what happened to the various teams after 1955, when for various reasons they failed to aggregate the interests of organized labor at the political level.

Intermediate Power Levels and Informal Leaders

The politico-administrative guidance of society is conducted not only through the governing team that occupies the highest positions, but also through the intermediate levels of power. These intermediate levels are in the hands of persons who hold a series of key administrative positions that are not so prestigious as the ministerial portfolios, but many times equally, if not more, important.

Within the intermediate levels of power we may place the undersecretaries of all the ministries, the presidential secretariat,[8] some general executive offices, the office of the federal chief of police, the intelligence service, certain autonomous entities, and the Central Bank.[9] They do not countersign executive branch decrees, as the ministers do, but in some cases they prepare the decrees and in others they are directly responsible for enforcing them. In still others they hold the most secret and intimate reins of government.

In the last analysis much depends upon the quality and ability of those at the intermediate levels of power: efficiency, in the case of a technical body; or political and party organization, in the case of a party group; complete identification with the governing elite and the faithful transmission of the commands of the former or, on the other hand, the permanent tergiversation of these commands if those on the intermediate level do not interpret them correctly or oppose them.

In short, those at the intermediate levels of power determine the average quality of the whole governing team, and they, more than the figure-heads and well-known personages so much in evidence, are the true depositaries of the decisions to be taken. Whether a minister can routinely sign anything presented for his signature or feels he must delay the conduct of business depends on his assessment of the loyalty and faithfulness of those at the intermediate levels of power. On those at the intermediate levels depends the internal climate which surrounds the working of the government, influences the soundness of the objectives, or fosters the appearance of cliques and intrigues and the spread of sordid interests. It is on them that the building up of unity in the government depends. Conversely, such unity is broken up by the investigations conducted by those at the intermediate level, to which the persons, acts, and even the opinions of the members of the team are subjected.

Presumably Gaetano Mosca was referring to both levels when he spoke of the "political class." The term is improper because it introduces the "class" element, which belongs only to social stratification. In any case, it is true that there is always a "political team." The political team is made up of the politico-administrative elite and administrators of the intermediate levels of power. According to the hypothesis of the Italian classic, the formulation of each "political team" should correspond to a "political formula," that is, to a new base of legitimacy, which in some cases may mean a slight alteration of the one used by the preceding political team.

Passing from hypothesis to facts and applying the hypothesis to events in Argentina, it may be possible to find a correlation between hypothesis and facts, but another interesting aspect is that in Argentina this correlation coincides with a third element: the role played by informal leaders in the constitution and consolidation of the intermediate levels of power. Two relevant cases could be pointed out in the 1936–1961 period, and if the analysis were extended to 1964, an extra one would be added.

Formal leaders are those who occupy official positions, such as members of the cabinet or presiding officers of the Lower House of Congress. It can be said, then, that Eva Perón's leadership was informal, since she did not hold any government post that could be considered equivalent to her influence. But from the point of view that now in-

43

terests us, without considering other roles she may have played, her function consisted in determining who would occupy the intermediate levels of power in her husband's administration.

Needless to say, hers was not an explicit function nor one that was rationally determined. It arose from events, from the performance of her duties viewed in historic perspective. In this sense, as will be shown later, it was the first of the three cases of informal leadership within the period under study which had the task of "putting together" the intermediate levels of power. It would be interesting to know whether these three cases indicate the beginning of a constant factor to be considered within the functioning of the political system.

Perón's wife became a screening agent for many of the possible contacts of the chief of state and a channel for modifying and adapting some of the important decisions taken by official organizations. But for our purpose here her function was that of determining who were to make up the confidential staff that was to be with the president throughout his two terms. The incorporation or exclusion of individuals always depended on the personal attraction or revulsion they might exercise on Eva Perón, who had undertaken the task of selecting them, on the basis of a very strong intuition and always resulting from considerations of an emotional nature.

The unofficial leadership of Eva Perón tended to separate the techno-administrative government functions from those intrinsically political. Leaving aside the former, the informal leader came to monopolize the latter. Relying completely on the above mentioned criteria for acceptance and rejection, rewards and punishments, she chose the higher administrative cadres. She eliminated many of the original leaders—some of the labor leaders and almost all of the former members of the Radical Party who had joined Perón—and replaced them with more obscure figures raised from the party bureaucracy. But she always operated through pre-existing groups and within the options that might arise within those groups.

Next, she concentrated her attention upon those occupying the intermediate levels of power who, because of the increasing personalization of the regime, found their roles reduced to that of "channels for the transmission of orders." Eva Perón did not appoint the technocrats, for they were beyond her scope; but even the technocrats had to have her approval to function as such. To all who had to be "transmitters of orders," the unofficial leader applied a basic criterion for selection: first the degree of loyalty must be ascertained and must be guar-

44

anteed in some fashion. Such loyalty had to be twofold, for ultimately it had to be strictly and permanently given to Perón himself, but at first it had to belong directly and personally to Eva Perón.

By means of an emotional rapport, the wife of the president selected personnel without reference to the technical, moral, or intellectual qualities of the candidate. In this way the political leadership of Eva Perón became the example closest to the ideal type of "charismatic domination" which had been seen in Argentina for a long time. I say only close to charismatic domination since it was exercised within an administrative framework of a rational type. This type of domination, exercised within the framework of a bourgeois economy, took form partially outside the traditional guidelines, since it incorporated certain aspects of maecenaship, offering both salaries according to impersonal bureaucratic standards and the advantages of a sinecure. As indicated by Max Weber, the sinecure was additional and somewhat contingent, as seems customary in the case of these charismatic leaders.[10]

By creating a twofold set of loyalties, Eva Perón strengthened her husband's power over the intermediate levels of power, thus creating a solid sense of cohesion in the governing team. Therefore, whether they liked it or not, both the political elite and those at the intermediate levels had to accept the situation and by this means were united by a "solidarity" and homogenization of groups that was imposed rather than freely accepted.

That this leader had imposed the principle of "reverse selection" again raises the question of whether the criteria she used were or were not nonrational, since there is the possibility that the criteria were logical and coherent. This depends on the objectives sought: if it was only the reinforcement of personal leadership, it was natural to reduce the power of those who shared the responsibilities of government and might one day oppose the will of the chief of state.

It is impossible to ascertain all this from the facts and the documents, and there is only a slight chance of obtaining true answers from those who took part in the events. Since it is impossible in this case to apply with a minimum of certitude the techniques of investigation employed by the social sciences, attention should be directed to the observable facts, to the continuity of behavior, and to the few available opinions of those well-qualified to judge, which seem to uphold these conclusions.[11]

Rogelio Frigerio, the other informal leader who selected holders of the intermediate levels of power during the Frondizi regime, did hold

45

an official position: in 1958 he was presidential assistant for economic and social affairs. While his personal influence suffered ups and downs because of the changing politico-military situation, he reappeared as an informal leader in the last twelve months before the fall of President Frondizi. Aside from having oriented part of Frondizi's economic policy with complete public support from the president, Frigerio had another role relevant to this study. The role was that of selecting the holders of the intermediate levels of power (at least those holders who were identified with Frondizi and who stayed with him until after his fall). The role was the same as that of Eva Perón, but his method of selection was radically different.

Both created the system of twofold loyalties which were not mutually exclusive but rather reinforced each other. Impersonal loyalty to the governing regime and personal loyalty toward both the president and the informal leader were required. This system of loyalties, functionally important in establishing the government, was reinforced at the intermediate levels of power: undersecretaries, private secretaries, general bureaus, and many of the offices considered to be key ones for the conduct of economic policy.

The ministers, on the other hand, might be named for different reasons, which could be technical or meant to satisfy the demands of some power sectors. However, there was a great loophole: the control of those involved in intelligence work, who remained outside the team thus structured. Frigerio played a decisive role in selecting the team that directly supported the President; that is to say, within the various succeeding teams and cabinets, Frondizi always worked with a "basic team"—sometimes in the majority, sometimes in the minority, at times minimal.

Within the three classical types of domination, that of 1958 came to be identified as the one most truly exemplifying "rational domination" within the categories established by Weber. Based on a normative order it functioned as a double bureaucracy. It was undoubtedly a state bureaucracy, but at the same time it was structured according to bureaucratic order and rank for the purposes of the internal life of the president's supporting team.

The "group bureaucracy" was then organized on a concrete ideological base: singleness of mind as to objectives, means, and the stages indispensable to the promotion of a certain policy and very close interaction and community of interests. It differed from the first type in that, while the rewards continued, it did not have the corresponding

46

punishments which Eva Perón employed. Rewards usually consisted of promotions and support for advancing the *cursus honorum* of the bureaucratic personnel subject to the double play of loyalties. At the same time the rewards and promotions were subject to the eventuality that once the informal leader fell or was dismissed the whole group would fall together.

In this type of group bureaucracy it was accepted that rules would be followed for judging and evaluating beforehand the qualifications of the personnel to be selected, for setting bureaucratic standards of conduct, and for insuring impersonality. The possibility of the fall or dismissal of each member of the team was foreseen and no resistance was offered to this.

Arturo Illia, standard bearer of the People's Radical Party and winner of the presidential election of July, 1963, provided Argentina with the third consecutive case of a political regime that structured its intermediate levels around a twofold system of loyalties: loyalty to the regime and loyalty to the party from which it arose. In this case the president of the party had taken on the role of the informal leader who assembles the political teams. He played an important part in the final makeup of the intermediate levels, though he lacked any official position.

The interesting fact in this case is that again it seems specific criteria for selection have come into play. They will not be those employed by the charismatic leadership of Eva Perón, nor will they be as rational and authoritative as in the second case. The standard seems rather to be based on long-term party involvement. In fact, it would seem that devotion to party solidarity when occupying important posts in the party structure is the most important qualificaion for the advancement of the official. Continuance of that solidarity and also belonging to certain inner circles of party life brings this instance of selective criteria close to some of those presented by Weber in his classic model of "traditional domination."

Notes

1. Gaetano Mosca, *Elementi di scienza politica*, (Turin, 1923,) 2nd part, Chapter I, where he refers to the "residual powers" of the former governing classes. See also Wilfred Pareto, *Tratatto di sociologia generale*, Barbera, 2nd ed., (Florence, 1923) Vol. III, pp. 2026–2029. See his theory of the "circulation of the elites" and the idea of "history as the cemetery of the aristocracies."

2. "Introduction: A Functional Approach to Comparative Politics," in Gabriel A. Almond and James S. Coleman (Eds.), *The Politics of the Developing Areas*, (Princeton, N.J.: Princeton University Press, 1960), 3–64. Professor Almond identifies four input functions of a political system: political socialization and recruitment, interest articulation, interest aggregation, and political communication.

3. The Argentine minister of the interior should not be confused with the American secretary of the interior; the former is strictly a political figure who, among other things, oversees the organization of elections and is directly in charge of the federal police. C.A.A.

4. The "Bemberg group" is, or used to be, a conglomerate with widely diversified investments in Argentina, mostly in commerce and international trade. Perón actually expropriated lands owned by it. C.A.A.

5. The IAPI, which could be translated as Argentine Institute for the Promotion of Trade, was an organization created by the Peronist regime for the purpose of controlling the activities of importers and exporters. It had authority to issue permits without which merchandise could not be cleared; although its declared aim was to supervise, attempts were made to convert it into an import-export monopoly. C.A.A.

6. They were Emilio Donato del Carril, Alvaro Alsogaray, Roberto T. Alemann, Carlos S. Coll Benegas, Jorge Wehbe, Federico Pinedo, again Alsogaray, Eustaquio Méndez Delfíno and José Alfredo Martínez de Hoz.

7. I am grateful to newspaperman Horacio Daniel Rodríguez for the information given on the makeup of the cabinets from 1958 to 1962, and especially for his study of some curious professional and commercial coincidences, among the succeeding members of those cabinets. Part of the material was published under his name in *Vea y lea*, No. 410, Buenos Aires, April, 1963.

8. The secretariat of the Argentine Presidency could be considered similar to the Executive Office of the United States Presidency. C.A.A.

9. The Argentine Central Bank has many of the powers held in the United States by the Federal Reserve Board and the Federal Reserve Bank System. C.A.A.

10. See the classical "domination" typology formulated by Max Weber, in the Spanish translation, *Economía y sociedad*, 1st part (theory of social organization), (Mexico, Fondo de Cultura Económica, 1944), Vol. I. Max Weber distinguishes three basic types of domination: a) rational, or bureaucratic and in accordance with impersonal norms; b) traditional, based on the sanctity of tradition, on respect for tradition, and for traditional authority for the sake of tradition itself; c) charismatic, or produced by leaders whose characteristics are very special.

11. On the role of the intermediate levels of power as order transmission channels, see Juan Perón, *Conducción política*, his courses taught at the Escuela Superior Peronista, (Buenos Aires, Consejo Superior Peronista, 1951).

3. THE ARMED FORCES—PART ONE

The Armed Forces and the Institutional Framework

IT WOULD be absurd to study the role of the armed forces in Argentina solely within the official normative framework, partly because recent experience has shown that the letter of the law establishing the supremacy of the civil government is inoperative and partly because the Argentine case is not isolated. In some countries, the responsibilities of world leadership force the military to take extreme precautions. In many underdeveloped societies, however, only the armed forces can be said to be truly modern institutions with a rational structure. The fact is that in both types of countries the role of the military exceeds the limits fixed by constitutions and regulations.

The intervention of the military in government and in civilian affairs is a widespread contemporary phenomenon. What interests this writer is the type of intervention undertaken by military men and in what way and for what reasons they intervene. Today sociologists and political scientists of widely varying orientations are deeply interested in this subject.[1] Consequently, we will analyze an inversion of the usual order—the normality of the abnormal. What is truly anomalous, however, is that military intervention should occur just when an ideology opposing it seems to be in effect. This study will try to view the intervention of the military as it appears in Argentina.

Some typologies have been set up to cover the various aspects that military activity may take vis-à-vis the civilian authority.[2] The extreme positions those typologies include have not been recorded in Argentina. In fact, in the institutional history of the country there is not even one instance of "militarism," meaning by this term a historical period during which the military, being in control of all the resources of command, has used them to foster a warlike spirit in the population, with a view to future conquests, as was the case in Sparta and in Paraguay

49

under the López family.[3] Nor have there been cases of "praetorianism" in Argentina. "Praetorianism" is the system imposed by the Roman legions when, having deposed one government after another, finally only their military chiefs came to hold power.

A third type, which also has not existed in Argentina, would be that of an intimate institutionalized relation between the leaders of a totalitarian state and the armed forces, this joint participation having the exclusive objective of eventual expansion, as was the case in Germany up to the start of World War II.

These three extreme possibilities are excluded and so is a fourth one, that of "Bonapartism," or the case of a charismatic leader who, relying on the armed forces (to which he belongs) succeeds in getting them to legitimate pseudo-democratic procedures that will allow him to reach power or to prolong his exercise of it.

In analyzing Argentine history from 1936 on, however, and setting aside these extreme categories, other levels of military intervention can still be pointed out.

The armed forces have four times exercised official power directly after deposing the existing authorities by force. At the time of the 1943 Revolution, the two men appointed to hold executive power were military men, one from the Army and the other from the Navy. When the Navy man died unexpectedly, the post was filled by an Army general. Some ministries, the Federal Police, and the *intervenciones*[4] in nearly all the provinces were filled by military personnel.

After some time had elapsed and after some military officers were relieved (who had been active only during the beginning of the revolution) almost all the ministerial portfolios and all the provincial *intervenciones* were filled by civilians—professional politicians—who were in agreement with the ideology of the leader of the moment. But up to the end of the Perón period and including the elections with which that period ended, responsibility fell exclusively on the shoulders of the military. In other words, the military as an "institution" had complete charge of the political outcome.

In 1955 there was a confrontation between military factions prior to the takeover of political power. It was not the armed forces that reached power, but only a faction which was opposed to another and to the holders of official authority. In regard to the mechanics of the takeover, the process was quite similar to that of 1943, with the Presidency and Vice-Presidency held by an Army and a Navy man, respec-

50

tively. As in 1943, when the President was removed, another Army officer, not the Vice-President, eventually filled the Presidency.

In 1955, it was the exception to find military men occupying important political posts. These posts were held by civilian political groups having close affinity with the military. Only the major *intervenciones* in the centers of power of the previous regime remained in the hands of the Navy and some provincial *intervenciones* in the hands of the Army.

Until the end of the period the civilians remained in important positions. However, the armed forces, as in 1943, assumed the responsibility of leadership, and they agreed to allow an electoral outcome, as they had before. This electoral outcome was conditioned and limited. It differed from that of 1943 because the Ministry of the Interior— which together with the military was responsible for the return to constitutional government—was in the hands of civilians and party men.

In 1962 the three branches of the armed forces jointly deposed the president, but, apparently worried about ideology, or rather by the requirements of the ideology they invoked, they tried to maintain certain appearances: The executive branch was not taken over completely. The president was a civilian, and almost all the ministers and provincial *interventores* were also civilians. But a restricted cabinet was set up composed of the three ministers of the armed forces, which in the last resort was the depository of the functions of leadership.

The president's role was reduced to that of a symbol of institutional continuity, similar to the role of the president in a parliamentary system. In 1962, for the third time during the period under study, the armed forces collectively undertook to guarantee the change of power through elections. As in 1955, when they exercised a *de facto* right of veto, the military made possible a conditional and limited electoral outcome. Again as in 1943, by taking direct charge of the Ministry of the Interior and of the country's political machinery, they assumed complete charge for the period of transition.

In these three instances of military intervention, the same processes have been accompanied by differing ideological attitudes. Similarities may be seen: (1) in the mechanisms; (2) in the original illusions; (3) in the parceling out of offices among the services; (4) in the working together with friendly civilians; (5) in the final loss of popularity; (6) in the increase of criticism of the government, both from within and from the related civilian groups; (7) in the emergence in the final

51

stage of repeated replacements of military groups; and, finally, (8) in the almost unanimous desire of offering a constitutional change of power in the country.

The difference between these three instances is in the scope of action that changing ideologies have allowed. In 1943 full freedom of action was in accordance with the ideological climate of the times. In 1955, action was justified or explained as unavoidable. In 1962, action was limited by the inhibiting brakes of the constitutionalist ideology that military men thought they were serving. The fourth case is discussed in chapter 13.

The second level of military intervention in decision-making is shown by the intervention that started around the middle of 1959 and lasted until President Frondizi was deposed. During that period the armed forces jointly exercised an "indirect control" over the civilian authorities, but one that was absolute and had the right of veto. The veto was used only on specific subjects, such as national and international policy, but especially for the appointment of key officials.

The two levels of intervention we have pointed out could be called "direct exercise of power" and "absolute indirect exercise, with veto rights." The period from May 1, 1958, until the middle of 1959 belongs to a third level. We might label this as one of "indirect and incomplete" control over the civilian authorities.

During this period the armed forces, which had made possible an electoral transfer of power, remained in control only of those sectors considered essential to them. The control of these sectors by the military could not have been interpreted as interference. At the same time, the military was able to guarantee the continuation in key positions[5] of those senior officials who shared the ideology widely subscribed to among the military establishment. This guarantee went beyond the constitutional provision that makes the president supreme commander of the armed forces.

Both the fourth and the following levels of intervention are minimal forms transcending the institutional forms and are confined to the strictly personal. Starting on June 4, 1943, and lasting until September 1955, a type of relation between Perón and the armed forces, what may be called a community of interests, became institutionalized. The real importance of this community of interests, beyond any formal appearance, was basically of a personal nature.

Perón's personalistic leadership reached all levels of the armed forces, and a solid aggregate of interests was created around him. The same thing happened at the top of the military command with respect to the political group and the leader who guided the country. Out of about a hundred generals of the period, in the opinion of well-informed judges, barely fifteen were both personally and institutionally committed to Perón's doctrines.

During this period the armed forces as an institution were not, strictly speaking, a power. A man who had come out of the armed forces governed the destiny of the country, and thus the military obtained favorable budgetary treatment that allowed increasing and modernizing equipment. But outside the institutional order, personal identification made the armed forces, together with the labor unions, the great pillars on which Peronism rested. In the case of the armed forces this was an implicit function, not an explicit one as in the case of the labor unions.

The fifth level of intervention that may be included within the framework of our analysis is the one that began in 1932 and lasted until 1938. During that period a military man exercised official authority. He had in a way risen from the group that had previously exercised direct power. Without approaching the identification that would occur during the Peronist period, General Justo, a military man who had become president and a president who continued to be a military man, also created a sort of link on a personal level between the seat of political power and the military establishment.

Starting in 1932, General Rodríguez, the minister of war who was called "the man of duty," gave primary importance within the armed forces to a "professional" ideology with absolute disregard of party politics. This ideology served only to hold the armed forces back temporarily, as it neutralized them precisely when democracy was said to be functioning by means of mechanisms that in fact were the most flagrant contradiction of democracy. The repeated violations of democracy perpetrated by civilian groups would finally provoke a change in the professional mentality of the military, which would bear fruit in the period immediately following.

The typology of the relations between the civilian authority and the military authority just outlined leads to the elimination of two possible means of analysis. The first would be that of analyzing the formal civil-military relations as outlined by the constitution and in both civilian legislation and military regulations. This sort of analysis would be feasible in a limited number of countries: in the more developed, "more modern," those having behind them a more complete historical

53

evolution, it would be possible. Those are the countries labeled by one specialist[6] as having a "mature political culture," because, no mattter what political formula prevails, its legitimacy is undeniable, and the resulting legality makes it impossible for the military to have access to power.

In those countries having a "mature political culture," the action of the military is reduced to influencing the civil power. Its influence will be the greater the more critical the situation the country may find itself involved in because of its international influence. But in those mature countries, although the armed forces may influence, there is substantial respect for legal forms. It is only in those countries, therefore, that the analysis of the behavior of the senior officers may be reduced to the terms of the legal regulations.

This is not the case in Argentina, which is a "modern" country, but is not sufficiently developed. Social and political processes (such as the gradual broadening of public opinion) similar to those of the more advanced nations have occurred in Argentina, but its institutional political order has failed to stabilize.

This delay in the growth of political stability is one of the many to which Argentina is subject because of the lack of "synchronization" of the processes of change, and it gives rise to the claim by the British scholar S. E. Finer that "Argentine political culture is low,"[7] though he reminds his readers that the "Argentine case" is anomalous, since by all the indices of development and modernity apparent in Argentina, it should have a more developed political culture.

The second means of analysis that must be discarded because of the relations bewteen the military and civilian authorities is that of considering the armed forces as a pressure group. In Argentina, the armed forces do not act as a pressure group. Pressure groups are ephemeral and their action is directed toward obtaining specific ends. They do not attempt to change the official structure of authority nor to supplant it; they wish only to achieve their immediate concrete objectives. Having accomplished this or having failed to do so, they fall or disappear, or become what they were before, mere interest groups.

In Argentina, the armed forces are a power factor, as they may be in those societies where political culture is "minimal," "low," or simply "less developed" in accordance with the typology already mentioned. The objectives of the power factors are permanent, and so are both their explicit and implicit functions and the interests they embody. Other power factors exist in "politically mature" societies, but

54

what distinguishes the armed forces from the rest is the means by which the permanently articulated interests of the armed forces are aggregated into the system.

Societies with "less political maturity" are not dealing with occasional "pressures" or "influences" but with the fact that the armed forces make the weight of their own points of view felt permanently within the structure of authority. The pressure of their permanent or of their *ad hoc* points of view is exerted either by totally controlling the formal structure of authority, by exercising the right of veto, by becoming a pillar of a Bonapartist civil regime, or simply by supplanting civil authority.

These cases can occur in those states not having reached a "mature" degree of political development. In Argentina, the intervention of the armed forces in political life has always been stimulated by the legitimacy crises that have periodically shaken the country or by occasional power vacuums. One such crisis of legitimacy occurred in 1943, when the country was defenseless (had it not been for the intervention of the military) while one of the grossest falsifications of democracy was about to be perpetrated. Another occurred in 1955 when, under the pretext of respecting democratic forms and expressing the desires of the lower class, the government contemptuously disregarded intermediate groups and institutions. A power vacuum was experienced after the March, 1962, congressional and provincial election.

Thus the assessment of the "Argentine political culture" reveals a vicious circle. It is not possible to ascertain whether the level of political culture is "low" because of repeated interference by the armed forces in the government, or whether such interference arises more or less unavoidably given the type of society that produces it: a society upset by value crises, and split into water-tight compartments, where different sources of legitimacy are upheld simultaneously by contending groups using mutually exclusive arguments.

Recruitment of the Senior Officers

In 1869, President Sarmiento sponsored the law creating the Military College, thus establishing the foundations for the profound transformation that was to take place in the armed forces. Four years later the first cadets were graduated with the degree of second lieutenant. This system replaced that of the original "levy" or the "impressment" of candidates.

Only 15 cadets were graduated in 1880; in 1890 there were 54, and this total remained the same with slight variations until well into the 1920s. This increase reflected an important transition: a replacement of one type of officer by another one, the passage from one type of army to a new one, from "militarism" to "professionalism," from the *condottiere* to the career officer. In 1872 the first military service law was passed; in 1880, the Escuela Superior de Guerra (Higher War College) was created, and in 1882 the law covering promotions in rank which institutionalized the "career" was passed.

The transition from "militarism" to "professionalism"[8] caused a series of transformations: regulation of entrance into the officer corps; a full-time military profession; budget provisions for the payment of salaries, equipment, and maintenance of status; the proliferation of military schools; the creation of objective standards for promotion; and the growth of a specific bureaucracy.

The senior officers included in this study were the product of that new framework. Recruited, accepted, and socialized within a period of intensive "professionalization" they bore the hallmark of the type of education given them and of the German model which—with several adjustments—was established at the beginning of the century. In 1900 a war with Chile seemed unavoidable, and so German instructors were brought into the country to improve the training of young officers. In 1939 when World War II was declared, 17 of the 34 generals born after 1875 had taken further training in the German army and had seen service in some of its regiments.

These senior officers were the product of the very solid training given from the beginning of the century. That type of professional instruction provided the core of a force that guaranteed the predominance of civil authority during the first thirty years of the century. It was the only force of a secular type in a new society that was going through a period of adjustment and still lacking well-consolidated institutions of its own.

In 1900, with the Escuela Superior de Guerra in operation, four of the ten instructors were German (those for tactics, artillery, fortification, and military history). The foreign language studied was French, but after 1905 it was German. In 1906, 33 officers went to Germany for training. In 1908, 13 officers took an examination in German in order to take further training in that country. In 1910, 26 officers took the German examination.

In 1912, 10 of the 36 professors of statistics were German. In 1914, 24 officers were assigned to serve for two years in the German Army. When the contract of the last German professor of the *Escuela Superior de Guerra* was cancelled in 1919, "professionalization" in Argentina had had a clear and undeniable model, a model that had inculcated its values, had taught discipline, and had given an example of subjection to the legal authority.[9] Of course, in the Germany of the Kaiser it was he who interpreted military values.

The generals on active duty in 1943 belonged to the classes graduated from the Military College between 1900 and 1910, which coincides with the height of the influence and prevalence of a professional consciousness. The senior officers in 1936 had been graduated between 1896 and 1904. In contrast, generals on active duty in 1956 had, with only two exceptions, graduated after 1920, that is, at a time when, after the German military defeat in Europe, its influence had decreased.

From the time the Army institutionalized the professional traits of its European model, it was structured as an authoritarian organization (to explain it in sociological terms) capable of imposing undeviating obedience on its members within a rigorously stratified system. Both the system and its members had an abundance of standards and symbols, which both facilitated communication and made the official structure visible.

The normative system in the Army, with some basic values as its core, performs functions of general cohesion and emphasizes the predominance of the senior personnel. Having accepted the norms that establish stratification, there are no conflicts visible at the structural level, and those who hold the highest institutional positions exercise leadership both formally and informally.

The esteem in which an officer is held within his service is known as "prestige." It is one of the elements that contribute to achieving the highest positions within the service, although personal relations and influence occasionally, but infrequently, account for some cases. Official and unofficial standards for promotion require as attributes of prestige the practice of certain archetypal values of the profession. Thus the officer who does not achieve the prestige that enables him to reach preferential positions gradually becomes peripheral and is assigned second level positions, what in military jargon is called "*tagarna*." The total loss of prestige identifies an officer as "burnt," a situation that precedes dismissal or early retirement.[10]

Thus the military leadership of the armed forces is highly structured and always belongs to the highest hierarchical positions in the service. This is why this study will center its attention on the generals who are both the official and the unofficial leaders. Although in certain critical situations lower ranking officers—colonels and lieutenant colonels as regimental chiefs and majors as heads of batallions—may be the ones who control local situations, in the overwhelming majority of the cases the highest hierarchical authority prevails. This study employs a sample made up of all the generals on active duty from 1936 to 1961, taken at five-year intervals.[11] Since 1946, the year the Air Force was created, its generals are included, as well as a sample of two different groups of admirals.[12] Conclusions which may be reached will apply specifically to the highest armed forces level and should not be construed to include the rest of the officer corps in any way.

The Recruitment Bases for the Senior Officers

The general belief is that most of the Argentine generals come from the traditional families of the interior. Nothing could be less correct. Those born in the Buenos Aires metropolitan area vary, according to the graduating class, from 38 to 47 percent. All those born in the "traditional provinces" amount to only 29 percent of the total. A similar percentage is apparent for generals born in the interior of Buenos Aires Province and in La Pampa and Mendoza.

TABLE 3.1

Place of Origin of Generals by Regions and Periods

Birthplace	Generals on Active Duty In:				
Region	1936–41	1946–51	1956–61	Total	% of Total
Buenos Aires (city and environs)	16	42	48	106	42
Entre Ríos, Corrientes	7	17	8	32	13
Córdoba	–	6	10	16	6
Northeast, traditional provinces	5	7	12	24	10
Remainder of the country	14	31	24	69	29
TOTAL	42	103	102	247	100

TABLE 3.2

Senior Officers of the Armed Forces by Service and Birthplace

Birthplace	Chiefs of the Armed Forces: Percentages		
Region	Air Force Generals	Admirals	Army Generals
Buenos Aires (city and environs)	64	67	42
Entre Ríos, Corrientes	7	4	13
Córdoba	1	4	6
Traditional Northeast	6	5	10
Remainder of the country	22	20	29

The percentage of those from the city and province of Buenos Aires is greater in the Air Force and in the Navy. Only in this sense could it be said that the Army, at its highest level, is comparatively more provincial. If the group of generals on active duty and retired at the beginning of World War II is employed as a control group, similar percentages are found: born in the Federal Capital and environs, 50 percent of the generals; in Entre Ríos and Corrientes, 16 percent; born in Córdoba, barely 4 percent; and in the provinces of the Northeast, 13 percent.[13]

Apparently this pattern has prevailed since the first classes graduated from the Military College. In fact, in 1872 when only 58 students were registered at the College, 31 of the 53 scholarship holders were from

TABLE 3.3

Nationality of Parents of the Senior Officers by Periods

Father's Nationality	Generals in Active Service			
	1936–41	1946–51	1956–61	Total Cases
Argentine	24	45	70	139
Italian	5	20	11	36
Spanish	1	10	8	19
Latin American	3	3	2	8
German	1	6	—	7
Various and no data	8	19	11	38
Total	42	103	102	247

the Federal Capital, 5 from Córdoba Province, and 4 from Entre Ríos Province. Today as yesterday generals come basically from an urban milieu, half of them from Buenos Aires and environs.[14]

Let us use a second control group: of the 1958 generals, both those on active duty and those retired, 54 percent were born in the Capital, 11 percent in Entre Ríos and Corrientes, 8 percent in Córdoba, and 6 percent in the Northeast.[15] The figures reflect some structural changes that have taken place in the country. The 1936 and 1941 officers had graduated from the Military College during the last years of the nineteenth century and the beginning of the present one. Five were the sons of Italians who must have come to the country as immigrants at the latest during the first Presidency of Roca.[16] This shows that from its very inception the military establishment was an open group and that recruitment took place as much from the families that had recently settled in the country as from the traditional Creole ones.

Since at that time almost all the cadets were on scholarship, the military career was a channel of upward mobility, even for those coming from the very new middle sectors and the lower-middle class strata. The fact stands out clearly from the figures for the generals in the 1946 and 1951 periods, which cover the Perón regime; as shown by Table 3.3, over half were sons of foreign-born parents. It is very unlikely, not to say impossible, that percentages such as these have occurred anywhere else in the world at the highest military levels, since they indicate that the process of assimilation was very rapid and that recruitment was not restricted to closed sectors or based on military families. These generals—twenty of them the sons of Italians—had been born between 1888 and 1902, and so their parents must necessarily have come as immigrants.

The subsequent increase in the sons of Argentines is logical. That 70 percent of the 1956 and 1961 generals were sons of Argentines is due to the fact that between them and the original immigrants a local generation of parents had grown up. The generals of the last period had entered the Military College between 1916 and 1932. Around the 1920s the immigrant European bourgeoisie had become established and could offer their children other opportunities aside from a military career. It is also interesting to point out that the similarity of percentages for the Army and the Air Force shown in Table 3.4 reappears consistently throughout the study.

There is little data available on the socio-economic level of the families of Army and Air Force generals. Only 33 percent of the dossiers of the Army generals and 45 percent of the dossiers of the Air Force generals of the sample give information on the father's occupation. Table 3.5 has been prepared on the basis of the documentation obtained and of a first simplistic division as to the prestige of various occupations.

TABLE 3.4

Birthplace of Parents of Senior Officers, by Branches of the Service

Nationality	Generals in %	Air Force Generals in %
Argentine	62	68
Italo-Spanish	24	20
German	4	2
Various and no data	10	10

TABLE 3.5

Occupation of the Fathers of the Senior Officers, Classified by Social Class

Assumed Class Level	Occupation	Army Generals	Air Force Generals	Total
Upper Middle Class	Rancher	5	5	10
	Merchant-industrialist	18	10	28
	University professional	12	2	14
	Military	16	4	20
	Executive	1	2	3
	Independent	4	–	4
	Builder	–	1	1
	Idle well-to-do	2	2	4
Dependent Middle Class	Newspaperman	1	–	1
	Photographer	1	1	2
	White Collar Worker	17	4	21
	Farmer	3	–	3
	Retired	1	–	1
Lower Class	Mechanic	1	1	2

From these data it is apparent that 73 percent of the Army and Air Force generals studied come from families belonging to the well-to-do

61

bourgeoisie, 25 percent to the petite bourgeoisie, and only 2 percent to families of working-class origin.

Twenty generals are sons of military men, which is not a very high figure compared to those in European countries. In France, where the officer corps is recruited within a provincial milieu, military families are significantly more important. This is not true in Argentina because of the nature of recruitment, which was open from the beginning to people of immigrant stock[17] and was encouraged by the scholarship system. In some years the scholarships covered almost all the available enrollment.[18]

A typology of the family background will enable us to distinguish different groups of origin:

—— A group of generals born within the traditional families of Buenos Aires,[19] together with another group from traditional military families of senior officers: the sons or grandsons and great-grandsons of officers of equivalent rank.[20] To them is added, at the top of the pyramid, another group related to the Buenos Aires upper class.[21]

—— A group derived from the traditional families of the interior. For this class the army career was indeed a natural channel for upward mobility, together with the legal profession.[22]

—— A third first-generation Argentine group, sons of Italian immigrants.[23]

—— A smaller number of sons of Spanish immigrants; in 1961 the highest figure was that for the grandsons of immigrants, especially of Basque origin.[24]

—— Last, a group of senior officers, sons of Germans.[25]

—— There is only one case of marginality, that of a senior officer born in a Syrian home.

The sample of the Air Force Generals shows:

—— The sons of the traditional families come from the interior.[26] There are also five related to the "Buenos Aires upper class," and only one is the son of a military man.

—— The families from the interior not included in the first group are less numerous than those strictly traditional.

—— Several Air Force generals are the sons of Italian immigrants.[27] This group is equal to that of the sons of Spaniards.

—— The general rule among the Air Force generals in active service in 1961 was the same as that for the Army; they were second-generation Argentines.

—— Those who were marginal because of national family origin were one son of Swedish parents, another of Germans, and a third of Syrians (Abrahim).

Turning from the Air Force to the Navy we find that, in essence, the same categories may be found:

—— A group from the traditional families, mostly from Buenos Aires;[28] some from a military environment (Campos Urquiza); one from the Air Force (Brown), or from the Navy branch itself (Izquierdo Brown). Few admirals are from the traditional families of the interior.[29] The rest is made up of those who within Buenos Aires enjoy a degree of prestige equivalent to that of the upper class.[30]

—— A group that does not appear in the other branches of the service is the one made up of sons of Frenchmen,[31] an interesting anomaly not only with relation to the other branches of the service, but also because French immigrants are a small percentage of the Argentine population.

—— Those with Italian immigrant origins are as numerous as in the previous cases.[32]

TABLE 3.6

Family Background of the Higher Officers of the Armed Forces

	Army Generals		Air Force Gen.		Admirals		Total	
	Cases	%	Cases	%	Cases	%	Cases	%
Buenos Aires traditional families. The same from the interior, Creole families	56	23	15	21	20	25	91	23
Immigrant Italian background	68	28	21	30	13	17	102	26
German and Saxon immigrant background	23	9	5	7	10	13	38	9
Families of French background	8	3	5	7	14	18	27	7
Families of Spanish background and others	92	37	24	35	21	27	137	35
TOTAL	247	100	70	100	78	100	395	100

—— The same is true of the sons of Spaniards, although as a reflection of structural changes and of the passing of the generations, the admirals are second-generation Argentine, coming from Italo-Spanish groups. As is true of the generals from Spanish families, the most numerous group is made up of descendants of Basques.[33]

—— Another variant with reference to the original family groups: those of English origin predominate[34] over those of German origin. There is no record of a senior officer born from a Syrian family.

Table 3.6 summarizes the family background of senior Army, Navy, and Air Force officers, according to paternal affiliation.

Notes

1. Morris Janowitz, *Sociology and the Military Establishment* (New York: Russell Sage Foundation, 1959), John J. Johnson, *The Role of the Military in Underdeveloped Countries* (Princeton, N.J.: Princeton University Press, 1962). See also the special issue of the *Revue française de sociologie*, Vol. II, No. 2 ("Guerre-societé-armée"), etc., April-June, 1961.

2. See especially, G. Germani and K. Silvert, "Politics, Social Structure and Military Intervention in Latin America," *Archives européennes de sociologie*, Vol. II, No. 1, 1961; and Lieutenant General Benjamin Rattenbach, "El sector militar de la sociedad," *La Nación* (Buenos Aires), November 24, 1963.

3. The text refers to the militaristic family which governed Paraguay in the nineteenth century. Francisco Solano López led his country to war with Argentina, Brazil, and Uruguay at the same time; as a result, his country suffered almost total destruction and its male population was decimated. C.A.A.

4. See p. 9. C.A.A.

5. Such as direct command of troops, military districts, bases, direction of the main cantonments, *et al.* C.A.A.

6. S. E. Finer, *The Man on Horseback. The Role of the Military in Politics* (London, Pall Mall Press, 1962). The British scholar thinks he can distinguish four levels of political culture. In the countries with a "mature" political culture, legitimacy is unquestioned and is consubstantial with legality. No one questions the principles which constitute the political foundation. The resulting government is wholly civilian, and the armed forces act only within their specific field and within the institutional channels. In the countries with a "developed" political culture—the second level —the principle of legitimacy is very important and is based substantially on the legal order. The level of intervention of the armed forces in internal politics is limited, but it may go beyond constitutional provisions through strategic programs or problems resulting from the cold war. In countries with a "low" political culture (the author includes Argentina, together with Brazil, Spain, and Portugal, here), "legitimacy" is fluid and while the

principles of "legality" are argued, no group seems ready to commit itself in defense of their application. The resulting government is cyclical, sometimes military, sometimes civilian, because the armed forces can overthrow civilian governments without encountering significant resistance. Finally, the author believes there are countries with "minimal" political culture, where the question of legitimacy does not even arise, let alone that of legality, and where military dictatorships or dictatorships by groups controlling the exercise of force are, in the light of historic experience, the "normal" form of government.

7. *Ibid.* But the British specialist explains that the case of Argentina is exceptional in the light of its "parameters."

8. For the concept of "militarism" as opposed to "professionalism," as well as to understand at what moment the change from one type of army to the other occurs, see Edwin Lieuwen, *Arms and Politics in Latin America,* revised edition (New York: Frederick A. Praeger, 1961).

9. Extracted from the annual reports of the Escuela Superior de Guerra.

10. Virgilio R. Beltrán, "El ejército, ¿Grupo de presión?" (Unpublished research paper presented to the seminar on pressure groups, held at the Institute of Sociology of the School of Philosophy and Letters, University of Buenos Aires, in 1963). The information contained in this paper is widely used in this chapter.

11. All the analyses employed in this and the following chapter on the elements determining the status of the senior officers and their type of career come from the data taken directly from their individual files. The data was supplied by the personnel bureaus of the Army and Air Force ministries, at the author's request, and through the good offices of the then Ministers, General Fraga and Air Force General Abrahim, to whom profound gratitude is expressed here.

12. The source of information for the Navy officers is different: The information gathered on "prestigious" admirals has been analyzed and processed; that is, those whose biographies appeared in the various editions of *Quién es quién en la Argentina* (Buenos Aires: Editorial Kraft, various years). The author is grateful to the director of personnel of the Ministry of the Navy, Navy Captain J. C. González Llanos, for his generous assistance.

13. *Quién es quién en la Argentina,* 1st Edition (Buenos Aires: Editorial Kraft, 1939).

14. Extracted from the annual reports of the Colegio Militar.

15. *Quién es quién en la Argentina,* 7th edition (Buenos Aires: Editorial Kraft, 1959).

16. Julio A. Roca served from 1880 to 1886 and from 1898 to 1904. C.A.A.

17. The decrease in the number of "military families" seems to be a universal phenomenon. In France, where there were believed to be over "several thousand" such families around the middle of the last century, they have decreased to a few hundred at present; see R. Girardet, *La societé militaire dans la France contemporaine* (Paris: Plon, 1953). Unfortunately there are no data on any Latin American army which might serve

as a frame of reference. In Argentina there is only one case—that of a recent service minister—whose family has had 17 Army officers.

18. According to the annual reports of the Colegio Militar, which brought this information together, in the 1920s and 1930s the children of military men accounted for from 10 to 20 percent of the total number of graduates. In the Escuela Naval in a graduating class of 80 taken as sample and corresponding to present day Navy Captains, 8 were sons of Navy men, 4 of whom were noncommissioned officers. According to the study carried out by the Bureau of Educational Institutes of the Air Force Ministry, most of the fathers of cadets in the Air Force School are white collar workers; in other words, the recruitment is currently from the lower-middle class.

19. Guido y Lavalle, Huergo, de Vedia y Mitre, Solanas Pacheco, Lagos.

20. Arana, Rawson (there are two Rawsons in the lists, also two Generals Fraga, two Generals Toranzo Montero, sons of the General, and so on).

21. Reynolds, de Biedma, Pizarro Jones, Merediz.

22. Martínez Pita, Molina, Espíndola, Calderón, Vargas Belmonte, Velazco, Lucero, Zerda, Nazar, Videla Balaguer, Cornejo, Alvarado, Sosa, Zenarruza, Ardanaz, Sueldo, Salas Martínez.

23. Pistarini, Rocco, Monferini, Tonazzi, Bassi, Rossi, Manni, Guglielmone, Checchi, Martini, Raggio, Bertollo, Perazzo, Baldasarre, Polero, Colombo, Cuaranta, D'Andrea, Lorio, Piantamura, Picca, Túrola.

24. Onganía, Elizondo, Labayrú, Martijena.

25. von der Becke, Trotz, Rattenbach, Streich, Rottgardt, Wirth.

26. Alsina, Llerena, de la Colina, Vélez, Olmedo, Vedoya.

27. Piccione, Fabbri, Parodi, Civati, Bernasconi, Romanelli, Bertoglio.

28. Malbrán, Rosas, Saénz, Ugarriza, Videla.

29. Rojas, Toranzo Calderón.

30. Vernengo Lima, Castro, Lynch, Merlo Flores, Pérez del Cerro, Rivero de Olazábal, Villanueva, Zuloaga.

31. Daireaux, Domecq, two Lajous, Martín, Renard, Vincendau, Bonnet, Brunet, Clement, Chretien, Lestrade, Maleville.

32. Fincatti, Repetto, Scasso, Storni, Bianchi, Basso, .Chierasco, Garzoni, Macchiavelli, Olivieri, Panzarini, Tozzini.

33. Beascoechea, Guisasola, Arambarri, Baroja, Estevarena, Estévez, Ibarborde, Jáuregui.

34. Two Fliess, Stewart, Frasch, McLean, etc.

4. THE ARMED FORCES—PART TWO

Specific Socialization

THE CADET—the future general—entered the armed forces between the ages of 15 and 19, after taking an entrance examination. In all cases entrance to the Military College was subject to the candidate's having passed examinations in algebra, geometry, geography, biological sciences, ancient and medieval history, drawing, and French. The degree of academic knowledge depended on the previous preparation of the cadet, who generally received instruction at a specialized academy, regardless of the formal schooling completed.

TABLE 4.1

Level of Schooling Prior to Entrance to the Military
College in Percentages

Schooling Prior to Entrance	Generals in Active Service		
Last Year of Study	1936–41	1946–51	1956–61
Some university studies or senior high school	60	59	31
Some junior high school	28	37	61
Last two grades of elementary school	12	4	8

From the foregoing it is apparent that the levels of previous schooling of generals in active service in the first two periods of the sample were higher than that for the last one. The theory that the military government of 1930 wanted to broaden the recruitment base by lowering the entrance requirement levels is not proved.

During those same years, from 1927 to 1934, recruitment was mostly from among those who had finished the first or second year at an academic high school. After that and up to the present, the normal pro-

67

cedure has been for the cadet to enter the Military College after having completed the fourth year of high school.

It is interesting to note the variance in previous education among the senior officers in 1936, or those who had entered the College during the first years of the century. While some had obtained normal school degrees, others had finished only the fifth grade in elementary school.[1] A comparative analysis of the levels of previous schooling of the senior officers of the Army and Air Force appears in Table 4.2.

TABLE 4.2

Previous Levels of Schooling at Time of Entrance,
by Branch of Service, in Percentages

Levels of Previous Schooling	Army Generals	Air Force Generals
Some University or senior high school	47	40
Some junior high school	46	50
Last two grades of elementary school	7	10

Early entrance into the Military College is beneficial from the professional point of view because it maximizes the process of specific socialization within the military order and values. But it may be a handicap when the former cadet, now a general, has to interact with the other civilian governing groups. Having entered early, after one or two years of high school, he has had less time to build close bonds of friendship with those who (after the passage of time) might come to occupy responsible positions in the economic, political, or intellectual leadership of the country.

It is difficult to ascertain what percentage of the applicants for admission to the Military College was admitted in each instance. Everything would lead us to suppose that, in selecting among the applicants, universal criteria were applied (such as superior performance in the entrance examination) together with particular criteria with respect to the sons of military personnel. But the number of candidates who applied each year seems to have varied, due, in part, to variations in the popularity of the military in the country. Table 4.3 shows some sample years.[2]

These figures need to be explained. The number of candidates in 1956 was almost the same as in 1920; however, the number of students who could have been candidates in those two years was extremely different. The second consideration is that the opportunities for success

68

TABLE 4.3

Number of Candidates to Military College by Year

Year	Total Number of Candidates
1920	344
1930	557
1932	688
1933	215
1941	385
1943	1,877
1946	389
1947	799
1952	460
1955	370
1956	354
1961	771

and promotion in other fields were much more diversified in 1956 than in 1920. The third factor is that in the 1950s the Air Force School was already in existence and attracted many candidates with aviational and technical vocations who had formerly entered the Military College.

The variable of the fluctuating popularity of the armed forces is still apparent, nevertheless, and these figures for the candidates may be valid as indices. Note the increase of candidates during the early days of the military and civilian government led by General Uriburu. On the other hand, the number of candidates decreased in 1933 after the erosion of the popularity of the government.

On the eve of the Revolution in 1943 the highest figure for applicants yet known at the Military College was registered. At the beginning of Perón's presidential term in 1947 the totals were high in relation to the years before and after. Around 1955 and 1956, in the midst of the institutional conflicts the Army was undergoing, the total decreased significantly.

Aside from the objective requirements of recruitment, the continuance of the cadet's career depends upon two factors: his finding that the military career satisfies his vocation and whether the climate existing in the country is favorable or unfavorable to the military group. This too can be ascertained by studying the total number of second lieutenants graduated after four years of study.

During the dominance of Peronism and up to 1952, over 200 second

69

lieutenants were graduated each year. But in some cases the curriculum was made easier, the courses being accelerated to the detriment of professional qualifications. From that time on a decrease in the figures commences, becomes more pronounced in 1959, with only 80 second lieutenants, and reaches its low point in 1960, with only 68 second lieutenants. These were the cadets who had entered from 1956 on, who had personally experienced the deterioration of popularity of the armed forces.

Promotions during a military career are made on the basis of a series of strict standards. But besides the official standards, there are also unofficial ones. One of these is that in order to be promoted to general, the individual first must complete higher studies. These studies may be either those of the Escuela Superior de Guerra, which make the military man a general staff officer, or those of the Escuela Superior Técnica, which qualify him as a military engineer.

TABLE 4.4

Generals and Higher Studies

| | Generals in Active Service in | | | | | |
Higher Studies	1936	1941	1946	1951	1956	1961
Escuela Superior de Guerra	18	27	36	53	32	28
Escuela Superior Técnica	–	1	1	12	6	18
Special Courses	–	–	–	4	5	6
Without Higher Studies	1	4	4	13	14	8
Total	19	32	41	82	57	60

Thus, 90 percent of the generals in active service in 1936 and in 1941 were staff officers or military engineers. That percentage is reduced to 82 percent of the generals of the Perón period, and to 71 percent of the generals in active service after the Revolution of 1955.

It is clear that the unofficial requirement of higher studies was observed more during the first two sample years than in the following ones. The generals in active service in 1936 and in 1941 had experienced solid professional training, based on the pattern set by German instructors at the beginning of the century. In 1946 and in 1951, however, "particularist" criteria began to diminish the institutionalization of standards in the services. Friendships and enmities took on a larger role in promotions, as did loyalty toward or incompatibility with the

70

established regime. Beyond the official standards of the service, those factors either made easier the promotion of those who did not meet all requirements or speeded them into retirement.

After the Perón period particularism continued, but in reference to an opposite political allegiance. After the Revolution many officers were reinstated and "revolutionary merits," and especially "1951 pre-revolutionary merits" counted for as much or more as objective qualifications, and officers who before 1955 had been retired because of their anti-Perón activity were promoted and permitted to bypass certain grades. These officers were excused from completing higher studies. Although it is understandable that there were special circumstances at the time, these promotions downgraded the institutional standards of the service, producing tensions that would have visible outward effects in 1962 and 1963.

One change over the years has been the increasing number of military engineers with regard to the total number of officers with higher studies. Graduates from the Escuela Superior Técnica (who before its creation received their training at the University of Buenos Aires) were as follows:

1946	1 out of 41
1951	12 out of 78
1956	6 out of 52
1961	18 out of 54

Thus, in accordance with the latest figures, a third of the generals are military engineers. The change is logical and, while it reflects a passing from the strictly military to the technical at the highest level, it also reflects the transformations that have occurred in the functions of the armed forces. Military factories, blast furnaces, steel mills, powder magazines, and the manufacture of synthetic toluene require new specialists.

These entrepreneur-generals or military entrepreneurs with ambivalent roles and ambivalent attitudes towards their status are the ones who can introduce a change of outlook into the armed forces. If it is assumed that the armed forces are an essential instrument for the expression of national cohesion, that the officers as a whole are the depositaries of the patriotic legacy of the preceding generations, and that the commanders identify the institutional continuity of the Army with the historical continuity of the nation, then only the technical-engineers and the engineer-technicians can make the armed forces equal to

71

the solution of the immediate problems of the society in which they live.

Few of the senior officers in the sample years received specialized training abroad. Practically none of those in active service in the sample years 1936, 1941, and 1946 did so. However, three of those in the 1951 sample had been trained abroad, one in Germany and the other two in France, as were two of the generals in active service in 1956, one in Germany (he was later to be Army minister), and the other in the United States. The percentage of those who were trained abroad is not too significant, perhaps because it represents those in power in the intermediate period. Before 1936, 12 of the 44 senior officers from a sample studied had gone through general staff school abroad at a time when the Imperial German Army was considered the great model. At the present time the percentage of senior officers taking special training and finishing their professional studies abroad is again above that shown by the samples. But since 1945 the United States military establishment has replaced the German one as a model.

Out of the 70 generals who make up the Air Force sample, only 4 had had higher training abroad, all in the United States; two graduated as aeronautical engineers, one received a Bachelor of Science degree, and the other specialized in flying. The percentage is very low, particularly if we consider the high degree of specialized technical training required by the Air Force that cannot be obtained in Argentina.

To a greater or lesser degree some Argentine airmen have entered the air forces of other countries for the purpose of receiving training to make up for deficiencies in Argentine training. In 1959 there were 31 commanding Air Force generals: 1 had been in the German air force, 2 in that of France, 5 had taken a short special training course in Spain, 1 had studied in Italy from 1931 to 1935, and 2 had been in the British RAF. The diversity in the models is understandable: the Argentine Air Force is a new service which separated from the Army in 1946, and the special training of pilots could be accomplished only through the opportunities offered by countries with a more advanced technology.

Contrary to what is commonly supposed, senior naval officers did not train in Great Britain. The British navy has been a remote model, but technically not the immediate model of Argentina's. From the British navy not only Argentina's but all the navies of any importance at the beginning of the century, including the American, adopted the British naval code of honor, a specific value system, and a substantial respect for ethical and official standards of conduct which would later come to be identified with navy status.

Argentine Navy personnel, however, had to seek specialized training in other countries. The British navy has opened the doors of its academies only to candidates from the other British Commonwealth nations. In the 1939 sample, only 5 of the 26 admirals (some in active service, others retired) had studied abroad, 4 in the United States, where they specialized in submarines and where they remained until the outbreak of World War I, and one in France.

Twenty years later, on the basis of a sample of senior Navy officers both in active service and retired, of 55 admirals, vice-admirals, and rear-admirals only 6 had received their higher studies abroad, in the United States and in Italy, and the countries that served as models depended on the navy equipment used in Argentina and the source of the ships and weapons.

The lowest percentages of Naval officers studying abroad are found, as in the other branches of the service, in the intermediate periods. Special training was made difficult both by the world war and by the relative isolationism through which Argentina passed at the war's end. At present the percentage of Navy men, particularly submarine and marine officers, receiving specialized training in the United States, is high.

Subsequent Career of Senior Officers

On the basis of the sample, it appears that in recent years the opportunities to reach the highest rank in the armed forces have come earlier in an officer's life. Considering the minimum age in each of the periods analyzed, it was possible to become a general at:

54 in 1936
52 in 1941
51 in 1946
48 in 1951
46 in 1956
44 in 1961

During this quarter of a century the minimum time required to reach the highest rank in the service had been reduced by ten years. The same is true of the next higher grade, general of division and of the mini-

73

mum age of generals of the Army. Of course, in the Argentine Army the latter rank is not normally attained; this grade is exceptional. Looking at the ages of the generals of the Army in the sample years, one finds:

1936—no generals of the Army
1941—same as 1936
1946—the general of the Army was 57 years old
1951—the general of the Army had reached the rank at 61
1956—at 55. The oldest was 60
1961—at 51

The general of the Army in 1961 was the same age as had been required a quarter of a century earlier to reach the rank of general. This "rejuvenation" of the higher echelons, which seemed to impair professionalization, is to be understood in the light of the changes in warfare which require younger senior officers capable of assimilating the new techniques. In any case, this premature "rejuvenation" becomes a drawback when the senior officer is retired and must face the civilian world, where he must make his way. In some analyses of military sociology this phenomenon has already been studied: the psychological problems which face the retired individual, the difficulty he finds in channeling his activities and maintaining an economic status corresponding to that he had formerly held.[3]

From the point of view which interests us in this study, however, that officers enter the ranks of the retired in full early maturity usually has implications for politics. It is not true that the rank of general opens the doors to political activity, but the fact that this has happened in some well-known cases, even though in the minority, may give a general the conscious or subconscious expectation of continuing a public career by other than military means.

The generals in our samples who after their retirement went on to occupy posts of political leadership, either as presidents of the republic, ministers, or elected governors, number 39 out of a total of 276, or 14 percent. On the other hand, those who after retirement were appointed ambassadors—a discreet way of rewarding them or of removing them from the political centers—number 19, which means that the embassy "reward" was achieved by only 7 percent of the generals included in the samples. Retired air force generals show even less official participation, both as to political power and diplomatic representation. Of the admirals included in the samples, 13 became ministers of the Navy,

74

2 became vice-presidents of the country, and another one was designated to that office in 1943 but did not have time to occupy it. Of 58 senior Navy officers, only one headed a ministry other than that dealing with his own service, and 7 were appointed ambassadors after their retirement. This is 12 percent of the total, a percentage comparable to that of the Air Force generals.

These indices of official participation may lead us into error. They do not reflect the exceptional relevance of the armed forces in the administration of public life. The indices are valid especially for one purpose: to indicate that the degree of formal participation in power by military leaders has been less than their real and actual influence on basic decisions. Also, because they refer to the highest posts, the indices may distort an appreciation of events, since it is not always at the highest official levels that crucial power is exercised. For example, the armed forces have reserved for themselves key control sectors that have greater significance than any ministerial portfolio.

The Intelligence Service, which has implicit veto power over the appointment of upper- and second-level officials, has always been in the hands of the Army. Without ignoring the many valid reasons that may justify this control—such as the universality of the practice, the professional military training of the specialists in that service, the necessity of having the personnel subject to a strict regime of loyalties and to a solid discipline, the identification of the values of the Army with those of the state independent of any political change, and so forth—the fact is that the armed forces have a virtual monopoly of official intelligence services.

The Federal Police, the second permanent factor in the control of key posts, has always had a military officer at its head, with the single exception of the last Peronist period. It is interesting that for a long period its holder was a Navy man, evidence of the decisive power of this branch of the military.

For these reasons, that a retired senior officer goes to fill a public post is a matter of secondary importance, and the low percentage of participation recorded may lead us on a false trail. In describing individual and isolated facts, the observer may lose sight of the permanently institutionalized relations between the military and the political sector.

More significant than the retirement of an officer who has completed his career is the retirement of those who unexpectedly find their hopes of promotion and their expectations of advancement frustrated,

75

especially when retirement is made en masse and takes place during crises. In these cases, the officer may become resentful both against his own institution and against the holders of political power responsible for his being forced into retirement. Because of this resentment, he may become a troublemaker and may undermine military discipline.

Something of this sort happened as a result of the mass retirements that took place in 1951, 1955, and 1962–63. In 1951 the officers who were retired after the abortive revolutionary movement of General Menéndez created strong anti-Perón feelings. The Peronist officers who retired in 1955 followed General Valle in the cruelly repressed attempted coup of June, 1956.[4] Those forcibly retired in 1962 and 1963 all aligned themselves, disregarding ideological differences, with one of the parties that competed for military and political power.

In all these cases those who were involuntarily retired may have had valid reason for resentment, or it may also be that they projected on the community the reasons for their discontent. Be that as it may, the fact remains that the promoters of some localized crises have not been the members of the armed forces in active service, but precisely those officers who had recently been forced into retirement.

Studies of the origins, backgrounds, and family environments of senior military officers justify discarding the idea that there might be a "military caste." This hypothesis is not acceptable in view of the origins of the officers. Should a "military caste" hypothesis be seriously posited, an explanation must be given using a more liberal meaning of "caste," perhaps by exploring the possibility of a status mentality being created in the military itself. To be called a "caste" in the strict sense of the term, the military establishment would have to be totally closed to outside recruitment, or at least recruitment would have to be conducted as a function of the future officer's ascriptive status. The Prussian *Junkers* would fit that category, and so would a good many French officers during the nineteenth century and up to the time of World War II. A caste could have developed in some European armies where a whole family group took on military status and accepted responsibility for carrying on the service.[5]

This is not the case in Argentina; in fact, the situation appears to be the opposite. The Argentine armed forces have always been open groups and have served as channels offering opportunities for upward mobility both to the provincial Creole sectors and to the native-born sons of immigrant parents. The scholarships offered at the Military

76

College, which were especially numerous in the first few years, made higher studies possible for many who could not have afforded them outside the service.

It is a different matter to say that after entering the armed forces, that is, after being recruited from a wide field, a specific status mentality is fostered in the military individual as part of the system of socialization in the services. A boy is taken at a very young age, cast into a specific mould, and taught the belief that a military career, by identifying the individual with the highest degree of patriotism, converts him into a depositary of national values. The military does develop a status mentality, then, in its recruits, as do other professional groups. The military status mentality tends to become identified with "national truth," just as that of intellectuals does with "intelligence and critical reason," and that of businessmen with the economic support of society.

The formation of a specific status mentality varies with the service and with the history of that service within the nation. Hence one service may show greater cohesiveness than another, one may give greater emphasis to its values, may be more cautious and prudent in making public the tensions between its members, and may have more institutionalized group norms. This is true of the Argentine Navy.

The problem of cohesiveness has been especially acute in recent years among the Air Force officers. The generals included in the sample had graduated from the Military College and not from a specific school. In 1946, when the new branch of the service was established, the officers were recruited from various sources. Almost all came from the Army, as has been indicated above, but some came from the Navy Air Force, and some (like three generals in the sample) from the noncommissioned officers who were allowed to enter the officer corps. Thus the Air Force did not have time to set up unofficial standards nor to develop homogeneity within its ranks. The critical period of this service began in 1951, almost at the time it was established, and culminated in 1955. This critical period affected the generals in the sample, who, in addition to the original ambivalence of their roles at the Military College, where they were as military as the cavalry and as civilian as technicians, experienced an institutional split in a service that had just been born.

In the Navy the situation was different. It is much more cohesive and institutionalized to such a degree that in the midst of the upheaval caused by the division of almost all the groups in the country, it preserved its ranks and its value system intact. Everything indicates that the type of values inculcated into the cadet from the moment he passed his entrance examination accounts for the cohesion of the Navy. Beyond his professional training, the Navy cadet was taught a code of honor, to "handle ships, lead men, and defend the country," to adjust his life to an ethical code, and to observe strict loyalty to his branch of the service. The Army cadet, in contrast, was being prepared for barracks life within a garrison and to settle in some place in the interior of the country.

Loyalty to the Army is a product of military discipline and the hierarchical position of the individual, while in the Navy it is an act freely consented to, to the extent that a value taught as a belief is freely consented to. The differences in the basic military socialization of Army and Navy recruits have positive and negative effects which reveal themselves as officers advance in their careers.

The life of the Army man will be spent in the garrisons of the interior of the country and there he will have ready access to civilian groups. The smaller the local upper class social group, the more outstanding will be his role and the greater will be his opportunities to interact with the local leaders. Military values and loyalty to his branch of the service, since they are expressed through hierarchical channels, will be reserved for life within the service, that is, for life in the barracks. As the hierarchical order and the authoritarian relations do not exist outside, the Army man will be, particularly in some places in the interior, anxious to enter into dialogue with nonmilitary elites. Transferred to bases located in such provincial towns as Santa Rosa, Curuzú-Cuatiá, or Tandil, he will have to make new friends and enter into new relations, and he will seek contact with the leaders of local society.

The life of the Navy man, on the other hand, is spent on ships and in coastal towns, particularly at the great Navy base of Puerto Belgrano. And while the few who are isolated in Tierra del Fuego, Puerto Madryn, and Mar del Plata are driven, like their colleagues in the Army, to live with civilians, the majority assembled within the bases tend to confine themselves to the Navy "endogroup." Cabins, staterooms, casinos, and bases tend to isolate them from a society they do not always find made to their image and likeness. This isolation is no obstacle from the professional point of view. On the contrary, it strengthens the system of loyalties towards the institution. Thus in times of crisis the Naval service has shown a uniformity of conduct that is unknown in the Army.

The comradeship produced by shipboard life, which leads Navy men

78

to argue that three social levels are found on board and that there is solidarity among the three because all their lives are equally at stake, strengthens the "endogroups." While it permits the officers to become acquainted with the problems and needs of their subordinates, it leads the latter to identify with those of the officers who serve as their examples.

All these factors strengthen professional cohesion; but they are drawbacks when Navy men, as has happened several times during the last quarter of a century, put aside their specific tasks and take over political roles. It would appear that intimate and constant living together has impaired knowledge of other groups. The values that have been inculcated into the Navy man, unobjectionable in themselves, are counterposed to those of a society that is ignorant of them, and these differing values have operated as mechanisms of psychological segregation.

The practice of those gentlemanly standards, the collective acceptance of a strict code of honor, and the enduring respect for "good form" lead Navy men to feel personally identified with the highest social stratum, because only the values of this stratum are identifiable with the Navy value system. This identification, as we will see later, takes place through a respect for good form, and it has led many senior officers and Navy ministers in recent years to assume representation of a social stratum which they did not even know. They came to know it after 1955.[6] It was not the service (in itself apolitical), but the new personal relations outside a strictly professional field entered into by some senior Navy officers who, taking advantage of the Navy's political inexperience, involved the institution in doubtful ventures.

Things, men, and ideas may be understood through the heart or through the intellect. Intellectuals accustomed to being guided by their logical faculties find it almost impossible to fully perceive this dichotomy. But the senior officers who had identified emotionally with a political position and sought advice and enlightenment from the intellectual spokesmen of the liberal faction, could not be prevented from risking everything for the position with which they had become identified. Since the service is very cohesive, it followed the officers as a unit. And as the system of loyalties is wholly impersonal, the dissident Navy men confined any criticism they might have to conversation with their peers. Thus, from 1955 on, because of the activities of the leadership, the Argentine Navy became identified by public opinion with a position which was ideological and political at the same

79

time. This position was not held by the Navy as a whole, however, and the political involvement of the service was contrary to the Navy's professional code.

An Explanation for Civilians and an Epilogue for the Military

It is not always easy to overcome the communication barriers that separate civilians from the military, but this problem is not peculiar to Argentina; it is universal. Military men can learn to understand the rules of the game of the political world, and they can even overcome their inevitable professional limitations and learn the most arduous and complex diplomatic rules. What is difficult for the civilian, and especially for the intellectual, is to penetrate military psychology and value systems.

To overcome barriers between civilians and the military, both groups must make an effort they are seldom disposed to make, and they should avoid projecting their own values on the other's field. Military men, for example, overrate efficiency whenever it is the result of unity of leadership, of the organization and perfect articulation of cadres and of a more or less long-term strategy. They believe that efficiency in action results from setting all these wheels in motion. Hence the inefficiency of civilians, the inefficiency of politicians engaged in sterile discussions of past events startles them. When they behold the deficient operation of the administrative machinery, the plurality of leaders, and the prevalence of a critical attitude, they tend implicitly to underrate leadership solely and exclusively by political men. Their attitude is very similar to that of technocrats—engineers, mathematicians, physicists—when they judge political events.

The military man, however, can adapt to politics, and can become a "political man" (some of the great statesmen of Argentina such as Roca, Mitre, and Justo, not to mention those in our times, have come from the armed services). But to do so, he must overcome his natural penchant for seeing men, ideas, and things in black and white, and must retrain himself to distinguish shadings in political events.

It is much more difficult for the intellectual to identify with the military and to arrive at an understanding of military values, symbols, and even language. This difficulty arises partly because the intellectual is projecting some of his own values—such as the constant exercise of the intellect, the sharpening of his critical faculties, the relativity of his cognitive faculties—on an organization which is organic, disciplined, vertical, and authoritarian; and partly because subconsciously he lets himself be swept along by prejudices that arise from the ideological currents that have shaped his thought.

For these reasons the barriers to communication have seldom been overcome and the efforts of each to understand the language and thought of the other have been minimal. When language and thought have been understood and the military man has become a political "fox," the governments he has established have usually been the most stable and enduring. It is not necessary to confine ourselves to the examples in Argentina such as Roca, Mitre, and Perón, who, though deposed from power, has yet continued to threaten Argentine political life for the last twenty years. It is just as true elsewhere and the history of the world and contemporary European events afford many examples of this.

The opposite is true of civilians. The most astute civilian political "foxes" rarely have understood military men. This basic incomprehension cost a former Argentine chief of state and a former Brazilian president their terms of office, since, forgetting or overlooking the existence of military hierarchical standards, they thought that by addressing themselves to the sergeants, they could override the position of the high commands. Both presidents attempted in vain to undermine the military hierarchical order; the result was total rejection, even by those officers who had been uncommitted.

"Pure" intellectuals are in the same situation. They worry about identifying the ideologies that influence the military and tend to believe that such ideologies arise from pure intellect, from the depth of the creative intelligence, or from a certain level of abstraction. They do not stop to think that military thought processes arise from the military condition itself, from the military profession and its standards of conduct. It is therefore time to have a sincere understanding between the two parties; it is time for military men finally to realize that they do not possess a monopoly of organizational efficiency, that they are not the sole remaining depositories of patriotism; and it is time for the intellectuals to fulfill their role by casting aside the hackneyed statements they have employed with regard to military men and by proceeding to an authentic "demythification."

There seem to be two universal constants in military behavior. In highly developed countries that are deeply involved in world leadership, the armed forces, concerned about the conduct of a subtle diplo-

81

macy they do not understand, believe more in the efficacy of their own security apparatus and formulate their policies of world strategy and professional alliances. In less developed countries, especially in the Arab Middle East, the armed forces are the most rational and modern expression of all the native groups and see themselves as the only ones capable of guaranteeing the efficacy of the bureaucratic apparatus.

Whether in highly developed or relatively underdeveloped countries, military men see themselves as the guarantors of the continuity of the spirit of their fatherland, as the legatees of historical tradition and of the heroic virtues of their ancestors, and as the custodians of national values.

It is also time that intellectuals come to understand that, while it is true their profession enables them to analyze the ideologies of other groups and especially of the military, their analyses should be free of value judgments. They should first prove the surgical cleanliness of their cognitive apparatus lest others perceive in their analyses traces of ideologies that influence their preferences and phobias. In this respect the analyses of military behavior in the various countries of the world now being made by contemporary sociologists show a desire for maximum objectivity and a capacity to understand military rules which is worthy of praise.

An initial analysis of the conduct of the military leads us to perceive both manifest and latent functions in the institution. The manifest functions of the armed services are always the same at all times in all countries and under all historical circumstances: they are the armed branch of the state. The latent functions are those of protecting patriotism and those related to it: to provide national cohesion and integration for the various graduating classes that pass through their ranks and to see themselves as the perpetuators of the glory and tradition of the nation.

In Argentina, where there have been no foreign wars for a century, the Army has had no occasion to carry out its manifest functions nor to put into practice the operational plans it has prepared. On the other hand, there are always occasions and opportunities to carry out whatever is included within its latent functions.

Aside from the values they inculcate into the citizens who go through military service, in most cases the armed forces' excercise of latent functions has determined their institutional behavior; or perhaps it should be said that the subjective belief that some of their latent functions were at stake has often driven the military hierarchies to take the steps they have taken. It does not matter whether this subjective belief is objectively true. What matters is that it be subjectively true to the military or to the military commanders of the moment. If the armed forces overthrew a civilian government in 1930, it was because subjectively they thought this government lacked efficiency and that the exercise of their latent function, that is, the protection of patriotism and national tradition against the disintegrating cliques that surrounded the president made their public intervention imperative.

If in 1943 they overthrew a second government, it was again because subjectively they believed that military efficiency might solve what the interminable party and legislative quarrels had failed to solve, and that, on the eve of a monstrous electoral fraud, military intervention was unavoidable as a patriotic imperative.

If in 1955 a whole military sector overrode another with relative ease, it was again because its "legitimacy" claims were more valid: the reasons of those who were protecting themselves from the government were more valid, in view of the administrative disorder, the burning of the national flag, the attacks on the religious values inbred in the nation, and the hierarchical insubordination the other branch intended when it accepted the idea of handing out arms to workers' militias.

If in 1962 the armed forces deposed a constitutional authority it was also because subjectively they were fully convinced that a government that authorized the electoral rehabilitation of those recently defeated was not efficient, and that those who acted to sow discord between the services, seeking to make them lose prestige and trying to estrange the masses could not be patriotic.

In these cases the conduct of the military was determined not by a specific ideology, which was different in each instance, but by the continuity of the same attitude. There are two constants that govern military conduct: complete commitment to efficiency as opposed to inefficiency and complete conviction that as protectors of patriotism they must go to its defense each time they think it is endangered. In each case the conduct of the military was sincere, the result of a subjective evaluation of the situation. Whether or not that evaluation reflected the real situation is a different matter. It is difficult to pass judgment on it; in any case, such judgment is beyond the scope of this study, which is only to point out a causal relationship.

If subjective considerations, such as efficiency and patriotism, are the constants, the variables were the ideologies that in each case fell on fertile ground. To interpret each event realistically it is necessary to

83

emphasize how military men saw their role on each occasion, in relation to the subjective responsibilities that accompany their professional status; only in a supplementary way should the observer consider the ideologies that may have had a bearing on each event.

A sociologist has pointed out[7] the influence Leopold Lugones' thought may have had on the chief leaders of the revolution in 1930. But the truth is that when Lugones convinced them with his eloquence that the "hour of the sword" had struck, he was simply putting the finishing touches to ground that had already been well prepared.[8] Sometimes events themselves and at other times the events magnified by a well-orchestrated press and by clever whispering campaigns convinced the military that it would be patriotic to depose a government identified with administrative chaos; that only the authoritarian apparatus the Army itself would impose could be effective; that the struggles between parties were unproductive; and that a "corporative" type of regime such as was then in fashion, which would totally do away with such struggles, would be much more efficient.

Almost all studies of the military ideology that prevailed in 1943 are somewhat biased; some because the authors own personal ideological positions led them to impute to military leaders an alleged adherence to totalitarian systems and others because their authors feared that beyond the confines of the country the Argentine military would be accused of having military expansion as their sole objective. Still other writers, a minority, narrowed all the problems of ideology to a secret military lodge that was presumed to have been the nucleus for all the higher command posts.

In the absence of any conclusive proof as to these ideological leanings, the fact remains that on more than one occasion the behavior of military men has refuted the first two charges. Accepted documentary proof such as revolutionary proclamations and later declarations do not support this alleged identification with totalitarian regimes, although from documentary proof cited (but not accepted), such as the alleged declaration of the United Officers Group (*Grupo de Oficiales Unidos*) a militaristic call to expansion might indeed emerge.[9]

"Chosen affinities" sometimes are more reliable indicators than many documentary proofs. It is true that the 1943 military group surrounded itself with nationalistic civilians, some of whom sympathized with the Axis countries. But when in January, 1944, the military government broke relations with the Axis powers, the nationalistic civil-

84

ians retired and part of the military governing group continued at the head of the government.

Facts are the proof and the best indices. The alleged expansionist policy of the United Officers Group was never corroborated by facts, although the officers who are said to have drafted the manifesto retained almost all government posts, as well as the command of the military establishment. What is beyond dispute is the natural sympathy that the Army command felt for the German military machine. On the one hand, this sympathy was the result of a formative inheritance and on the other, of strictly professional admiration of a model.

Official Army literature affords an objective index of this attachment. A study of the titles and authors of all the books published up to 1943 by the *Biblioteca del Oficial* shows that the themes were limited to technical and professional matters such as operations, strategy, logistics, troop command, military history, and so forth. Almost all the titles published dealing with descriptions and technical analysis of World War I came from German authors.[10] As of 1956, the fortieth anniversary of the establishment of the *Biblioteca del Oficial*, it had published 448 titles. Aside from the translated works already mentioned, almost all the technical analyses covering action in World War II had been written by North American or French sources. The German authors, in contrast, rather than covering technical problems, dealt with the problem of the subjection of the German Army to the ideological party leadership which had hindered it. Some of their accounts, many of them in the first person, relate specific instances of conflict with Hitler, whom they considered a presumptuous and self-ordained military leader.[11]

In 1962 Argentine politics had changed, and it perhaps is possible to talk of a new specific ideology or counter-ideology emerging from the changing aspects of the situation in the armed forces, and also as a result of the world situation. A study would be possible because military materials, published by the armed forces and distributed through its official services (which is the only literature that can really serve as an index), were very clear in content.

The post-World War II period had modified the traditional terms of wars—their nature, the localization of conflicts, the quality of the enemy, and, especially, their technical nature. Above all, the sense of strategy had changed, and von Clausewitz had definitely been relegated to the classics. Strategy now assumed a global and total charac-

85

ter, localized wars over frontier problems seemed to have been banished definitively, and only total situations in response to conflicts between blocs were envisaged. On the universal level, even the idea of frontiers had disappeared: now war might be carried on within the frontiers, and the enemy was not a hostile foreigner but rather a fellow citizen serving the interests of the other bloc consciously or unconsciously. Subversive war became the new theme of military preoccupations. The enemy might be within, operating as an irregular army in the service of an ideology destructive of national values. The gradual contamination of all basic sectors of national life—labor, academic, political, religious, and even the military—together with core groups acting as irregular troops could lead to insurgent action. Psychological warfare would inevitably lead to revolutionary war.

The role of the Army would then have to change. Joined to other services in the common defense of the value system, it would undertake an engagement of a regional nature: to guarantee the "interior frontiers," to adopt all the precautionary measures possible to avoid the action of Communist groups and the spread of their antinational ideology. The country has had two perfect exponents of the new warfare problems in recent years, who have exhibited within the local armed forces the same concern shown by all Western armies. One of them contends,

> Within the new concept of war the intervention of the armed forces may not be essential . . . since all other elements may be able to construct the necessary framework to achieve victory indirectly through mass subversion of the population, which is the instrument of revolutionary warfare.[12]

From the professional point of view, the problems presented by the new revolutionary war are objectively certain and this is true in the ideological field too. The problem is that the subjective interpretation of possible subversive activities is left to the military. They are the ones who judge whether the possible decline of the popularity of the armed forces is due to their own behavior or to the concerted action of third parties consciously or unconsciously dedicated to slandering the armed forces, to setting one service against the other, and to upsetting the hierarchical command structure. They are also the ones given the power to judge whether the conditions of subversion and contamination have reached such a point as to make it imperative and

86

unavoidable for them "to take the offensive" in order to control the situation. In this case, a counter-ideology (rather than an ideology proper) is added to the professional adaptation to new situations that the guerrilla war demands. Thus, a professional situation, rather than a specific ideology, causes the Army to assume *de facto* a new guardianship function which is added to the traditional latent functions: that of guaranteeing the continuity of formal democracy, the solidarity of the Western world, and individual liberties.

This outlines, of course, only the theoretical situation. In practice, the Army has experienced all the stages of ambivalence and internal contradiction that seem to have pervaded all groups in the nation. Because the Army is based on the national community (at the same time it conditions it), it is also a reflection of the nation.

1. There is no such thing as a military policy, nor has there been. There has been no policy of the military for the military. This could have happened only within a society under a military regime. In 1943, ostensibly for the sake of efficiency, the military and their civilian advisers dissolved political parties and banned their existence. In 1955 they brought the parties back to power, opening all the doors for them, granting the party men key offices, and giving up control of the actual command positions for the exclusive benefit of the latter.

In 1962 and in 1963 when one military sector, showing singular professional cohesion and organization, defeated another sector by force of arms, it displayed a strictly military supremacy; however, the victorious faction was not able to forge a military policy. Basically, the policy of the military has been simply to fill the power vacuums produced by the incapacity of politicians. Military men have acted in the name of efficiency and have been fully convinced that they were the embodiment of legitimacy in accordance with the latent functions of their institution.

2. As is true in all sectors of the nation, the Army has demonstrated the coexistence at the highest level of "universalistic" and "achievement" standards with others of a "particularistic" type. In other words, in spite of the Army's being a functional unit with a command structure, that is, the product of a specific normative order, there have operated within the institution "interest cliques," or "ideological groups," just as in the other sectors of national life. In the Army's case, these groups have impaired professionalism and functional unity.

These inside groups or cliques have taken the place of "lodges." The

87

existence of formal or informal lodges since the 1920s seems to have been one of the elements that has distorted military leadership;[13] conflicts were then between groups within the services. Thus, it is difficult to contend, as people commonly do, that the Argentine military control politics. The truth, as shown by historical experience, lies in a pattern of interactions in which the political is paramount; consequently divisions initiated in the political realm run through all groups and institutions. The military is also split by political divisions, thus creating an anomalous situation since, according to its structure, it should be a functional monolith.

3. The third element to be taken into consideration arises from a curious duality which requires a deeper analysis than mere presentation of facts would allow. The result of the public opinion polls conducted by the intelligence services have not been made public, but it is possible to assume (however impressionistic and unscientific this opinion may seem) that the great majority of those Argentines consulted in July, 1963, expressed total opposition to military intervention in politics. But it is also true that many Argentines, minimally interested in public affairs during the last twenty-five years, have hoped at some time for military action, whether to depose Perón or to bring him back to power, that would satisfy their personal point of view on national problems. This strange ambivalence between verbal rationalization and the intimate "living feeling" which has at some time or other been experienced by every uneasy Argentine is one of the many dichotomies which, starting with each individual, split what might otherwise have been a political community.

Since the armed forces have not excercised their manifest function of defending the country in war, the war apparatus of the military has been visualized by all political groups as an instrument potentially useful to satisfy other political objectives. Thus, aside from all the explanations presented, resort to the armed forces as a source of legitimacy has been a tacit rule of the political game in Argentina. This is an aspect of political life of which nobody expressly approves, but from which all the political groups have profited at least once. All will publicly deny this rule, but in private Argentine politicians cannot ignore that, at one time or another during this quarter of a century, they have all knocked on the doors of the garrisons.

It has been stated above that, because of the new characteristics of warfare, as well as of the world situation, the Argentine armed forces reserve for themselves the guardianship of formal democracy. It is possible that they might engage in the performance of functions that would make them a tool of actual democracy. That is to say, the armed forces may actually enter the national development process, on the basis of the power they possess and of the constructive employment of the manpower which yearly enters their ranks. At the time of this writing, however, this new outlook can only be glimpsed in a barely perceptible statement of objectives.[14]

Notes

1. A brief description of Argentine education should clarify the meaning of the data provided above. Generally speaking, Argentine elementary schooling lasts seven years; high schools, known as *colegios* (a word used throughout Latin America, which has caused untold confusion and facilitated numerous educational frauds in the United States) usually require five years. Normal schools are specialized high schools which train elementary school teachers; here again, it should be pointed out that the training of elementary school teachers in Latin America seldom goes beyond the high school level and almost never surpasses one or two years of college. C.A.A.

2. From the Military College Annual Reports, various years.

3. Lieutenant General Benjamin Rattenbach, *Sociología militar* (Buenos Aires: Librería Perlado, 1958).

4. In June, 1956, groups of officers, noncommissioned officers, and civilians attempted a coup with the avowed objective of returning to Peronist rule. They failed and some of those apparently involved were executed. C.A.A.

5. In the French military establishment Salan, de Lattre, and Liautey had sons who were officers and died on the battlefield.

6. The Argentine Navy was deeply involved in the overthrow of the Perón regime in 1955; the upper class was interested in seeing Perón overthrown, although not necessarily for the same reasons. Naturally, the contacts between the Navy and the upper class increased markedly shortly before and after the 1955 revolt. C.A.A.

7. Darío J. Cantón, "Notes on the Argentine Armed Forces," paper presented in the Department of Sociology, University of California at Berkeley, in the course conducted by Professor R. Bendix.

8. The Argentine poet Leopoldo Lugones, who subscribed to a variety of political ideologies, made a widely publicized speech before the 1930 coup d'état, in which he encouraged the military to take over the government of Argentina and eliminate the vices of democracy. C.A.A.

89

9. The United Officers Group (there are disagreements about the correct name) was the Army lodge whose members launched the 1943 coup d'état that eventually opened the door to Perón's accession to power. Some of the manifestos traced to them show fascist and expansionist tendencies. C.A.A.

10. General Von Falkenhayn, *El comando supremo del ejército alemán, 1914–1918, y sus decisiones esenciales*, translated in 1920. Archives of the German State, *Las batallas de frontera en el oeste*, translated in 1927; General von Tschischwitz, *El ejército y la armada en la conquista de las islas bálticas*; General K. Krafft von Dellmensingen, *La ruptura*, with maps. Nine volumes of the official works edited by the German Army after 1918 were published.

Also, General von Poseck, *La caballería alemana en Bélgica y en Francia durante el año 14*, and *La caballería alemana en Curlandia y Lituania*; General von Hoepner, *La guerra aérea alemana*; Lieutenant General von Janson, *La cooperación estratégica y táctica del ejército y armada*, and others.

The most important publication of all published by the *Biblioteca del oficial* was von Clausewitz's military classic *On War*, two editions of which were made, the first a direct translation from the German and the second a translation from the French.

Not all publications are German, however; translations were also made from the French, Italian, Swedish and, very rarely, from some English author.

11. Until 1956 all technical works with reference to World War II were by American authors. Those translated from the German all reflect the resentment of the defeated officers who blamed the defeat on the interference of the National Socialists and of Hitler in military affairs. This is true in the translated works by von Lossberg, *En el estado mayor general de las fuerzas armadas alemanas*; General Siegfried Westphal, *El ejército alemán bajo Hitler*; General Guderian, *Memorias de un soldado*; *memorias del Mariscal Rommel*, and one of the most characteristic, *Los generales alemanes hablan*, translated from the English and with a journalistic flavor. All appear on the various volumes of the *Biblioteca del oficial*. The analysis of the contents has been carried out in volume 448, a compilation, published in April, 1956, under the direction of General Nicolás C. Accame.

12. General Osiris G. Villegas, *Guerra revolucionaria comunista* (Buenos Aires: Pleamar, 1963), one of the most complete books on the subject published in Argentina. Also see the second volume of Colonel Alberto Marini, *La guerra, la política y la estrategia* (Buenos Aires: Círculo Militar, 1962), published as volume 552 of the *Biblioteca del oficial*; and Carlos A. Florit, *Las fuerzas armadas y la guerra psicológica* (Buenos Aires: Ediciones Arayú, 1963); his prologue for civilians has the virtue, rare in Argentina, of facing the problem of lack of communication between the civilian and military sectors.

90

13. Such as the Lodge San Martín, the Group of United Officers, the "parallel commands," the "admirals' group," the *colorados* and others. On this subject see Juan V. Orona, "Una logia poco conocida y la revolución del 6 de septiembre," *Revista de historia*, No. 3, first quarter, 1958; and Orona, *La logia militar que enfrentó a Hipólito Yrigoyen* (Buenos Aires: Editorial Leonardo Impresora, 1965). Also consult R. Lanus, "Logias en el ejército argentino" (Lecture delivered at the Instituto Popular de Conferencias on June 30, 1950).

14. Speech by the director of the Escuela Superior de Guerra at the beginning of the 1964 courses. Also see the speech by the minister of national defense (May, 1964).

5. THE ARGENTINE RURAL SOCIETY

SINCE its establishment in 1866 the Argentine Rural Society has been considered the organization that best represents the agricultural sector of the country. It was the first such organization and has been the model for the other local rural societies created subsequently.

People have vague ideas about the Rural Society; they assume that its membership includes the largest traditional ranchers. This perception is accurate as far as it goes. The Rural Society was established by the largest ranchers of the province of Buenos Aires. The list of its founders includes the innovators of the period, the very ones who at about that time were introducing into the country new breeds of cattle for crossbreeding and were for the first time putting up wire fences around their landholdings in the *pampa*.

Since the Rural Society brings together the largest landowners and the most important ranches, it has been assumed that its members must be involved in the processing of foodstuffs and in the development of a domestic market, in the meatpacking industry and in export. How and in what manner these relations are established, to what extent the Rural Society participates in these activities, what economic power its members have, all this is what people do not know. In the absence of real direct knowledge, many myths are current.

It is known that some members of the Rural Society travel to Britian to take part in the great cattle shows in Scotland and that periodically they purchase prize stud bulls for the local ranches. They then pay back their social obligations, as is evident from the fact that their British friends turn up as judges at the Palermo cattle show.[1] It is common knowledge that during negotiations for the renewal of the meat agreements, the Rural Society has something to say on the subject. The opinions of the organization are given special consideration, and some of its members form part of the commissions that discuss the provisions, details, and percentages of future export quotas.

92

People have the impression that the Rural Society is identified with the Buenos Aires upper class. While the average person could not say who runs the organization and is not sure who are its most prominent members, he does know that its greatest festival, the Cattle Show, coincides with the only mass reunion of the Buenos Aires upper class. People identify one with the other and believe that the rural landowners are also the greatest financiers and that they are always related to important groups, such as the government of the moment, so that there is no doubt that the Rural Society is represented at the highest level. The people take for granted that the Rural Society participates at the government level in whatever decisions affect its members' interests.

These are popular beliefs. As will be seen later, these beliefs are plausible since they have both empirical and inductive bases. Other beliefs have been elaborated intellectually. On the one hand, we have the theories of some social historians who, after evaluating the negative role of the holders of *latifundia* in underdeveloped societies, extend their conclusions to many transitional societies. When they refer to Latin America they contend that the great landowners constitute a unit, part of old and unchanging traditional aristocracies, entrenched from the time of the Spanish colonies and that since these oligarchies are alien and impervious to social change, they would act as brakes on development.

To the popular versions and the working hypothesis of some theoreticians a third type of assumption should be added. Starting with actual facts—such as the high degree of concentration of rural property in very rich regions—some ideologues contend that in all cases property implies corresponding political and social power. From this it follows that to carry out any policy of a social character these holders of power must first be eliminated, since they oppose all change, and that to eliminate the power of the landowners private ownership of land must be abolished.

On this occasion, far from a priori rejecting or accepting any of these versions, advantage will be taken of them as working instruments, and they will be applied to the group which Argentines consider to be the holder of great rural property. The same method applied up to now will be employed here: the elements of status, family background, type of schooling, and economic and social bases of the official leaders will be observed. A statistical sample made up of all the directors of the Rural Society for the sample years adopted (1936, 1941, 1946,

93

1951, 1956, and 1961) will be employed. But the study will not be confined to an analysis of the sample. The complexity of the problem and the variety of hypotheses about the role of this group make it difficult to arrive at an explanation through the use of only one technique. Thus other supplementary techniques and all the available information and documentation will be used.

The Official Leaders of the Rural Society

In 1936 the Rural Society had 2,000 members. In 1961 it had over 9,000. The intervening increases did not take place suddenly: the institution had over 3,000 members in 1946, over 5,000 in 1954, and over 7,000 five years later, until in 1962 it reached 9,122 members.[2] During this quarter of a century it changed from a rather restricted group to a broader one. This gradual broadening of the membership base has relevance to the problem which engages us: the governing of the organization.

Anyone going over the rolls of the boards of directors during the sample years will be surprised to find that not all its members could be considered members of the Buenos Aires upper class. In fact, only 38 of the 97 directors could be considered to be members of this traditional group on the basis of objective criteria.

However, what gives those rolls their special character (to the point that the Rural Society becomes identified with the highest social stratum) is the fact that those traditional families constitute a "permanent team" within the boards of directors.[3] The government of the Rural Society is made up of the same individuals or of different ones from a basic group of families. This permanent team usually has filled somewhat over 50 percent of the posts in the various boards of directors. In 1946 the percentage was 38 percent. In 1951 it was the lowest, 7 percent. This figure for 1951 can be convincingly explained if we analyze it in the light of contemporary events: it was advisable at that time not to have well-known names appear on the board of directors.

Together with those traditional names we find others that appear with some frequency. They come from families with different backgrounds, but from an economic and social standpoint they enjoy comparable prestige. The traditional families are precisely those who own long-standing establishments in the province of Buenos Aires. On the

94

other hand, the others belonging to the upper, but not traditional, class own property outside Buenos Aires Province.[4]

If the permanent team is disregarded and attention is paid to the remaining members of the boards of directors, it is found that, of the 37 individuals whose most important ranches could be identified, 29 were located in Buenos Aires Province. Of the remaining 8, one was located in Entre Ríos, 4 in Santa Fe, and 3 in Córdoba. Thus, it would seem to be correct to identify, at the highest levels, the Rural Society with the cattle-raising and grain-producing landholdings of Buenos Aires Province.[5]

On the rolls of the full members of the board of directors examined in this study, no representatives of the corporations established within Argentina as subsidiaries of European financial groups were found,[6] nor were there members of corporations established with British capital which own land in Buenos Aires. The result would be different if the analysis were extended to those who represent some of the districts before the board of directors:[7] the representatives of the Patagonia district do appear to be corporation executives. Furthermore, it is not implied here that the interrelationships between these corporations and the other landowners should be overlooked. But the fact remains that no executives of those rural corporations appear in a personal capacity on the boards of directors.

Who are the leaders of the Rural Society? On the basis of the rolls within the sample analyzed various groups could be identified.

(a) First we have the traditional permanent team already mentioned, to which families that, although from a different background, enjoy comparable social prestige have been added. It has been indicated that this group contributes 38 percent of the total number of directors and that the norm is for these people to fill from 50 to 55 percent of the executive positions, with the exception of the 1946 and 1951 periods which lower the total average.

(b) A second group of leaders is made up of those from immigrant families who settled in the province of Buenos Aires around the end of last century. These families, whose characteristics would be those of all rising bourgeoisies, devoted themselves tirelessly to cattle raising, acquired a good economic position, increased their property, built up the number of cattle and crossbreeds, and sometimes ended up as dairy ranchers.[8] Their children, the first Argentine generation, in time came to have economic leadership and interested themselves in the

95

processing of the raw products. They appeared among the founding members of the Argentine Meat Producers Corporation and on later ruling committees; they also established the various cattle breeds associations.

(c) A third group with the same characteristics as the preceding one and also motivated by the same desire for economic upward mobility may be pointed out. The difference in classification lies in that the latter came from local regions, they are local ranchers who, unlike those in the other group, are not well known in Buenos Aires.

(d) A fourth group is made up of the leaders attracted from business. These are owners of sheds and warehouses for the produce of the countryside who, due to their economic success were able to expand their economic activities toward the end of the nineteenth and the beginning of this century. They were immigrants, mostly Spanish, and after they had established the original commercial firms they went on to purchase land and to administer it directly. Their children would later appear as leaders of the Rural Society. Now these firms carry on both commercial and agricultural activities.[9]

(e) A fifth group moved from the industrial or transportation and service field into rural enterprises, either for the purpose of economic diversification or to attain greater prestige (Fano, Mihanovich). For this group rural activity was a new venture.

(f) Last, and most marginal within the lists, we have the lawyers. These are professional people who, because of the success of their law firms, because of the kind of interests they have defended, and because of their professional connections with the Society, late in their careers became not only rural landowners, but also proprietors of some of the most renowned dairy ranches. In these cases it was the individual himself who moved up to leadership positions (Busso, Satanovsky), and there is no previous rural-based generation.

In view of the backgrounds of the official leaders, it is not possible to maintain that those from the traditional upper class govern the Society, since those from that class hold on the average only 38 percent of the official posts. All the others, by whatever means they have moved up, wherever they come from, whether they started as tenant farmers at the lowest levels of farming, or as successful merchants, textile manufacturers, or well-known members of the legal profession, are of immigrant stock. Their properties are not the result of inheritance through generations; their lands have been purchased, either by the immigrants themselves or by their first-generation Argentine sons, all motivated by the desire for economic success.

That most of the official leaders of an organization that represents large rural interests have relatively new roots should serve as a first warning before we extend the hypotheses that may be valid for other countries of Latin America to Argentina. However, a large number of the directors (at least those in groups b, d, and e) may feel without hesitation that they are included in the Buenos Aires upper class. As has been shown elsewhere,[10] this class is permeable; while a good many of its members consider that family background is the determining factor leading to recognition as members of the group, this factor is not crucial. Other factors are more determining, such as friendships, social contacts, and connections by marriage. On the other hand, differences of family background, though they may be pointed out, may be overlooked.

Many of the persons included in the Rural Society listing are identified as members of the upper class, despite their more humble family background, because other factors have gained them prestige. If their parents purchased land, if they were educated at the "proper" private elementary and high schools in Buenos Aires, if they have been professionals (if lawyers, all the better) and have kept up and increased their contacts, if they have accepted and adopted the mores of the more prestigious group, after they have obtained *entrée* to certain circles they can be acknowledged as equals. Once this happens, all differences disappear and unconsciously the acquisition of properties is attributed to earlier periods than the actual one. Confusion arises when these prestige seekers come to be identified as members of the traditional aristocracy.

Once members of this new group are assimilated and recognized, they develop a new status mentality. Since their determination to "belong" is great and since as an upward-moving bourgeoisie they have a fortune to devote to conspicuous consumption, they end their upward climb as ranchers. It is in this role that they become identified with the upper class. Once they are recognized within the group, they strive to be recognized by those outside the group. They come to share certain norms of the traditional families, which they had no part in setting up, and believe in them with the faith of converts. They seem all the more anxious to display them, the more alien these norms are to their social origin.

The structure of the primary sector of the Argentine economy and especially the origin and formation of the body of great landowners does not exactly fit the classical pattern of underdeveloped countries. It has been said that through analysis of the governing board of the Rural Society two important groups may be discerned. One is made up of members of traditional families who represent the local version of the true model for underdeveloped countries. The other sector, over half of the formal leaders, are the sons of Spanish merchants (mostly Basques) and of Italian, English, and Irish families.[11]

Many official leaders of direct European origin might be found in the recently independent countries of Africa. In those countries, the rural leaders are still Europeans and as such are marginal to the society and the area where they established their interests. The Argentine case is very different, since those of European origin are citizens of the country, with permanent interests within the country, and with a vital commitment exclusively within its boundaries.

Of the 64 persons who signed the charter organizing the Rural Society, 15 were Englishmen and 2 were Italians. This was in 1866 before the deluge of immigration. An analysis of the successive rolls of directors after the first one shows that around 1922 it is possible to identify the pattern of percentages of "traditional" landowners and "new" landowners on the board of directors that would prevail during the 1936–1961 period. At this level the problem posed is different from a pattern construed on the basis of other Latin American models. The acquisition of "central" land took place much later in comparison to the other Latin American countries and also with relation to the rural areas corresponding to the traditional cities of the interior.[12] The ownership of *latifundia* in Salta and Corrientes Provinces does correspond perfectly to the pattern found in traditional societies.

In the central regions of Argentina the heavy concentration of land ownership was achieved by pushing into Indian lands, that is, into the desert. The first great owners of *latifundia* of the last century established themselves in the first great advance.[13] The *latifundia* owners of the end of the century date from the two subsequent advances into the desert. Many times they obtained only nominal control attested to by a deed, rather than direct control of the land. This nominal control resulted from either the political power they wielded or was due to the situation in which they found themselves. On this matter there is very ample documentation, so it is not necessary to go over the subject again.[14]

The original owners of these lands frequently lost legal control of their property because of the economic crisis of 1890, misuse of the property, gambling, debts, politics, excessive spending in Europe, or because leaders of expeditionary forces that went into the desert were not able to possess the lands granted to them, and for various other reasons. Different groups such as thrifty merchants, financiers, or foresighted speculators then obtained control. In the province of Buenos Aires very few farming colonies were established, in comparison to Santa Fe and Córdoba; therefore there was no subdivision of the land following coherent settlement plans. Historians are agreed in pointing out that the traditional aristocracy of Buenos Aires was opposed to farming colonies. While there were few farmers, many Europeans with foresight and financial means bought land from its nominal owners who had neglected their property and so were forced to sell. Thus, the transfer of ownership without subdivision occurred, a fact that is clearly reflected in the roll of official leaders of great rural properties.

There is not, at the level of the great landholders, then, a "non-modern" social structure. At the most, it would be an intermediate type. Paradoxically, what does exist among a good many of the leaders is a sort of "non-modern" attitude, which might be called "ideological traditionalism." The traditional attitude is an inner reality for traditional owners, but becomes an acquired attitude for a good many of the owners who have come into their property more recently. This moving up took place precisely because the structure of the rural sector of Argentine society was penetrable and fluid. At the beginning, therefore, it was relatively modern; this is shown by the fact that over half the leaders of the Rural Society were the product of this state of affairs. If later on a "sclerosis" of modernity set in, that is another matter.

The Interests Represented

A comparison between the rolls of the directors of the Rural Society and the roster of the largest landowners of the province of Buenos Aires, on the individual or family level, that is, without taking into consideration corporations in which they may also participate, shows that:[15]

99

On the 1936 Board of Directors, 12 of the 18 members were large landowners in the province of Buenos Aires

    1941: 14 of the 18 members were large landowners
    1946: 14 of the 18   ”   ”   ”   ”
    1951: 10 of the 18   ”   ”   ”   ”
    1956: 10 of the 16   ”   ”   ”   ”
    1961: 14 of the 19   ”   ”   ”   ”

On the other hand, reading the roster of members of the Rural Society in the 1960s may prove a surprise: after the changes made in the by-laws in 1948 in order to "incorporate the greatest number of producers," the rank and file of the Society came to be made up of the "local notables," which meant the producers, the largest producers of the central regions of the country, but many of whom had small-town backgrounds. It is very likely that the careers, backgrounds, and education of these local owners may differ widely from that of the "permanent cast."

Thus the Rural Society at present represents one sector: that of the large landowners, solely and exclusively. Within its ranks there is no room for the local medium and small property-owners, nor for the remaining farmers, leaseholders, or tenant farmers on the great landholdings. The Rural Society assumes representation of these large landowners as its official function. In the following chapter it will be seen how by virtue of its latent functions the Rural Society also assumes representation of a social sector, even though at present many of its members may not own a single acre of land.

Now that the group explicitly represented has been identified, it would be interesting to determine what significance the large properties have today in Argentina's agricultural economy. Thus it may be possible to arrive at an impressionistic estimate of the total interests articulated by the institution. Such an undertaking will necessarily prove difficult, for no preliminary studies are available. There have been no serious and responsible analyses of the degree of concentration of rural property, nor of its significance and proper evaluation within the total production of wealth. Statistics are incomplete and in this field any generalization is dangerous. The total figures for the country with reference to the average size of rural property are meaningless. Given the variety of products, of yield, and of cost per unit, they are figures that bear no relation to each other.

This first provisional analysis will be confined exclusively to comparing the size of properties in the interior of the province of Buenos Aires and to ascertaining their significance in the economy of the province. It is confined to Buenos Aires for two reasons: because it is the only province where previous basic investigation makes available real estate data on the landowners; and because the majority of the Rural Society directors analyzed have their properties in that province.

Table 5.1 outlines information regarding the tracts of land registered in the Real Estate Tax Register of the province of Buenos Aires in 1958. The "small and medium" heading includes all tracts of less than 2,500 acres; under "medium to large," those between 2,500 and 6,250 acres; under "large," those between 6,250 and 12,500 acres; and under "*latifundia*" those above the last figure. The figures used refer exclusively to the tracts into which the province is divided for real estate tax purposes. But, as pointed out by the Provincial Planning Board, the tracts do not represent economic units, and a single owner often holds several, thus the concentration of land is much greater.

TABLE 5.1

Ownership of Land in Accordance with the Size of Ranches
(Province of Buenos Aires)[16]

Size of Property	% of the Total	
	Individuals in Control of Property	Area
Small and medium	96.4	58.9
Medium to large	2.6	19.6
Large and *latifundia*	1.0	21.5
	100.00	100.0

The above data refer to legal ownership; however, what was crucial at the time the survey was conducted was actual possession of the land, since the law protected tenants from rent increases and eviction. For the purpose of correctly assessing rural ownership of land and its incidence over the total picture, it was important for the tracts to be free of tenant farmers, thus making possible direct possession by the owner. In spite of these limitations, Table 5.1 shows:

1. An overwhelming majority of small and medium ranchers whether as owners or leaseholders;

101

2. Concentration in the hands of very few ranchers (3.6 percent) of 40 percent of the area worked;
3. That the large landowners and the holders of *latifundia*, that is, those who normally would be directly represented by the Rural Society, jointly owned one fifth of the total area.

On the other hand, if we analyze the data supplied by a special list made up exclusively of owners of more than 12,500 acres, it appears that 536 groups (whether individual, family, or corporate owners) own 17.5 percent of the area of the province;[17] and 1,280 proprietor groups own 22.3 percent of the area of the province. Finally, using a third list of individuals or corporations that own over 6,250 acres, it is found that the area held in this type of ownership is a little less than 25 percent of the total area of the province.[18] The latter, then, would correspond to the properties whose interests the Rural Society represents. In 1958, when Argentina was just emerging from the frozen tenancy period, 77.7 percent of the land of the province apparently was held by others than the large owners.[19]

A number of indices, such as the unit value, the yield per acre according to the type of operation, and the minimum area which, varying from district to district, constitutes economic working units, should be taken into account in order to arrive at the specific meaning of "the large landed interests." The ministry of agriculture defines an "economic unit" as one providing the minimum needed to guarantee its proper operation and producing enough to maintain and provide for the development of a family of four. It should be emphasized that acreage, by itself, has no meaning. The same amount of land in San Antonio de Areco and in the district of Villarino, situated at opposite ends of the province, has different value.

The General Real Estate Bureau has divided the province into seven zones: the data published by the Bureau will be used and its zoning followed, but the total areas will be regrouped in accordance with the size of the ranches.[20]

Latifundia, that is, units over 12,500 acres, cover a considerable area only in the southern part of the province,[21] while in the rest of the province *latifundia* account for between 2 and 9 percent of the area. Medium and large landholdings (those between 2,500 and 12,500 acres) prevail in the eastern districts. Thus, it is only in the eastern part of Buenos Aires Province[22] that the combination of three types of landholding included in table 5.2 jointly account for nearly 50 percent of the usable land. Next is the western region in the districts adjoining

102

TABLE 5.2

Area Covered by Medium, Large, and *Latifundia* Ranches by Zones
(Province of Buenos Aires) in Percentages

Zone	% Area Covered		
	Latifundia	Medium and Large	Total
North	2	22.3	24.3
Northeast	2	18	20
West	8	36	44
Center	7.5	30.6	38.1
East	9	40	49
Southeast	4.2	34.2	38.4
South	21	18	39

the province of La Pampa. The lowest percentages of area held as *latifundia*, large and medium property are found in the northern and northeastern regions, which happen to be the richest in the country.

To evaluate the quality of the land correctly, reference will be made to the indices drawn up by the Real Estate Bureau of the Ministry of Economics and Finance of Buenos Aires Province. These indices, based on a maximum rating of 100, are drawn up in accordance with the ecological, topographic, and economic advantages of each district. In this case, however, the small economic units are not relevant to this study. On the contrary, in view of the interests being analyzed in this chapter, it will only be necessary to readjust the large landholdings to their potential rent parameters. Only through this procedure will it be possible to assess the large landholdings from a realistic viewpoint.[23]

TABLE 5.3

Relation Between Soil Quality and Area Covered by Landholdings
in Buenos Aires Province

Percentage of total area under medium, large, and *latifundia* units	Zone	Soil Quality		
		Average	Maximum	Minimum
24.3	North	81.0	86	72
20.0	Northeast	64.0	68	53
44.0	West	59.5	68	53
38.1	Center	57.6	69	50
49.0	East	50.0	83	29
38.4	Southeast	58.9	87	49
39.0	South	48.6	73	27

103

As may be seen, the variations in quality are very marked. The evident gap between the extremes (the quality of the districts in the north and of those in the south) makes it possible to adjust the figures for *latifundia* to their proper significance.

The results of two national censuses and those of a poll taken in 1956 by the Bureau of Statistics and Research of Buenos Aires Province on the ownership of cattle are outlined in table 5.4. The figures are consistent, so even if the medium, the large, and the *latifundia* units were added, it would be found that all these ranches together do not account for 50 percent of the cattle in the province. On the other hand, the small and medium owners together own more than half the head of cattle, but, of course, they also represent from 95 to 97 percent of the owners, according to the year.

TABLE 5.4

Ownership of Cattle by Unit Size in Percentages[24]

Type of Unit	1937 Census	1947 Census	1956 Estimate
Small and medium	55.95	53.45	57.2
Medium and large	26.75	26.80	27.3
Large and *latifundia*	17.30	19.75	15.5
Total	100.00	100.00	100.00

Assuming that the Rural Society includes the *latifundia* owners and only half of the medium and large owners, its members would have owned roughly 30 percent of the cattle in the province in 1937, 32 percent in 1947 and again 30 percent in 1956. But, since the total number of members of the Rural Society in the same years fell short of the total numbers of *latifundia* owners plus half of medium and large landholdings, it seems improbable that the percentage was that high.

In the final analysis, 84.5 percent of the cattle, representing the major portion of the livestock, is owned by ranchers who own units of less than 10,000 acres, which gives a ratio of approximately one head per two and one-half acres of land in units of less than 10,000 acres. In conclusion: (1) The large owners represent a small minority of the total cattle producers; and (2) the combined holdings of the large owners amount to 23 percent of the area of the province.

Though their properties are not so large, the medium-large owners having establishments in the northern zone of the province may be

104

considered to be on a level comparable to that of the largest land-owners, since that zone is the only one in which quality indices would compensate for the differences in size. Therefore, it appears that the "large owners" (that is, the interests represented by the Rural Society in the province) at best would own only 30 to 32 percent of the cattle in the province.

A similar result comes out of an analysis made jointly by the Federal Investments Council and the National Development Council in investigating land tenure.[25] The "large traditional ranch" (owned by a family or a corporation, devoted to cattle raising, using agriculture only for rotation of crops, given to extensive farming, underexploited, having mechanization below the indices for the zone, and containing a modest incorporation of technical advances) in the *Pampa* region would include only 0.8 percent of those farming, 17.1 percent of the land area, and 4.7 percent of the total labor force.

The Interests Being Articulated

In view of the above evidence, how can the hegemonic role played by the Rural Society be explained? In principle, the explanation may be found in the effective articulation of its interests.

Up to 1943 the large landowners of the province of Buenos Aires, especially the owners of winter pastures in the richest zones surrounding the federal capital, were the natural clients of the export meat-packing plants and the best known suppliers of the market in the city of Buenos Aires. In view of the high quality of their cattle, which export buyers frequently bought, these landowners played an important role in the fluctuation of prices, and they benefited directly because they had an intimate connection with the market. That has been properly documented before, and so there is no point in insisting on it.[26]

The group that made up the board of directors of the Rural Society during the first years of the twenties, when the Society had a clear awareness of its own interest, was convinced that the ranchers themselves must promote processing and marketing of their meat, activities that up to that time had been the exclusive province of the meat packing plants owned by British and American capital. This board of directors promoted a policy tending to keep a percentage of the processing in its own hands. Thus what later came to be known as "the meat war" started.[27]

105

Soon thereafter the members of the Rural Society became divided. Some wanted to expand their share of meat processing, others considered the maintenance of the status quo simpler and more advantageous. The former, the more progressive faction, was defeated, and subsequent boards of directors adopted the opposite attitude.

When the Argentine Meat Producers Corporation was founded in 1934, the various points of view had been reconciled. Both internally, because of the great depression, and externally, due to the Ottawa Treaty,[28] circumstances led the more recalcitrant to formulate a new statement of the problem. The new Meat Producers Corporation was then left in the hands of the directors of the Rural Society. The variant phases of this institution, which was subjected to successive government takeovers and to economic pressure from rival meat packing plants, cannot be outlined now. However, for the purposes of this study it should be pointed out here that the management has always continued to be identified on a personal basis with the directors of the Rural Society. The 1936 Argentine Meat Producers Corporation Board was the same as the original one. In the 1941 board, 6 of the 14 members had been or would later be members of the Rural Society. After the government takeover was rescinded in 1956, the first president chosen had previously been a director of the Rural Society. Of the 16 directors listed on the Argentine Meat Producers Corporation board of directors in 1961, 4 had had corresponding positions within the Rural Society.[29]

Since the Corporation represents all the producers, even though members of the Rural Society are among its stockholders, it is clear that the former (which promotes processing and commercialization of the raw products) surpasses the Rural Society in membership. The highest membership figure for the Rural Society has been only 9,000.

Among the Corporation's stockholders are many members of the local rural societies, the agricultural cooperatives, or the Agrarian Federation, which means that there are producers of varying importance. In its latest list of stockholder delegates (153 in the 30 districts) only two persons have occupied executive posts in the Rural Society within the last quarter century. Regardless of certain institutional relationships, it might be said that those who belong to the Rural Society also belong to the Argentine Meat Producers Corporation, which they themselves founded; it might also be said that the Rural Society's executives are also high-level executives of the Corporation; on the other

106

hand, it might be said that the Rural Society members have very little influence at the intermediate levels of the Corporation, that is, among the representatives of the stockholders from all over Argentina, since the scope of the Corporation exceeds theirs.

In a market such as that of Liniers,[30] where 400,000 producers offer their products, a figure as small as that of the 9,000 members of the Rural Society would be submerged, were it not for the importance of their ranches, the extent of their institutionalized relations, the volume of their operations, and the traditionalism which exists in this economic activity. It is known that they are not submerged, essentially because, even though the Rural Society is limited to representing solely the small group of large landowners throughout the country, the total number of their herds is significant.

There seems to be no way of evaluating these facts quantitatively, the only figure available being that possibly 30 to 32 percent of the cattle are found in Buenos Aires Province. The percentage cannot be applied to any of the other central lands. In the province of Córdoba and in that of Santa Fe, the subdivision of land is much greater than in Buenos Aires. And, conversely, the members of the Rural Society have their greatest concentration in Buenos Aires.

In the absence of any estimate, one fact is obvious: the Rural Society members benefit from the advantage that control of the marketing of cattle gives them, an aspect which is often neglected by the medium and small rural owners, when it takes place beyond their immediate direct range.

The large landowners are therefore the classical example of being clients of both the Corporation (which they control) and the meat packing plants (which also buy from them). If their present situation is advantageous, it would become even more so if the Corporation could fulfill the purpose for which it was conceived. If they could break the meatpacking monopoly and obtain better prices for local production, the Corporation would transfer a considerable amount of income to them, and thus the economic power relations would be changed and the cattle-raising sector would be even stronger than it is now. The beneficiaries would be both the few large and the many small and medium producers. What is interesting is that the level of the economic aspiration of the large landowners seems to have reached the upper limit. Only surveys and studies in depth on the basis of the economic behavior of specific groups could provide an answer with the

107

necessary minimum of scientific precision. It would be necessary, for instance, to ascertain whether there is a difference in attitude bearing relation to the size and the type of property owned.

While there are large unproductive *latifundia,* there are also large properties worked and developed on an industrial level for maximum income. While there are small areas under intensive use by ambitious owners with a high level of aspiration, there are also barren medium and small properties, and leased properties frozen in the hands of tenant farmers not possessing economic foresight.

In the absence of an in-depth study, the reduction of cattle stocks as a result of an irrational policy that led to the slaughtering of breeding cattle would justify assuming that the economic aspirations of a good many of the large landowners must have been satisfied. At least they must have been satisfied by the prices being paid for their cattle. The policy of compensatory support prices would have served as an incentive to increase cattle stocks in the case of a rising bourgeoisie (those incentives work with medium and small landowners). On the other hand, when such a policy affects large landowners, as in this case, the effectiveness of the incentives decreases. The economic satisfaction of the large landowners can be taken as an indicator that their interests are effectively articulated, regardless of whether they do or do not satisfy the nation's needs.

Interests not Adequately Articulated

It is not by accident that certain interests are well-articulated, as they are in the case of the large rural landowners and in that of the export sectors connected with them. Sometimes the power they wield is due to their own merit and sometimes it is acquired by default, that is, by default or bankruptcy of the other groups that might be expected to have similar or corresponding power. But in the case of rural property, only the large landowning interests seem to be well-articulated.

On the local level, all the interests of the landowners of a certain importance are expressed by the corresponding local rural societies. These rural societies operate only in some district capitals and within a narrow field of action. They are federated, but their activities do not have either the importance nor the range of the Rural Society. The latter has been the model imitated as the ideal prototype, the opinions and directives of which set the general "tone" for the others. The na-

108

tional organization is only a superstructure, and the member units have significant power of their own. Within the local organizations, however, the outlook is parochial, the horizon of their directors being confined to the narrow compass within which they move.

Below the level of the large landowners, the problem of deficient articulation of interests becomes evident. While the cooperative movement is quite developed in some regions of the country (the more "modern" ones, those more open to new currents within the agricultural world) it articulates interests around certain basic products such as milk, cotton, or wool.

Aside from the cooperatives created around a product in order to protect it, transport it, industrialize it, compete on the market with it if possible, as in the case of the dairy cooperatives, most are simply consumer cooperatives. While undoubtedly useful, they do not influence the national economy, nor identify with similar interests, nor create a system of loyalties among producers, nor can they assume representation of the immense and scattered majority of the medium and small owners.

The Argentine Agrarian Federation (*Federación Agraria Argentina*) was founded in 1912 to interpret agricultural interests and especially those of the small owners and tenant farmers of the period. After half a century of existence, however, it fell out of step with respect to the group it presumably represents and the ideology to which it claims to subscribe.[31] There has been a gradual change in the situation of the federated farmers as a consequence of structural changes that occurred when many *latifundia* were divided by the 1956 agriculture transformation plan.[32] A credit policy was instituted by federal banks in 1957 and 1958 which granted the occupants credits for 100 percent of the amount needed to buy those lands. As a result, landholding patterns in the central region of the country were transformed.[33] This greatly favored the Santa Fe and eastern Córdoba agricultural owners and other farmers and sons of farmers, who were traditionally members of the Federation, but the organization found itself displaced, since it could not adapt its historical objectives to the situation of a good many of its rank and file members. Although the status mentality of the former leaseholders was changed, the Agrarian Federation remained the same; while it was meant to represent the weaker farmers, there was now a great mass of those who had recently moved upward; while it had to proclaim itself the defender of the leaseholders, almost all its officers had become property owners and some of them even

109

large landowners. The Federation upheld the principles of agrarian reform, but such reform had taken place, and it had benefited precisely those who might be expected to use it as their ideological banner. This ambivalent situation has weakened the organization. The Federation has been unable to set up new norms and, aside from participating as consultant to governmental organizations, has been unable to reassume any form of rural leadership.

Leadership exists as long as, and to the extent that, the group identifies with the leader and the leader is capable of interpreting the objectives, purposes, and tensions of the groups. This does not occur at the medium and small levels of cattle-raising activity. Like all new groups, they have not matured sufficiently to acquire an objective consciousness of their true interest, and they are guided by changing frames of reference, alien to their own substantive reality.

Since the middle levels lack real leaders, the well-articulated aggregate of large landed interests is all the more visible. The great majority of the producers have ended by abdicating in favor of the latter, tacitly yielding to their experienced hands the direction of the whole agricultural and cattle-raising sector.

Notes

1. Palermo is a sector of the city of Buenos Aires where the Rural Society holds its yearly national cattle shows. C.A.A.

2. The information on the Boards of Directors of the Rural Society and on the members has been taken from the Annual Reports of that entity, from their publication, Anales, and from the lists of members.

3. Includes such names as Herrera Vegas, Pueyrredón, Pereyra Iraola, Guerrero, Martínez de Hoz, Peralta Ramos, and Ocampo.

4. Examples of this upper, but not traditional, class, are the Menéndez Behety and Braun Menéndez families, which own property in the Patagonia region, and the Firpo family, which has landholdings in Córdoba Province.

5. Beginning in 1951, twelve members representing that many districts were added to the Board of Directors. These new members are not included in the sample.

6. Such as Bunge y Born, Dreyfus, de Ridder, and Bemberg.

7. The Rural Society has divided the country into districts; the districts select representatives which serve as contacts between regional and national organizations.

8. This group includes the Galli, Campion, Duggan, Harriet, and Genoud families, among others.

110

9. They include, among others, Echesortu, Lalor, Elordy, Jorba, and Zuberbühler.

10. J. L. de Imaz, *La clase alta de Buenos Aires* (Buenos Aires: Instituto de Sociología, Universidad de Buenos Aires, 1962).

11. The Basques include Gaztambide and Aldazábal; those of Italian descent include Firpo, Galli, Vetrone, Gregorini, Poggio, Ginochio, Guastini, and Bruzone; of English and Irish origin are, among others, Cook Kelsey, Cavanagh, Duggan, Harriet, Harrington, and Kenny.

12. Such is the case of Salta, Corrientes, and Córdoba, where the "traditional society" settled in the highlands rather than on the flatlands.

13. They include Rosas, Anchorena, Terrero, and Leonardo Pereyra.

14. J. Oddone, *La burguesía terrateniente argentina*, (Buenos Aires: Ediciones Libera, 1967), third edition. This is an important study which shows how public land was gradually acquired, being granted to a few, precisely to those who were in the political "situation" of the moment.

15. We have used the "Registro de propietarios de más de 1,000 hectáreas," 1957 (manuscript) – drawn up by order of the Economic Planning Board of Buenos Aires Province in 1958. Profound appreciation is expressed to Alfredo Eric Calcagno, who made available this single copy, a most valuable unpublished source of information, used fully through this chapter and the next.

16. Economic Planning Board of Buenos Aires Province, "Distribución de la propiedad agraria en la Provincia de Buenos Aires," in *Revista de desarrollo económico*, Vol. 1, No. 1 (La Plata, Argentina) October–December, 1958.

17. *Ibid.* On the basis of the list drawn up by the General Real Estate Bureau of Buenos Aires Province.

18. Economic Planning Board of Buenos Aires Province, *op. cit.*

19. These figures show that there has been subdivision of the land in the province of Buenos Aires, although it has taken place slowly from the time of the original grant. Taking into account only those holding over 2500 acres, it is found that:

in 1914: 220 groups owned 19,335,000 acres
in 1958: 108 groups owned 4,315,000 acres

To compare present figures to those given by the Third National Census, see S. Bagú, *Evolución histórica de la estratificación social en la Argentina* (Buenos Aires: Departmento de Sociología, Facultad de Filosofia y Letras, Universidad de Buenos Aires, 1961).

20. Economic Planning Board of Buenos Aires Province, *op. cit.*

21. Including the districts of Patagones, Villarino, Puán, Coronel Rosales, Tornquist, Saavedra, Coronel Suárez, General Lamadrid, Laprida, and Coronel Pringles.

22. Such as the district of Magalena, Chascomús, Castelli, Dolores, Maipú, and Madariaga.

23. This table was drawn up with the information supplied by the Economic Planning Board of Buenos Aires Province in the article cited.

24. *Ibid.*

111

25. In *Tenencia de la tierra. Aspectos de la estructura agraria y su incidencia en el desarrollo agropecuario* (mimeographed), joint work by the Federal Investments Council and the National Development Council, vol. I, 1963. The "Pampas Zone" is divided into seven sections, six of which lie within the province of Buenos Aires. In each of these sections there are four categories: sub-family, family, medium multi-family, and large multi-family units. In each of the sections, the "large multi-family" ranches account for:

	Percentages of the Total of		
Regions within "Pampa Zone"	Operators	Area	Labor Force
Southern Agricultural (Buenos Aires Province)	0.6	18.0	6.5
Breeding (Buenos Aires Province)	0.2	6.8	2.5
Winter Pasture (Buenos Aires Province)	2.4	26.7	14.6
Northern Agricultural (Buenos Aires Province)	0.6	18.1	4.3
Dairy (Buenos Aires Province)	0.2	2.7	0.9
Mixed (Buenos Aires Province)	3.2	19.8	6.5
Diversified (Chaco and Santa Fe Provinces)	0.9	21.0	3.1

26. The most important study published on this period is that of Nemesio de Olariaga, *El ruralismo argentino* (Buenos Aires: El Ateneo, 1943). A most useful work in which the author includes his own experiences, but no similar studies have continued this line of research.

27. Horacio V. Pereda, *La ganadería argentina es una sola* (Buenos Aires, n.p., 1939).

28. The Ottawa Treaty, signed in 1932, established discriminatory preferences which threatened Argentine access to the British market and to a certain extent limited such access for the benefit of members of the British Commonwealth. C.A.A.

29. The analysis of the members of the CAP board was made possible by an earlier work, the paper by Hugo Berlatzky, "Investigación sobre la CAP como estructura de poder," presented to the Seminar on the Sociology of Power held at the Institute of Sociology of the University of Buenos Aires in 1961.

30. Liniers is an industrial suburb of the city of Buenos Aires where the slaughterhouses are located. C.A.A.

31. What little has been published on the birth of the Agrarian Federation is not objective. The best known book was written in the light of a partial focus vitiated by ideological elements. The information employed is derived from *La Tierra*, official publication of the Federation; its 1961 and 1962 volumes were compared with those from the earlier period, when the edition was bilingual (articles in Spanish and Italian).

112

32. By virtue of this plan, those tenant farmers whose leases had been frozen heretofore by law became owners of the lands they occupied.

33. There are not enough studies to make possible evaluating this fact "documentally." Besides, everything depends on the zone. As an example of transfer of property in the central zones and of the consolidation of a "property-owning middle class," see J. L. de Imaz, "Estratificación social del sector primario en Ucacha," *Desarrollo económico* (Buenos Aires), January–March, 1962, Vol. I, No. 4. For the "marginal zones," see the same author, "Pucará y Jasimaná: El desarrollo económico y social en dos comunidades indígenas," IDES, Conferencias (mimeographed), a lecture delivered at IDES, Buenos Aires, in 1963.

In the study by Roland Gioja and Héctor J. Cantón, "Distribución de la tierra en Juárez," paper presented to the Institute of Sociology, College of Philosophy and Letters, University of Buenos Aires, in 1964, the authors show that in the Juárez district of the province of Buenos Aires: 1) In twenty years the number of landowners had increased; the transfer of property had occurred slowly, but in 1958 the properties were smaller and the average area was less than in 1938, and 2) the increase in land owners occurred among the "small" and "medium" landowners, to the detriment of the large. For a comparative analyses consult the above mentioned, *Tenencia de la tierra.*

6. THE LARGEST LANDOWNERS

SOME TIME ago the Planning Board of Buenos Aires Province prepared a register of rural property owners whose tracts exceeded 2,500 acres. The register was set up to determine real estate taxes on the basis of cadastral data. Grouping the tracts together according to surnames and groups of owners and taking into account only those family units which total more than 25,000 acres, we find:

82 "family groups" (That is, basic surnames, since members of the group may be only distantly related)

17 agricultural companies (Some are corporations, others partnerships)

20 individual owners (These are surnames which appear only once on the tax list as owners of 25,000 acres)

Among the family groups the size of holdings varies a great deal. The family group at the head of the tax list owns a total of 300,000 acres; the next in order of size, 237,500; and the third, 150,000. There are two groups of owners with holdings of from 125,000 to 137,500 acres. The sixth group in size covers a total of 105,000 acres and so on, in decreasing order. Within these 82 family groups the greatest concentration is found among those whose holdings total 25,000 and 50,000 acres.[1]

By themselves the figures can give the observer an impressionistic overview of the original size of the family property, but not of the present situation. The "family group" is employed as a category for purposes of classification, but it is very unlikely, not to say impossible, that it be an economic unit. In some cases the relationship between the family group and the economic unit may be intimate and direct, in others so remote that there is hardly any trace of it. This assumes that those with the same surname are descended from a single line.[2]

114

The problem becomes more complicated when one must distinguish those who share a patronymic but are not related. For example, along with the traditional family named Anchorena, we find other landholding Anchorenas who descend from more recent Basque immigrants and who are also large landowners but have not the remotest kinship with the former.

A group that shares the same surname may in many cases be a cohesive economic unit, but in other cases it may be a simplistic methodological abstraction to consider those who share the same name as a group. Families with the same ancestry have now branched out and have divided their properties. Conversely, those with different surnames may act as a cohesive unit as in the case of collateral relatives and, as often happens, through marriage. In following the trail of the patronymics, one might lose sight of a substantial reality not apparent from the tax list. Be that as it may and whatever the kinship bond that today may unite them, the 82 basic family groups are clear proof of the high degree of property concentration that existed early in Argentina's history.

Fifty-six of the 82 family groups bear the names of the members of the upper class of the city of Buenos Aires. Twenty of these 56 come from traditional families of long standing in Buenos Aires province.[3] This traditional group, which has acquired its properties by inheritance, is also the one most subdivided by the different combinations of second surnames and by kinship, marriage, and the high birthrate of the group.[4]

While today the remaining 36 which complete the 56 upper class families enjoy prestige comparable to that of the traditional families, they have lesser historical roots. It is easier to discover the source of their present agricultural fortunes: the present owners' grandparents, who came to Argentina as Spanish immigrants, were the ones who made the money (families such as Pereda, Santamarina, Unzue).

Aside from these 56 basic families that in one way or another— whether through tradition or success in rural enterprises—have reached the highest position within the social structure, there are 26 family groups whose surnames have not been identified as enjoying social status similar to that of the other families.[5] They are "unknown" families, which in itself is significant. This leads to the supposition that either their scope of activity is strictly local (an unlikely possibility, in view of the size of their property), or that they habitually reside

115

abroad. Twenty-six of the 82, one third of the total, is a significant figure when it involves families owning large properties.

We have said 17 companies own over 25,000 acres. It was possible to obtain information about 12 of them, specifically those that have adopted a corporate form of organization. The others are partnerships, and there is no public information about them due to the present legal system, which exempts noncorporate agricultural activities from the provisions of the Commercial Code. In the absence of any information and considering the lack of legal requirements that apply to them, it could be concluded that these five large landowning partnerships are the result of undivided family estates.

The officers of 7 of the 12 corporations are members of the same families which have already been mentioned as owning large properties.[6] The official stockholders of 4 of the other 5 do not come from an agricultural background. One of the 5 corporations has headquarters in the city of Olavarría and belongs to Fortabat, the most important industrial and commercial complex of the region. Two of the other corporations were organized in the city of La Plata, and they are headed by businessmen of Buenos Aires province. The fourth has the city of Tandil for its headquarters, and its official stockholders are ranchers of that region. The fifth corporation is made up of merchants from the city of Buenos Aires.

The 20 property owners whose ranches do not form part of family complexes have been classified in a third group. At least the surnames of their owners appear only once on the tax list. They are regional owners, since their ranches constitute a unit within the district, or running over into a neighboring district, but not located in different districts.

Even if some of these owners are known in business circles, especially at the highest levels of the livestock business, they do not enjoy social recognition commensurate with the size of their properties.[7] The names indicate that these individuals who own large landholdings have nothing to do with the traditional aristocracy. If they have acquired large areas it has been by purchase from the original grantees. These property owners are typical examples of change of ownership; their economic success was also the result of the structural socio-economic changes which were in process.[8]

The World of the Rural Leader

Thirty-seven percent of the officers of the Rural Society are professionals with university degrees. As will be seen in later chapters, this percentage is quite similar to that for officials of other organizations representing management, such as the Argentine Chamber of Commerce and the General Economic Confederation; it is slightly higher than that of the Industrial Union. Of 36 professionals, 23 are lawyers, 7 are agricultural engineers, and 6 are engineers; clearly, lawyers account for two-thirds of all the professionals. This fact is in accord with the significant number of lawyers found in all of the leadership circles in the nation during the twenty-five year period under study. Lawyers account for one-third of the professionals even in the very specific industrial sector.

A review of the sample list of 97 leaders of the Society shows that, 38 actually are also members of the boards of directors of various corporations. Within that total, however, 26 serve exclusively in agricultural corporations; 2 serve in both agricultural and commercial and industrial ones; and finally, 10 leaders serve only in commercial, industrial, financial, and governmental enterprises.

Except for three marginal cases, the Rural Society officers act mainly within enterprises directly interested in primary production. The marginal cases are one president who is connected with the textile industry (Fano); another former officer who is involved in construction, electricity, and pharmaceutical companies (Sánchez Elía); and a third who is on various boards of printing, import-export, and metallurgical concerns (del Carril).

The rule is that officeholders in large rural concerns have organized their management units according to the modern corporate form, and in general they act exclusively within corporations. Thus, the following names appear on the boards of the corporations listed:

Leloir	Cabaña Santa Sergia
Herrera Vegas-Pereira Iraola . .	Pampas y Hacienda La Rueda S.A. Quemú-Quemú Estancias Querandíes La Marieta La Defensa
Santamarina	Santamarina e Hijos

117

Bengolea and others	Los Toros
Pueyrredón	{ Nahuel Rucá El Campamento
Bioy Casares	La Martona
Sánchez Elía	El Bagual
Leloir	{ Estancias y C. Macedo Estancias y C. Centella Manantiales
Lalor	{ Estancias Juan Lalor El Simbolar Tres Pozos
Pereda	13 de Abril
Duggan	Bernardo L. Duggan S.A.
Harriet	{ Juan Alberto Juan A. Harriet S.A.
Jamieson	{ Estancia Moy Aiké Ganadera Cancha Distante Ganadera Hill Station
Brain Menéndez	{ Estancia Mauricio Braun La Ganadera Argentina Ltda. Estancias Sara Braun Estancias Puerto Velaz Estancias Puerto Loyola Ganadera Nueva Oriental Locavan Auca Mahuida

The list in each case is far from being complete. In turn, almost all the officers of the Rural Society enter the entrepreneurial field, but only as directors of corporations devoted to agricultural activities.

Some of the owners of large rural properties, however, appear on boards of corporations devoted to different activities. For example, a Pereyra Iraola is president of ALA Airline, a member of the board of the Atlantic Bank, of the La Patagonia Insurance Company and of the Pérez Company Shipping Line. A Herrera Vegas is a member of the board of Radio International Company; a Santamarina, of the Southern Argentina Company; a Pueyrredón, president of Indoamerica, an oil producing company. But very often the participation of

118

these prestigious figures in business is more nominal than real, since they agree to lend their names to the boards of directors because of the confidence the names inspire.

So the search for correlation between land ownership and other activities at first may seem fruitless. The large landowners (those whose holdings exceed 25,000 acres) do not appear on the boards of industrial corporations, nor can it be proved that the officers of the Rural Society take part in organizations representing management other than in their own specific field. As in all cases, there are some exceptions: two of the officers on the sample of the Rural Society participated in the management of the General Economic Confederation (Sojo and Solari), but they did so as representatives of the cattle raisers.

However, for the purpose of this study, these slight results are useful parameters, even by omission. They indicate that the Rural Society officers act only within their specific environment, but that, on the other hand, industrial executives (Firpo, Fano, Sánchez Elía, Echesortu) also turn out to be officers of the Rural Society. It should be repeated once more that this sort of analysis must be subject to numerous qualifications.

In any case, we are dealing with nominal relations, for the name of a director gives us no information as to how much control he may exercise over the enterprise. On the other hand, in the role of stockholders and in financing industrial companies, the large landowners of the Rural Society may very well play an important part without this importance necessarily being apparent from the makeup of the board.

This difference between official leadership and institutionalized relations becomes more evident if the observer leaves the plane of the relations between various economic groups and passes to that of the relations between the landowners of the Rural Society and official political power.

A comparison between the list of Rural Society directors and that of ministers of agriculture for the period 1936–61 shows little correlation. Only one of the 97 officers was minister of agriculture (Cosme Massini Ezcurra), and only one was undersecretary of that ministry (Casares). However, it is known that the norm in Argentina is for the heads of the ministry to have come from the ranks of the Rural Society. The first and second ministers of agriculture during the Perón regime were members of the Society. The third minister was a notary

119

public[9] who after being sworn into office became a member of the Society. Only Horne, the minister in Frondizi's cabinet, was never a member. The next minister (Urien) was a member, though the one who temporarily replaced him, who claimed representation of the cooperatives, was not. The secretary of agriculture (later minister of economy) under President Guido was a member of the Society, and also was the son of the Society's former president and a direct descendant of one of its founders.

In any case, analysis of the official leaders of the Rural Society and of their links with public office seems to lead nowhere. In effect, this type of analysis points to two conclusions about their political activities:

1. Neither the large landowners nor the official leaders of the Rural Society have occupied high public posts, with the exceptions already noted, to which we must add that of the minister of the interior during President Aramburu's term and that of a senator for the province of Buenos Aires until 1943 (Santamarina).

2. These large rural landowners and these leaders did not participate publicly in party politics. Two congressmen out of a total of 97 officers is not much, especially if one considers that both served before the Revolution of 1943 and that they both were conservatives (Ussher and Casares). The only officers who have been active party men have belonged to a party which after 1943 lost control of the leadership of national politics.

The hypothesis that during this quarter of a century the Rural Society never ceased to govern cannot be explicitly confirmed through personal identification of its members with the official political power. The hypothesis arises from events and from real and objective findings.

For example, during the Perón era, very few of the Society's officers or former officers had direct relations with the regime in power. Two were ministers of agriculture, and one of these was also later on the Boards of the Central Bank and of the Argentine Institute for the Promotion of Trade. An officer of the Rural Society participated actively in setting up the General Economic Confederation, and another was President of the Producers' Confederation. But as public representatives of the Society's interests, these officers became marginal because they had rejected the collective position taken by the members of the Rural Society, and they served the Society only as contact men when needed.

120

However, what is not explicitly evident from a study of individual careers becomes more clear from a study of events. The Rural Society came through the Perón period basically unaffected both as an entity and as individuals. The interests of the group were not damaged during the Peronist regime, even though the ideology of the latter would have warranted the opposite assumption and even though it came to power precisely by opposing the "oligarchical" control of the previous regime.

Shortly after the Perón regime fell, a movement was organized within the Rural Society to remove those then serving as officers on the charge of having "collaborated" with the regime. Whether the charge was true or not, the fact is that explicitly or implicitly a *modus vivendi* had existed with the regime that allowed the Rural Society, and especially the great agricultural interests it represented, to go through the most critical period in its history unscathed.[10]

Next, the problem of the relations between the cattle owners' group and official political power must be analyzed by means other than that of simple analysis of personal relations between the leaders of the Rural Society, the large landowners, and the holders of political power. First, however, it may be useful to restate the much publicized theories regarding the role of the rural landowners in underdeveloped countries, in order to see whether the pattern is or is not applicable to the case of Argentina.

The Large Landowners in the Transitional Period

If events in Argentina before World War I had conformed to the model of the "traditional society,"[11] the governing elites should necessarily have been of the "traditional type." But such was not the case in Argentina, nor did the traditional elite play a traditional role. This group exercised leadership functions before and during the period when certain structural changes took place in the social, political, and economic sectors. This elite cannot be labelled tradition-bound; on the contrary, it was an innovating elite. Nor can the government itself be called traditional, even though until the passing of the Sáenz Peña Law the problems of government were solved by a few. Moreover, the national economy was not static, the technological level of the country was not low, and the national income was not stagnating. These factors which shaped the economic dynamics of the country at the end of last century and well into the 1920s have been studied analytically by econ-

121

omists to an extent that makes any explicit reference unnecessary here.[12]

Had those in power been truly a traditional elite in accordance with the model,[13] they would have proved hostile to any process that might imply even a minimum of modernization, and they would have considered the traditional norms sacred precisely because they were traditional. Although such traditionalism has dominated and still dominates in some provinces such as Salta and Corrientes, where leadership of the traditional sectors is based specifically on upholding the status quo and on exclusive adherence to form, these are exceptional cases in the more marginal regions.

At the beginning of the century Argentine society throughout the Pampa region was no longer traditional, nor could the governing group that guided it from Buenos Aires be considered so. On the contrary, this group initiated the modernization process over a period that covered nearly half a century, from 1880 to the 1920s. If it was not the direct agent, it did open the way for modernization.

The ideology of the dominant group during this period seems to have been the decisive factor that promoted modernization. Throughout the period of consolidation of the nation, the traditional upper classes of the provinces—its agricultural sectors and its lawyers—were basically conservative, and the Buenos Aires upper class, its agricultural sectors and its lawyers, and the people from the interior who had settled in the city of Buenos Aires were basically liberal.

The ideology of the generation of 1880,[14] never fully made clear but widely shared throughout the Buenos Aires upper class, in a way provided spiritual sustenance for the liberal group. Every country has its ideological "North" and "South." In Argentina, as in the United States, the struggle between the two was decided by force of arms and in both cases the ideology of the "North" won. As a result of the battle of Pavón[15] a political group with concrete and specific ideas emerged. The group had one ideology and, as had happened and would continue to happen, it imposed its ideology, in such a way as to exclude others. Its political liberalism à outrance allowed no compromise with the vestiges of a traditional society which it wanted to leave behind for good.

Military victory gave the liberal group political power, and the politico-military power thus obtained after the beginning of the desert campaigns resulted in economic power. The doors of the *latifundia* world opened as a reward for the military who had driven out the Indians,

122

for the politicians who were prepared to take advantage of the victories, for the families close to political power, for those who controlled finances, and for the importers connected with European interests. Thus, in Buenos Aires one did not proceed from the *latifundia* world to political power, but from political power, or from circles in some way connected with it or having primary contacts with those who held that power, to the *latifundia* world. This was true during the period of organization at the national level; during the Rosas regime of 1835–1852, the process had been the reverse.

Political and economic liberalism appears as the common denominator of all the factions of the period, even when these factions were in conflict. Like their European counterparts at that time, the elites adopted this liberalism, internalized it, made it their own. While in Europe the victorious ideology rested on a complete economic system, capitalism, in Argentina the elites of the time could only make it coherent on the basis of expansion of the *latifundia*. The mores of the then emerging European bourgeoisie were analogous in Argentina, in accordance with the economic condition of the country, with the "economicist" motivations and the agricultural expansion of its small ruling elite. Hence, since a great many Argentine *latifundia* owners had previously accepted the requirements of modernization and economic growth that would lead them to seek their own individual expansion, they could hardly be accused of being hostile to change and modernization, at least as long as they exercised leadership.

The structural changes which the landowners themselves precipitated finally influenced their membership. It has already been indicated that *latifundia* still exist, but a great many of the largest landowners have nothing to do with the original group of owners. The *latifundia* owners themselves transferred enormous areas almost undivided to new owners. Thus the structure of the large properties was and is both in the hands of the "old" and of the "relatively new" owners.

As long as the group of large landowners who belonged to the Buenos Aires upper class exercised leadership, that is, while it was the ruling class, it gave evidence of a certain ability. It numbered within its ranks some exceptionally versatile individuals who will be discussed again at the end of this work, and it permitted inclusion of individuals by achievement, rather than ascriptive, criteria in its ranks. To employ the Machiavellian simile, it was the happy result of a discreet combination of "lions" and "foxes." Thus, as long as it was the ruling elite, it accepted and granted a certain recognition to individuals from a different social background, provided these individuals placed their intelligence at the service of the permament interests of the group and accepted the channeling of their ambition within the options the group offered.

There was some "circulation of elites" within the group, partly because its origin in Buenos Aires was very recent and not adequately consolidated, and partly because the ideology of liberalism it had adopted brought with it certain demands: merit had to be rewarded, and the family groups that supported unchanging values had to be circumvented. Also, the weakening of moral fiber resulting from economic well-being induced the group to delegate functions to new and more active spokesmen.

Argentine society differed from the model of "traditional societies," for since it was, around the turn of the century, fluid and in full growth, it was open to recruitment of leaders. The ruling class itself even prepared and approved the legal instrument by which the leadership would be renewed, i.e., the Saénz Peña Act.

Only as an intellectual abstraction could the precise moment of the crisis in this leadership be determined. Although this crisis began to acquire a definitive form in the 1930s and was clearly discernible in politics by 1945, in other parts of society it had come earlier.

The "circulation of elites," which is so beneficial for normal institutional continuity, gave rise to serious difficulties in the continuity of leadership: while members of the "old" upper class adapted themselves to change, a great many of the "new" members opposed change. The original mores had been flexible, for liberalism was converted to an instrument of development. Those of the "new" upper class became inflexible; that is, the same liberalism became an immutable dogma. While the "old" had been anti-conservative and anti-traditional—with resulting harm to the historical continuity of the nation—the "new" stiffened their attitudes by adopting a conservatism and a traditionalism which were not inherent in the ideology. This ideological traditionalism in the end became one more mode of distorting original upper class ideas.

There were no industrial leaders in either group, but the "old" upper class, as will be seen, participated in establishing the Argentine Industrial Union and in the creation of the Industrial Bank, and they facilitated the activities of the immigrants. Although the Argentine *latifundia* owners looked down upon the immigrants, they could not fail to feel secretly satisfied with the foreigners' efforts. The "new" elite on the other hand, converted their own preference for agriculture

124

and imported manufactured goods into a battle cry against domestic industry. Both groups had confined themselves to a single economic theory for what they wanted the country to become, but while the "old" correctly interpreted the coming tendencies in economic development, the "new" entrenched themselves and adopted a stance outside the historical mainstream of events.

Finally, while the "old" elite, knowing that their era of power was ending and wisely trying to forestall events, signed their own political death warrant by extending the voting franchise to the whole population, the "new," on the other hand, invented palliatives and substitutes to try to reconcile as much as possible the dichotomy between the system of government which their ancestors had bequeathed them and their inconsistent decision to accept the rules of the game.

Thus, in the mid-1940s when the "new" had demonstrated its inability to realize that the incorporation of the masses into socio-political processes was irreversible, the latent crisis became manifest. As in other historical processes, the "merit elite" was reduced to a "nominal elite."[16] When the crisis materialized, the elite found itself replaced by a completely new leadership, although the former was never left completely devoid of power. There are always "residues" of power, and while a new leadership exercises new functions, an old or "nominal" elite may yet control some specific functions.

The "Residue" of Power of the Nominal Elite

The old elite, now a nominal elite, is still accorded a prestige based on the past and holds control of some basic elements of the economy other than those related strictly to cattle-raising.

A large part of the private finance system in Buenos Aires is controlled through a network of financiers who head banks created at the time of great expansion,[17] notwithstanding the share of bank stock held by foreign investors. The same is true of many of the insurance companies originally financed by domestic capital, within the limitations arising from subsequent agreements and from reinsurance.

A look at the lists of directors of these banks and insurance companies makes it possible to perceive the interlocking memberships that exist between these directors and the group enjoying the highest social prestige. Nevertheless, owing to the modern distinction between administration and ownership of corporations, it is not possible to as-

125

certain beyond doubt whether the old elite really owns and controls this traditional sector of Argentine private banking or if they simply appear as stockholders for the record, thus concealing the real owners. The old elite had also completely controlled the governmental banking system until 1943; it regained control in 1956 and, with some interruptions, has continued in that position until this day. Such control has, generally speaking, coincided with periods of disruption of the nation's institutional order, either by revolts or by military pressures. On some occasions after 1956 the holders of political power have themselves forestalled events and, being doubtful of the very bases of their legitimacy, have surrendered control of the economic sector and governmental banking system to members of the old elite, hoping thus to obtain economic and social backing from the group, with all the advantages that such backing implies, especially in international relations.

Almost all the federal appellate judges, the federal judges, and judges of other jurisdictions, with the single exception of the labor courts, have been recruited from the Buenos Aires upper class. Others have been members of the provincial upper classes, especially those from the Córdoba upper class who have become residents of Buenos Aires because of appointments to the federal courts and subsequent transfers. Even though the percentage of upper-class judges decreased during the Perón regime (only one Supreme Court judge was from the upper class), all the intermediate levels of the judicial apparatus continued to be overwhelmingly the prerogative of this social class.

Some of the judges may not have shared the same upper class background, but these have not altered the dominance of the upper class. On the contrary, since the federal judiciary is staffed almost exclusively by this class, the sort of interaction that arises from joint participation in certain tasks leads to social intercourse and eventually to identification with the upper class, this identification being the result of the upward movement of those promoted. The slow course of advancement in a judicial career results not only in changes in status, but also leads to changes in status mentality. Also, the end of the career usually coincides with the most propitious moment for anyone who did not originally belong to the upper class to become identified with it.

Diplomacy, that is, the corps of "career" diplomats, would seem to be the career for those of the upper class who have no land and no law degree (or those who become lawyers and then realize they have no vocation for the law) and have no relatives in financial circles.

126

Whenever any political change takes place in Argentina, especially if this change is due to military intervention, the members of this group claim ascriptive right to enter diplomacy. This does not happen when the political change comes about through constitutional elections, since the upper class has been identified with electoral losers for the last twenty years.

As long as professional competence was not demanded, or rather, except in those "abnormal" years in which it was strictly required, members of the upper class have filled vacancies in the diplomatic corps. They had the necessary connections to do so and in public they were capable of satisfying some of the incidental and subordinate requirements for a good diplomat: *façons*, or manners. This situation became evident when Perón was overthrown, but even during his administration the basic staff of the foreign ministry, the non-political officials, were individuals of the highest social origin who, willingly or unwillingly, had adjusted to the Perón regime. Apparently, they had discreetly applied to the domestic environment the "personality type" mechanism which diplomats develop in their professional roles.

In any society in which change is in prospect (disregarding at this time the Argentine case) it might seem strange for the upper class, or nominal elite, to remain in control of certain strategic economic and governmental sectors. What must be taken into account is the lack of synchronization of changes in all sectors of the society and also that the victory of more modern groups does not neccessarily require the destruction of the traditional in all societies. On the contrary, if change has come about without serious cleavages, the traditional elite, after having lost political power, withdraws to the exercise of specific functions, thus facilitating the necessary process of social adjustment. The exercise of diplomacy by this class, for example, far from being an exclusively Argentinian phenomenon, seems to be typical of all European aristocracies removed from political control. In Europe, however, these aristocracies have channelled their experienced abilities into efficient public service.

The Buenos Aires upper class has not given any of its members to the clergy, and its members have had little or nothing to do with the establishment of a modern entrepreneurial group. Although there is a small minority in the armed forces, there have always been (and here lies the great difference between the military and the entrepreneurs and clergy) senior officers who have come from that class. These relatively few senior officers can be, when the time comes, functionally

127

useful to their class, particularly in moments of political confusion or latent or overt crisis. In these cases the upper class always has some relatives in the armed forces who can be influenced, either to hasten military intervention (in most cases), or to prevent such intervention, or once it has taken place, to facilitate a return to civilian administration.

The most typical aspect of this concentration of special roles to which the old governing class has gravitated is that almost all the writers, novelists, apologists, and essayists of a liberal cast of thought have come from its ranks.[18] In this sense, it would seem that the spiritual maturity of the old ruling class, which for three or four generations was devoted almost exclusively to military activities or to personal enrichment, produced its best fruit at the time when the class had lost political power.

That upper-class intellectuals appear in the liberal camp is not without significance. The Buenos Aires upper class was never authentically conservative, and the intellectuals who had previously come from its ranks were always inspired by the same liberal attitudes.[19] Nor is it irrelevant that the other writers, intellectuals, and essayists closer to traditional values and more concerned and alert to all that might imply national historical continuity, have come from the *provincial* upper classes that have settled in Buenos Aires.[20] But intellectuals have no power in Argentina unless they are historians or historical novelists like Manuel Gálvez. Besides, local novelists or essayists are not usually the ones who strengthen ideologies.

Thus, generally this great number of writers has not provided the group anything but some spiritual enjoyment and satisfaction, and a certain intellectual glow to replace its former political power. Some of them, who have known the upper-class family environment thoroughly, have presented to the outside world a rather unedifying image in the portrayal of their kind. Contrary to what is usual among modern promoters of unknown debutantes, they have surrounded the fall of their class with the grace of the death of a swan.

The upper class liberal intellectuals have not devoted themselves to aesthetic values only. When several of them have joined to devote their concerted efforts to creating a great newspaper enterprise, the result has been very effective for the group. The two largest traditional morning papers in Buenos Aires[21] are the most perfect supporters and best broadcasters of the activities of the liberal intellectual group and of the opinions of the Buenos Aires upper class.

128

Again, what must be kept in mind is the asynchronization of changes; as the loss of political power does not necessarily mean the loss of economic power, the loss of one of the economic sectors (the upper class's reluctance to enter the industrial sector) does not necessarily have to be followed by the loss of political power. Between the economic and political spheres there is a gulf to be bridged. This subject will be considered later. Now an attempt will be made to ascertain on what basic factors the upper class's continuity in power rests, so that despite its having ceased to be the ruling class and having been reduced to the exercise of only some functions, it continues to play such a decisive role in the nation.

There is group cohesion within the Buenos Aires upper class. Despite some occasional differences, this cohesion continues to operate on basic matters. The upper class is made up both of families of traditional origin and of immigrant stock. There is almost no "family memory" within the group capable of conceptualizing the double source of recruitment. The author has demonstrated elsewhere[22] that although a substantial number of the members of the upper class maintain that "family origin" is the determining factor for recruitment, they accept as equals individuals whose origin is completely different. Actually, family origin is overlooked, and what identifies members of the class definitely are certain commonly shared "external rules of behavior." There are no group values or common ideology.

Members of the upper class possess a type of prestige which is valid within the group, or at least serves the group as the criterion in recognizing the individual as a member. But their political power varies greatly, being almost nil in many cases. The range of economic standing of members of the group also includes many levels from the very highest to the lower level of the middle income groups.

The ownership of large areas of land does not identify members of the group. It is possible to be a large landowner in Buenos Aires province and also belong to the group; it is possible to own as much or more land and still not be accepted. It is possible to be a great rural landowner in some far off place such as Patagonia and still be a member of the class, provided the umbilical cord connecting the landowner to the nation's capital has not been cut. It is possible to be a small landowner in any place in the country and still be a member of the group. It is possible to own no land and still feel that the Rural Society interprets one's interests. (The Society's manifest function is to defend and represent the great landowners, but it also has a latent function: that

129

of representing a whole social sector, the Buenos Aires upper class, even when it owns no land.) It is possible to become a judge without land and without one's family owning an acre of what it once possessed; one can be a career diplomat on a meager salary in Buenos Aires; one can be a laywer without lawsuits or a notary without business in the capital; but if one is a member of some "upper class in the interior," one is immediately accepted as a peer. What counts is the upper class status, the prestige that the group assigns the individual when he is accepted as a peer.

Some members of the upper class, however, do wield power and that power, whether permanent or temporary, will be used whenever possible to benefit their own kind. A transcending solidarity is sometimes manifested in a negative way in these officials' behavior towards their upper-class peers: not to touch, not to make difficulties, not to bring up acute problems. The upper class citizens who were persecuted during the Perón regime knew that they could count on coming through any difficulty unharmed due to the benevolent protection of their peers who were in office. The members of the upper class who were persecuted for political reasons after November, 1955,[23] knew that the same machinery would be set in motion and the same tacit solidarity would spring into action to temper for their exclusive benefit the rigors of a general policy.

It is evident that the cohesion of the group transcends ideological differences. The cohesion is "functional" and tends to increase to the maximum the scope of the influence of the group, which takes advantage of occasional power vacuums to fill a vacant office with one of its candidates.

The cohesion of the group is based on various intangible factors—a special culture which in the last analysis is nothing but an internalized group culture, a given set of manners, and the frequenting of the same social circles. The frequenting of the same social circles is the basic factor which makes it possible to transcend differences of origin, and all the subordinate variables arise from this. The social foundation is laid at the time of one's formal education, that is, is based on where and how the child, and later the adolescent, was educated, what type of school he attended at the proper time.

There may be no more than five private schools in Buenos Aires where those who will turn out to be members of the upper class are recruited. It is necessary to say "those who will turn out to be" because to those who are already members by parental ascription one must add

130

those who do not start out as members but end as such due to the friendships started at school and to the primary type relations kept up after graduation.

This sort of school-centered relations, continued at some "key" rowing, polo, rugby, golf, and yachting clubs, will create the foundation for solid cohesion later on. This cohesion goes back to a common point of departure and will transcend the variables which might tend to separate, such as ideological differences, different standards of living, and different interpretations of reality. Thus, this socialization process carried on continuously from the time of entering school, as long as it is expressed through external symbols, through "manners," operates as an indicator of recognition.

Operating throughout different occupational groups (though ranchers, lawyers, or financiers make up the basic ones) the Buenos Aires upper class is the only cohesive group in the nation that possesses "horizontal social mobility." This means that within the same social level they interact with their peers in different sectors of economic activity. Thus, the members of this "class devoid of power" get support from their peers through "elective affinities." They will always find someone to sponsor and support their acceptance anywhere whenever the occasion arises.

Of course, the upper class is not the only cohesive group in Argentine society. Other classes and groups also carry their members along, pushing and supporting them. But some of these groups are bound by a formal structure, such as the ecclesiastical group, or they are ethnic minorities which for the very reason that they are minorities support each other (the Jews, for example). The great advantage of the upper class groups lies in that their cohesion rests completely on informal elements and at the same time is expressed at the very highest interest levels.

This upper class, which has only "residual powers," and was formerly a merit elite but has now become a nominal elite, still has succeeded in articulating its own interests very well and in extending its scope of action beyond the social functions to which it is ostensibly confined. This is not due solely to its own merits, but also to the complementing bankruptcy of the other groups. The other groups and interests which hold economic power have not up to now achieved either prestige or status presumably equivalent to their real power, nor have they achieved united and cohesive articulation of their objectives, their points of view, and their interests. Whenever a power vacuum occurs,[24]

131

the upper class is in a position to fill it. It is able to do so because it is a cohesive group and because the many other rival groups which oppose it lack cohesion and apparently have little training and less vocation for the exercise of political power. But this subject will be treated in the following chapter.

Notes

1. The researcher traced only the main surnames under which the tracts are registered in the Registry of Real Estate Owners.

2. An example: under the common patronymic of "Alzaga" there are tracts totalling 238,445 acres entered in the Register. But the notations of property titles correspond to the following titleholders: Alzaga U.S. de; Alzaga de L.M. and others; Alzaga del C.D. de; Alzaga del Carril; Alzaga, Emilio F. and others; Alzaga and others; Alzaga U. D. and others; Alzaga U. D. de P. I. (there are three other parcels entered in a similar way); Alzaga U. de P. I. D.; Alzaga U. de V. I. M.; Alzaga U., Félix de; Alzaga U. J. de S. E.; Alzaga U. S. de; Alzaga U. y R. L. A. C.; Alzaga U y R. L. S .F.; Alzaga Unzué S.; Alzaga Unzué S. de; Alzaga Unzué R. D.; Alzaga y R. L. and others (there are three parcels more entered in the same way); Alzaga y S. Quesada; Alzaga y Sole M. L.; Alzaga y Sole C. A.; Alzaga y Sole de L.; Alzaga y Unzué D.

3. They include Alzaga, Anchorena, Elizalde, Guerrero, Martínez de Hoz, Peralta Ramos, Pueyrredón, Riglos, Sáenz Rozas, Uribelarrea, and others.

4. All the information has been gathered from the "Registro de propietarios de más de 1,000 hectáreas," unpublished manuscript drawn up by the Economic Planning Board of Buenos Aires Province, 1958.

5. The criteria used in determining social status can be found in José Luis de Imaz, La clase alta de Buenos Aires (Buenos Aires: Instituto de Sociología, Universidad de Buenos Aires, 1963). C.A.A.

6. The analysis of the members of the boards of agricultural corporations has been made on the basis of the information supplied by the Guía del accionista (Buenos Aires: Editorial El Accionista, 1960). This guide lists all the names of the directors of national corporations and contains a second attached list with the details on all the boards on which each entrepreneur appears.

7. They include, among others, Abin, Allievi, Andiarena, Azumendi (an officer of the Rural Society), Berrote, Bordea, Churruca, de Olaso, Dietrich, Dunoyer, Ibarnegaray, Larralde, Pepre, Reedy, Scarpesa, and Suirmusky.

8. The names of these owners were compared with lists of members of the highest social stratum, such as the Guía azul, and the lists of members of the Jockey Club in 1953 with negative results.

9. In Argentina, as in other Latin American countries, "notary public" is a professional degree, earned at the universities, considered to be somewhat below that of lawyer in prestige and training, but not necessarily in terms of income. C.A.A.

132

10. See the Rural Society's 1952 Annual Report.

11. For a "model" of the traditional society, see G. Germani, *Política y sociedad en una época de transición* (Buenos Aires: Editorial Paidos, 1963) chapter 3.

12. A. Ferrer, *La economía argentina. Las etapas de su desarrollo y problemas actuales* (Mexico: Fondo de Cultura Económica, 1963).

13. As described in Max F. Millikan and Donald L. M. Blackmer (eds.), *The Emerging Nations: Their Growth and United States Policy* (Boston: Little Brown, 1961), 3 and 5: "These are societies with hereditary hierarchical rule, living under the sway of custom rather than law. Their economies were static and remained at the same level of limited technology and low income from one generation to the next . . . they should be termed traditional since they were incapable of generating a regular flow of inventions and innovations and of moving into a phase of sustained economic growth. . . . The society had encountered a new condition to which it could not adapt. Old patterns of behavior persisted even though new circumstances required a changed behavior, and society ceased to function sufficiently well enough to prevent disaster." As may be noted, these characteristics of the model do not correspond to Argentine society.

14. O. Cornblit, E. Gallo, and A. O'Connell, "La generación del 80 y su proyecto. Antecedentes y consecuencias." (Paper presented before the Inderdisciplinary Seminar on Economic and Social Development in Argentina, Buenos Aires, 1961.)

15. The Battle of Pavón, fought on September 17, 1861, between the forces of Buenos Aires Province and those of the newly established central government, was won by the former and had the ultimate effect of transferring for the last time the center of power from the interior to the city and province of Buenos Aires. C.A.A.

16. The terms "nominal elite" and "merit elite" are used in their strict Paretian meaning. See Wilfredo Pareto, *Trattato di sociologia generale* (Florence: Barbera, 1916).

17. Such as the Supervielle Bank, the Argentine Bank of Commerce, the Popular Argentine Bank, the Tornquist Bank, and the Shaw Bank.

18. Jorge Luis Borges, Leonidas de Vedia, Victoria Ocampo, Silvina Bullrich, Bioy Casares, Mugica Láinez, and a long list of others.

19. Miguel Cané, Agustín Alvarez, and others.

20. Carlos Ibarguren, Martínez Zuviría, Ignacio Anzoategui, Manuel Gálvez, Julio Irazusta, and others.

21. *La Prensa* and *La Nación*.

22. J. L. de Imaz, *La clase alta de Buenos Aires*.

23. The military leadership which overthrew Perón in September, 1955, split in November of that year, and the "nationalist" faction was purged from the government. C.A.A.

24. Power vacuums have in fact occurred several times in recent years because the Argentine military, after exerting pressure on the government of the day, have not dared to carry through to their ultimate consequences the processes they have unleashed.

133

7. THE ENTREPRENEURS—PART ONE

The Members of ACIEL

THE TIME has come to study some aspects of entrepreneurial leadership, but not the entrepreneurial group as such, since the latter is not within the scope of this book. By "leadership" is meant those who appear to be the "formal leaders" because they are at the head of great organizations representing management.

There are two of these entrepreneurial organizations. The one known as ACIEL is made up of three entities: the Industrial Union, the Argentine Chamber of Commerce, and the Coordinating Committee of the Rural Societies. Consequently, ACIEL is a superstructure for entities which existed before it was established after the 1955 revolution. The Industrial Union dates back to 1887 and the Argentine Chamber of Commerce, to 1924.

The other great organization is the General Economic Confederation, which has a different structure. In this case it is the all-inclusive top that counts. Three different Federations are combined within this organization: the Industrial Federation, the Commercial Federation, and the Federation of Production. The provincial federations which coordinate these interests are also affiliated.

The same method of analysis that has applied in the preceding chapters will be followed in the study of the entrepreneurial leadership. Attention will also be paid to the entrepreneurs who founded great companies or who are the sons of the founders, though they may not be part of the leadership now. These entrepreneurs enjoy a prestige acquired in their economic activities. While their companies have now adopted an anonymous corporate structure and management has become impersonal, some of these men were still officers during part of the period covered by this study.[1]

Now there is a new generation of leaders at the corporate level; they are the managers trained at special institutions. It is clear that these men represent a new type of leadership within the impersonal corporate system. This subject, however, is beyond the scope of this work, which is not concerned with the structure of the industry, but only with ascertaining who represents the industry.[2]

As a rule, both the Chamber of Commerce and the Industrial Union leaders are native-born Argentines. In the sample used, 21 percent of the leaders of the former and 14 percent of the latter are foreign born.[3] The number of foreigners in the Chamber of Commerce has been decreasing since 1936. In the sample we find two Englishmen, two Italians from Milan, one Swede, two Spaniards, and so on. With the exception of a Frenchman and a Belgian, foreign industrial leaders are natives of the same countries as the businessmen with whom they are associated. In both organizations the Argentine leaders come from the Federal Capital or from the province of Buenos Aires. However, there is one important exception, Luis Colombo, president of the Industrial Union until 1946, who was born in Rosario and had his main business headquarters in Mendoza.

The industrial leaders could be classified in three groups according to their origins.

—— Twenty-one officers of the Industrial Union came from the well-to-do bourgeoisie, that is, they came from entrepreneurial families, and they have inherited a solid economic position. Five of these families were French and had come to Argentina before the end of last century; three were German; three, Italian, and five, first- or second-generation Argentine. Many of the "traditional" industrialists belong to this group.[4] In view of the comparatively recent appearance of the entrepreneurial group, those who can claim two preceding generations in the business are considered traditional industrialists.

—— A second group is composed of foreigners sent from their native countries as managers or representatives of companies who have become entrepreneurial leaders after having been incorporated into the nation's activities. In Europe the members of this group, or their families, had a socioeconomic status comparable to that of those classified under the preceding paragraph. This is apparent from their university degrees and from their fields of specialization. In the sample are five engineers who would belong in this category: two from Milan, one from England, one from France, and one from Belgium.

—— In the third group are ten entrepreneurs of very humble origin, half of them sons of Italian immigrants and the other half, of Spanish

135

immigrants. These leaders started their entrepreneurial careers at the bottom, and their careers, with but slight variations, follow the pattern of genuine self-made men.[5]

—— The same classifications might be employed for the family origins of the leaders of the Argentine Chamber of Commerce. In that organization, too, the largest group turns out to be from well-to-do bourgeois families of foreign extraction who have settled in Buenos Aires.

Of the 57 officers of the Industrial Union, 23 were officers only of long established firms which in some fashion bear the name of the founder, though they are now incorporated.[6] These officers constitute the generation of "sons." They are the heirs of the founding pioneers. Normally on the various boards of directors of the Industrial Union analyzed (1936, 1941, 1946, 1951, 1956, and 1961) they shared posts with the self-made men. It is only on the 1961 board of directors that a third group representing some of the large modern (generally foreign) corporations begins to emerge. The role of this third group— their authority to make decisions and to commit the company—is different. The others were completely identified with "their" company because they had personally founded the firm or because they had inherited an important share of the stock. Corporate officers, however, belong to an organization representing management because of the high degree of industrial, economic, or legal skill they possess.

Traditionally, textile, foodstuffs, and metallurgical entrepreneurs have been at the head of the Industrial Union. But on the last board (1961), 6 of the 19 members represented large metallurgical companies, while in 1946 there had been only one and one in 1936. This fact may be indicative of a change of base, both in the makeup of the body of entrepreneurs and in the preponderance of certain industries.

The leaders of the Chamber of Commerce are similar; there are those who are themselves the founders of their own business enterprises and those who are sons of the founders who come from established foreign bourgeois families.

A third group of technicians and economists is associated not with only one but rather with multiple commercial enterprises. A fourth group represents import firms (British, North American, and Swedish), but the members of this fourth group seem to be moving away from leadership positions. While on the first board of the Chamber of Commerce analyzed, representatives of import firms held one third to one-half of the posts, as a result of structural changes in the composition of the business group they do not appear on the most recent boards.

Last, it is possible to identify a fifth group made up of managers who have made a career by starting at the bottom within great foreign capital companies.[7]

The leadership of both entrepreneurial organizations showed growing oligarchical tendencies up to the time of the Perón regime. In each of these organizations, one group had ruled the destiny of the respective institution until 1946. In 1941, 16 of the 19 officers had been on the board of directors of the Chamber of Commerce since 1936. Ten of the 13 on the board of the Industrial Union in 1941 had been there since 1936. In 1946, 10 of the 17 leadership posts of the Chamber of Commerce were filled by the same people who had been there five years before. But in the Industrial Union in 1946, only 4 of the 11 member board had been on it five years before, and the president of the Industrial Union (who was the one who really counted) had occupied that office for twenty years.

In 1946 that trend ended. After that year's elections, the Industrial Union's board of directors, as a result of the part it had played in the electoral process, resigned as a body. A provisional board was appointed which stayed in office only three weeks. The Industrial Union was placed under government control and was inactive throughout the Perón regime. Not until ten years later was it able to reorganize and resume its institutional life.

In both organizations a substantial change of leadership took place in 1961. In fact, in the 13 positions in the Industrial Union and the 19 in the Chamber of Commerce, there is no case of a holdover of officers; all are new, as is shown by comparison with the other lists employed, made up at five-year intervals. But in both cases the changing of the guard did not mean a change of ideology, or of the concept of the role of the entrepreneur, or of the attitudes they adopted.

The Members of the General Economic Confederation

The General Economic Confederation (hereafter, GEC) brings together three federations established in accordance with their type of activity, whether industrial, commercial, or productive, and also numerous provincial federations.[8]

The GEC was established in 1951 as a result of the movement started by the entrepreneurs of the interior who were anxious to up-

137

hold their interests vis-à-vis those of the national capital and the east-central part of the country. It originally represented a reaction against the Buenos Aires leadership of the traditional industrial and commercial entities. This entrepreneurial movement later won the support and goodwill of the Perón regime, which tried to convert it into the legal representative channel for the entrepreneurs. The GEC was taken over by the government in 1956, but was able to reorganize two years later. Consequently, it has had a shorter span of activity, and it became necessary to make some changes as to the dates in which the samples were taken. The data employed apply to the leaders active in 1953 and 1963.

The percentage of foreigners in the leadership of the GEC is about the same as in the Industrial Union, that is, 14 percent. Of these, two are Poles and the rest, Spaniards.[9] The essential difference between the two organizations is to be found in the fact that only 41 percent of the GEC leaders were born in the city of Buenos Aires metropolitan area, whereas almost 100 percent of the leaders of the other management organization were born there.

Twenty-five percent of the leaders of the GEC included in the sample come from the Northwest, from such provinces as Tucumán, Santiago del Estero, Catamarca, and La Rioja. This is understandable when we consider the federated structure of the GEC. The city of Rosario takes third place after Buenos Aires and the Northwest as the place of origin of the leaders, with 4 of the 36 whose biographies have been analyzed.

At the highest executive level of the GEC there are six Jewish leaders (two born in Warsaw, one in Russia, and three in the Russo-Jewish colonies that have settled in Argentina, especially in the province of Entre Ríos), as against none in the sample for the Industrial Union and the Chamber of Commerce (this does not mean that Jews are excluded from executive posts in the other entrepreneurial organizations, as there are two Jews in the Industrial Union not included in the sample). It has already been noted that a prominent Jew figured on the board of directors of the Rural Society. On the board of the GEC, there is one Syrian director while there are none on those of the other organizations. As to origin, the majority of the Argentine leaders of the GEC (and of its member organizations) were born in the interior from well-to-do bourgeois families, especially from those of Spanish extraction.[10]

Aside from the Polish and Spanish immigrants (true self-made men)

138

on the board of the GEC, there are many leaders on the local levels in Azul, Tucumán, and La Rioja who have no national significance and who apparently do not head important companies. The fact that it has not been possible to obtain information on the business activities of these leaders after going through all available documentary sources in Buenos Aires is in itself significant.

Fourteen of the 45 leaders analyzed are engaged in commerce, 14 in processing industries complementing agricultural production; 6 in agriculture and cattle-raising or in grain and sugar production; 5 in printing, metallurgy and chemicals; 1 in savings and financing institutions; 1 in mining; and 2 are legal administrative officials without any other entrepreneurial involvement.

It is evident from the survey of the entities represented on the GEC boards that small and medium enterprises of a local nature have an undeniable numerical superiority. Eight GEC leaders, however, are affiliated with large enterprises. One is established in Catamarca at the head of important mining operations, and another owns a large store in Buenos Aires; a third is connected with various agricultural and cattle-raising enterprises and with insurance companies; a fourth heads an important cereal company, owned by Argentines; the fifth is president of the board of a modern television enterprise and also has other mass communication interests; the sixth represents the sugar industry, and the remaining two represent companies in the national capital.

There are, therefore, two levels in the GEC leadership: a minority at a very high economic level involved in enterprises of high economic concentration, and a local majority at a low economic level attached to small enterprises with an insignificant role. At least this is true on the national plane, though there seem to be some cases of leaders who have been very active in setting up local units. Thirty-two of the 45 leaders operate in the Federal Capital and 8 in the Northwestern provinces. Nine of the 59 GEC leaders had previously been active in labor unions, employers' associations, or in entrepreneurial groups before the advent of Peronism. They are the ones who made up the GEC board in 1953. Some leaders who had been active in the Industrial Union and some (like Sojo and Solari, the leaders of the Federation of Production) who had previously been active in the Rural Society joined that board.

Fifteen of the 59 leaders were active only during the Perón period and exclusively through the GEC channels. The rest of those included in the sample, that is, 35 of the leaders, continued to be active after the

1958 reorganization. The latter were men who had not been active during the previous period or had been so only at the local level, but not within the provincial or national federations, and so this was a new team.

The most pronounced differences between the entrepreneurs of these organizations are as follows:

—— The men of the Industrial Union represent the more traditional domestic capital companies, many of which were established around the turn of the century and are generally still controlled by the founding families.[11]

—— The largest companies, especially the metallurgical ones, belong to the Industrial Union.[12] Important economic groups are represented on the board of the GEC, but there are no firms with capital comparable to that of the Industrial Union companies. Ducilo and Fiat, the only large foreign capital companies represented in an entrepreneurial organization, are both members of the Industrial Union.

—— On the other hand, the new corporations, with a relatively large number of stockholders, in which ownership and management may be in different hands, predominate in the GEC. In general the newer entrepreneurs, with a shorter entrepreneurial career, belong to the GEC, though there are some notable exceptions such as its former president.

—— Only large companies are found in the Industrial Union, while the small and medium predominate in the GEC; the large groups in the latter are a small minority. The leadership of the Industrial Union is made up exclusively of Buenos Aires men. Due to the federal structure of the GEC, the interests of the interior seem to be adequately represented and those of the Northwest probably are over-represented.

—— Political factors have fundamentally affected these organizations. The Industrial Union adopted a very uncompromising attitude of opposition to Perón during the period before he came to power. Once Peronism became established, it gave the GEC official recognition and invested it with representation of the whole sector. The president of the GEC participated in cabinet meetings. Even though many of the GEC leaders were not Peronists, the organization came to be identified with the Perón regime to the point that, after the fall of his administration, the entrepreneurs who had belonged to the intermediate leadership levels of the GEC joined the "free enterprisers" in demanding a temporary government takeover of the entity. Throughout the Perón regime, the "political factor" continued to affect the government-controlled Industrial Union. The persecution of one of its former

140

leaders served to harden the group's attitude against Perón even more. After the situation changed in 1958, when a new generation of entrepreneurs that was free of earlier involvements came into the GEC, the "old story" and the "old charges" continued to have an effect out of proportion to their intrinsic merits.

——The two organizations are also separated by ideological differences. While both favor a "market economy" and the creation of conditions guaranteeing "free enterprise," the Industrial Union's statements and proposals seem to be identified with orthodox liberal economics. The declarations of the GEC, on the other hand, fit within the framework of the economic "structuralists" who are more closely identified with the directives of the United Nations Economic Commission for Latin America and favor jointly controlled planning by the private sectors, under the supervision of the state. Within the more complex organisms such as ACIEL, which is the superstructure of the traditional entrepreneurial organizations, both the Industrial Union and the Chamber of Commerce follow the "free enterprise" line of the Rural Society and the economic scheme and interpretations of events pushed by this top cattle-raising organization.

—— Economic power, when it is new, brings with it changes in status which are evidenced by outward signs such as a change of residence to another quarter more in keeping with the social prestige sought. All the Industrial Union leaders live in the "northern quarter" of Buenos Aires, or in Belgrano, San Isidro, and Acassuso.[13] Only 25 of the 42 GEC leaders who reside in the capital and environs live in comparable sections. The other 17 live in typical Buenos Aires middle class districts.[14] Many of these GEC leaders who do live in the northern district have moved there only within the last few years, which leads us to conclude that their money is "newer." Though the remaining 40 percent who live in characteristic middle class districts may come from the bourgeoisie, it would be from newer sectors than those from which the Industrial Union leaders come. Table 7.1 compares the social origin of the leaders.

TABLE 7.1

Origin of Entrepreneurial Leaders by Organization

	IU	CC	GEC
Traditional upper class	3%	14%	4%
Well-to-do bourgeoisie	60%	?%	64%
Self-made men	17%	19%	32%

These are only rough estimates because from the data available it is not possible to tell how many of the leaders of the Chamber of Commerce come from the well-to-do entrepreneurial bourgeoisie, but in view of the relatively small number of self-made men, it may be assumed that there must be a substantial majority of members from the entrepreneurial bourgeoisie. In terms of higher education of the leadership body, it is found that the number of holders of university degrees accounts for:

27% of the Industrial Union
47% of the Chamber of Commerce
37% of the General Economic Confederation

Lawyers make up a third of the university men in the last two organizations, while in the Industrial Union they account for 40 percent. These percentages confirm once more what has been observed throughout this entire investigation. This is a striking fact and especially interesting in this connection, since those now being considered are captains of industry.[15]

The Upper Level Entrepreneurs in Argentina

When the entrepreneurial elite is discussed, one may be referring to three different sectors, though there may be crossovers among the three. First, members of this elite are the leaders of the entrepreneurial organizations, whatever their personal merits or qualifications. The fact is that these men are at the head of the entities which represent all entrepreneurs and speak in their name and interest. More clearly, they are always depositories of a mandate. These are the members of the entrepreneurial elite already discussed in the preceding paragraphs. Personally they may have no power, little economic strength, and, in the case of those who own their companies, these companies may not be large, but these individuals "represent" the large and small entrepreneurs whether on a national or local scale.

Second, those who head the most important technologically innovative companies belong to the entrepreneurial elite. This study does not deal with them, but later in this chapter the author will make reference to the results of a sociological analysis carried on among those managers.

Third, entrepreneurs who have acquired prestige might be counted among the elite. They are generally the founders or the next generation which has carried on the enterprises and also some local managers of very important international enterprises.

These entrepreneurs who at present have prestige may no longer be in control of their factories, and they may even have retired. In any case, they are the product of a certain type of career, and they show a status correlation between occupation, economic level achieved, and social influence. It is necessary to pause here, since these careers reached their peak during the quarter of a century under study.[16]

TABLE 7.2

Nationality of the Prestigious Entrepreneurs in 1959

Original Nationality	Industrialists		Businessmen		Total Entrepreneurs	
	Cases	%	Cases	%	Cases	%
Argentine	106	61.5	50	44.0	156	54.5
Spanish	8	4.5	8	7.0	16	5.5
Italian	9	5.0	5	4.5	14	5.0
German-Swiss	13	7.5	11	10.0	24	8.0
French-Belgian	14	8.0	6	5.0	20	7.0
USA-English	13	7.5	15	13.5	28	10.0
Arab	3	2.0	3	2.5	6	2.5
Other	7	4.0	15	13.5	22	7.5
Total	173	100.0	113	100.0	286	100.0

Table 7.2 shows that the percentages of native industrialists is high, especially when compared with the low figures for the businessmen. In the industrial sector a high percentage of the Argentines are native-born children of the pioneer group. Some of these entrepreneurs have benefitted from the prestige attained through the efforts of the preceding generation.

Among the businessmen, the low percentage of natives is notable. This percentage would have been normal fifty years ago when all the large businesses in Buenos Aires were in foreign hands. Even today big business, that is, the principal firms, the subsidiaries of international companies, and the large importers, provide a channel of upward mobility for people who come from abroad.

143

The figures for Spaniards and Italians are also low when one considers the large size of the Spanish and Italian communities; in this connection, the percentages of German, Swiss, British, and American businessmen seem very high. Combining the figures for businessmen and industrialists, barely a little more than half are Argentines. The British and Americans are next with 10 percent, then the Germans and Swiss with 88 percent. It is possible to subdivide the Argentine entrepreneurial group by analyzing the biographical data for 69 industrialists and 50 businessmen.

One subgroup is made up of those from the established bourgeoisie that developed around the beginning of the century; this is a first-generation Argentine group. The parents opened the way and founded companies which their children later continued, modernizing and enlarging them. This foreign bourgeoisie enjoyed a solid economic position during the period before World War I, and so they were able to pay for their children's education, sending them to Europe for specialized training. Four of the entrepreneurs in the sample studied at the School of Higher Commercial Studies in Paris; seven in Switzerland, either in Zurich or Lausanne; three in England, one in Germany and one in Florence, for a total of twenty-seven. These individuals were most characteristic of their class; they were the children of the founders of the best-known and most prestigious enterprises.

A second group includes eleven members of the traditional upper class. It is hard to determine whether the entrepreneurial activities were their route to prestige; in most cases it would seem that their ascribed prestige might have served to increase what was gained within the company. The members of this subgroup, who process agricultural products (dairy items, sugar, vineyards), could just as well be placed within the agricultural sector, since they are also rural landowners.

The English in Argentina constitute a third subgroup. They are men born in Argentina of British families, who have studied in British schools and some of whom served as volunteers in the British armed forces during World War I. Their activities in connection with entrepreneurial organizations were basically channeled through the Argentine-British Chamber of Commerce. Sixteen individuals included in the sample belong to this subgroup.

The rest make up a subgroup, which includes those whose classification would be more difficult. Many of them come from Spanish, Italian, or Jewish families, and they have all "come up from the bottom."

144

The above information completes the report on 119 of the 156 entrepreneurs who appear in the register. Table 7.3 summarizes the information.

TABLE 7.3

Origin of Prestigious Argentine Entrepreneurs in 1959

Origin	Industrialists	Businessmen	Total	%
Foreign entrepreneurial bourgeoisie, founders of enterprises	28	32	60	50
Traditional upper class	8	3	11	10
Anglo-Argentines	11	5	16	14
Careers "from the bottom"	22	10	32	26
Total	69	50	119	100

Three-fourths of these prestigious Argentine entrepeneurs had a favorable family economic base. The self-made men accounted for about 25 percent. But this percentage might have been higher if we had obtained complete information on the 156 recorded cases.

It is to be remembered that self-made men account for 17 percent of the leaders of the Industrial Union, 19 percent of those of the Chamber of Commerce, and 32 percent of those of the GEC. All these percentages indicate a very significant upward mobility in the composition of the entrepreneurial leadership stratum. The percentage of self-made men is higher than that shown at the same level in the United States.[17]

American entrepreneurs on the list are the local managers of the large American companies.[18] There is only one marginal case, the sole owner of a large business concern in Buenos Aires.

The Italian entrepeneurs on the list are self-made men who came into Argentina as immigrants. There is one exception, the President of Pirelli Enterprises, who is a member of almost all the local boards of directors of the Italian industrial group. It is interesting that more individuals from the powerful Italian entrepreneurial group do not appear on the record. Perhaps this is because they have settled in Argentina quite recently, and prestige, especially when obtained by the entrepreneurial route, requires maturing.

The German entrepreneurs head enterprises that they founded or continued. Two exceptions are the managers of the Bunge y Born Corporation and of the Bracht group, both old enterprises solidly estab-

145

lished in Argentina and connected with rural production and export. On the other hand, none of the Germans from Mercedes Benz, or from recently established enterprises appear on the record. They are still "illustrious unknowns" as far as local society is concerned, even though they may head multi-million dollar concerns.

Prestigious Spanish entrepreneurs are owners and founders of their enterprises, with the exception of two who have made careers for themselves and are now managers of great international capital corporations. These are immigrants who came to Argentina with their parents, but can be considered nationals as far as their careers are concerned. With the exception of a high corporate official of the largest electric company, all these Spanish entrepreneurs typify cases of upward social mobility. They settled in Argentina at the beginning of the century, and so there has been time for their reputations to become socially established.

The British on our list are managers of British or mixed capital companies established in Argentina, especially in the meatpacking and dairy derivatives field (such as Dayrico). The French, on the contrary, head local companies, with the exception of the Bemberg Corporations and the manager of Fiat-Someca. This is also true of the Belgians.

All Russian and Arab entrepreneurs, as well as Sephardic Jews coming from Arab countries, personify upward social mobility situations achieved through their specific careers in the business world.

Most of those entrepreneurs who have higher education have received it in foreign countries. Table 7.4 shows them classified according to the country where their higher education was received.

TABLE 7.4

Prestigious Entrepreneurs with Higher Education in Percentages

Higher Education	Businessmen	Industrialists
Argentine Universities	3	5
European Institutes	25	28
American Universities	4	4
Total	32	37

These figures indicate two things: that the percentage of prestigious entrepreneurs with higher education is low and that it is lower than

146

that found among entrepreneurs in other countries that also have reached a stage of relatively advanced industrial development, as indicated in table 7.5.[19] These percentages also show that, despite the fact that these entrepreneurs have spent their lives in Argentina, the nation's universities have not contributed much to their professional training, in some cases because they are self-made men, in others because they have received their higher education in Switzerland, France, and Great Britain.

TABLE 7.5

Comparative Educational Levels of the Entrepreneurial Elites

Educational Levels Completed	Buenos Aires	São Paulo	United States
Elementary	22%	12%	5%
Secondary	33%	42%	28%
Higher	45%	46%	67%

Source: For Buenos Aires, Zalduendo, op. cit.; for U.S., Lipset and Bendix, op. cit., and for São Paulo, Fernando H. Cardoso, O empresário industrial e o desenvolvimento econômico do Brasil, (São Paulo, Mimeographed edition).

Since these percentages correspond to those who are prestigious today, they may represent those who were at the head of industries around the 1940s, a period in which the present entrepreneurial corps had not yet been clearly defined. It has been seen that the percentage of those with university degrees is higher at the level of the leaders of entrepreneurial organizations. Everything indicates that the changeover to new corporate entities, with the resulting decrease in self-made men and increase in technological specialists, will produce a greater percentage of professionals in the future. Table 7.6 classifies the present prestigious entrepreneurs according to nationality and place where they studied. As may be seen, the eductional level of non-Argentine entrepreneurs is higher than that of the natives. Only 28 percent of Argentine entrepreneurs have higher education compared to 40 percent of the non-Argentines. The greatest percentages of those with higher education are found among the French, Belgians, and Swiss.

The analysis of the 249 "case histories" of prestigious entrepreneurs made by the author indicates not only that these men are dedicated to the enterprises which absorb all their energies, but also that:

147

TABLE 7.6

Entrepreneurs and Their Education
By Original Nationality and Place Where Educated

| Nationality | With Higher Education | | | | Without Higher Education | Total Entre-preneurs |
	Argentine U.	Europe	U.S.	Total		
Argentine	10	22	2	34	85	119
American	—	–	8	8	6	14
Italian	1	6	–	7	7	14
German	—	5	–	5	9	14
Spanish	—	1	–	1	15	16
English	—	3	–	3	11	14
French	—	8	–	8	3	11
Belgian	—	6	–	6	3	9
Swiss	—	8	–	8	2	10
Syrian	—	2	–	2	4	6
Russian	—	–	–	–	6	6
Other	—	5	1	6	10	16
Total	11	66	11	88	161	249

—— They have not been active in entrepreneurial organizations, nor are they now. Only 13 of the 149, that is not even 10 percent of the total, are or have been significantly involved in such activities: 2 have held office in the Industrial Union, 3 in the General Economic Confederation; 2 in the Buenos Aires Stock Exchange, 1 in that of Rosario, 3 in the Argentine Chamber of Commerce, 1 in the Chamber of Corporations, and the other two at the level of their respective trade organizations. Qualitatively, these 13 leaders are very important. Quantitatively, they are too few to appear in a special prestige stratum.

—— They are not active publicly in political life, with the single notable exception of Rogelio Frigerio[20] and two minor ones, one a nonparty candidate in the elections of 1962 and one a leader of the Popular Conservative Party. There are no others on the list that have occupied official positions either in political parties or as candidates for public office.

—— With a few notable exceptions,[21] the economic prestige achieved by the entrepreneurs does not seem to have been accompanied by a corresponding degree of acceptance at the highest social level; in other words, incongruence of status seems to prevail.

In all these evaluations it must be borne in mind that foreigners represent such a high percentage of the total of prestigious entrepreneurs that nothing similar is encountered in any other sector of public activity. It has been indicated that the foreign entrepreneurs whose case histories have been analyzed do not belong to representative entrepreneurial organizations, even at the level of the chambers of commerce. It has also been indicated that they have not achieved significant social recognition; much less have they become publicly identified with any political institution of any type or ideology, thus respecting in this matter entrepreneurial standards of behavior.

Notes

1. A transformation would have gradually taken place in the enterprise which, in the opinion of T. R. Fillol, *Social Factors in Economic Development: the Argentine Case* (Cambridge, Mass.: MIT Press, 1961), would be characterized by "an evolution in administration, which had gradually passed from the stage of a personal adventure to that of nuclear family enterprise, then to the extensive family type and finally was turned over to professional administrators."

2. An analysis of the entrepreneurs may be found in E. Zalduendo, *El empresario industrial en la Argentina* (Buenos Aires: Instituto Torcuato Di Tella, Centro de Investigaciones Económicas, 1962). This author centers his analysis on the entrepreneurial function. "We therefore think of the entrepreneurs as a function imposed by technical progress which is more and more exercised, not in an individual or personal manner, but rather by a harmonious staff, by a group."

3. The analysis of the directors of the Industrial Union is derived partly from the research carried out by Ruth Sautú de Graciarena, within the Seminary which gave rise to this work. She extracted data from *Diccionario de la actualidad, Diccionario biográfico argentino contemporáneo, Diccionario biográfico contemporáneo del Río de la Plata, Diccionario contemporáneo sudamericano* and *Diccionario biográfico de hombres de negocios*, various years. The researcher also used *Quién es quién en la Argentina* (Buenos Aires: Editorial Kraft, 1939, 1943, and 1950).

4. Masllorens, Campomar, Llauro, and others.

5. Among these leaders one finds Luis Colombo, the son of Italian laborers who settled in Rosario; he was the guiding spirit of the Industrial Union and its president for over twenty years. Other examples are Pascual Gambino, also a former president of the IU; Blanco, who as minister under Frondizi represented that entity; and Miguel Miranda, economic czar during the early years of the Perón regime, who was the son of Spanish immigrants from Asturias.

149

6. Campomar, Fourvell Rigolleau, Herbin, Llauró, Pini, Tailhade, Vasena, and others.

7. Shell, Harrod's, Westinghouse, and IBM, within the sample.

8. Information on the directors of the General Economic Confederation as well as of the Argentine Chamber of Commerce has been collected by Jorge Balán. He used the news report *Veritas*, whose generous cooperation is deeply appreciated.

9. In Zalduendo, *op. cit.*, foreigners made up 29 percent of the sample of entrepreneurs at the highest corporate level. On the other hand, 70 percent of their parents were foreign-born.

10. Such as Muro de Nadal, García Oliver, Elordy, Sojo, Padrós, and others.

11. Campomar, Decker, Fourvell Rigolleau, Llauró, Pini and others.

12. La Cantábrica, Atma, Tamet, Fabril Financiera, Acindar, Fábrica Argentina de Cemento.

13. The area known as the "northern quarter" (*barrio norte*) has traditionally been preferred by Argentina's traditional upper class, as have certain parts of the Belgrano district. The suburban communities of San Isidro and Acassuso originally were weekend residential areas, but since the late 1940s they have become part of the Buenos Aires metropolitan area. C.A.A.

14. Almagro, Once, Caballito, Flores, Vélez Sársfield, Morón, and Matanza.

15. In Zalduendo, *op. cit.*, it appears that according to the sample 44 percent had a professional university degree. A third of the professionals were lawyers, a figure lower than that of engineers, but higher than that for economists.

16. The prestige referred to throughout this chapter is of a reputational nature: entrepreneurs included in *Quién es quién en la Argentina* (Buenos Aires: Editorial Kraft, 1959) are considered prestigious.

17. Seymour M. Lipset and Reinhard Bendix, *Social Mobility in Industrial Society* (Berkeley: University of California Press, 1959), point out that the greatest proportion of the entrepreneurs who make up the American industrial elite had, before their successful careers, favorable economic and social backgrounds. Only between 10 and 20 percent of the great businessmen come from families in which the father had been a laborer, a craftsman, a small entrepreneur, a white collar worker, or a small rural landowner. Of the American entrepreneurial elite born between 1891 and 1920, which is equivalent to the Argentines studied in this work, only 7 percent were the children of rural or urban workers, and 6 percent of low-level white collar workers. On the other hand, the sons of important entrepreneurs and rural landowners account for 74 percent. Although Lipset and Bendix may doubt the validity of the hypothesis for the United States, it is very likely that the percentages of leaders who are self-made men such as are found in Argentina may be possible only in the initial phases of development.

18. Such as the managers of Goodyear, RCA Victor, Esso, Packers Ltd., Swift, General Motors, the Bank of Boston, Peabody, and Armour.

19. The level of schooling of Argentine entrepreneurs is low, a fact clearly indicated in table 7.5.

20. He was adviser, confidant, and key member of President Frondizi's staff. C.A.A.

21. Dodero, Fortabat, Masllorens, Pasman, Bracht, Braun Menéndez, and a few others.

8. THE ENTREPRENEURS—PART TWO

Foreign Capital Companies

THE ANALYSES in the last chapter show that no one directly representing the great international capital corporations appears on the boards
of the entrepreneurial organizations. Or, to put it another way, neither
the directors of those corporations nor their managers or attorneys
take part at the highest level of their trade organizations. The 1961
Industrial Union board, on which Ducilo S.A. and Fiat S.A. board
members appear, is the only exception.

Who are the members of the local boards of directors of internationally financed companies. There seem to be three different patterns:[1]

—— The entire local board may be made up of foreign personnel,
and the managers may also be foreign. Only in exceptional cases does
one find a native director, usually the legal and public relations officer
in charge of liaison functions. For example, this is true of the great
American or English capital companies such as General Motors, Ford,
Duperial, and Esso; and of CIBA, financed by German capital, or of
some companies of the Italian group such as Pirelli, Techint, and
others. In some companies of the Italian group, the chief financial officer is usually Argentine.

—— The native-born may be in the majority both on the boards of
directors and among managers and heads of departments. But sometimes the participation granted the native-born on the boards of directors is only nominal. They are likely to be well-known people who are
accepted in order to give the company local prestige and to facilitate
necessary local relations. Occasionally, these people may be former government officials, or former diplomats who were active during the
period when the company was first established in the country. Italo,
the Standard Electric Argentina, the German DECA and Mercedes
Benz companies, and old export firms such as Bunge y Born and
Dreyfus are among the foreign companies that grant major participation to nationals. But official participation by Argentines on the board

does not indicate that they have freedom of action or the amount of dividends distributed within the country.

—— The third type of foreign capital company is that of the mixed capital companies established in recent years in the metallurgical and chemical fields. Since it is not possible to be certain what economic relations actually exist, these companies are classified in accordance with a common denominator: the presence of armed forces officers on the boards leads us to suppose that there is some type of institutionalized relationship.[2]

It was determined that, with the exception of the companies in the last group, the norm is that either there are no Argentines on the boards of directors (this is true of the American, English, and a large part of the Italian group), or they are mere figureheads, or they have been made members as a discreet reward for services already rendered, or they may be confined to government-related functions, as is the case with legal counsel and public relations men.

Given the evidence, is one then entitled to conclude that in these cases economic power may be converted into social or political power? It is hypothesized here that, in regard to the type of relations which may be established between the three fields of activity, the Argentine case is anomalous. In other words, what is anomalous is the relationship between the economic power resulting from ownership of the largest and most important means of production, the social power which such ownership might command within the community, and the political power which such economic and social power might consequently exercise over the government.

The problem is to ascertain, first, whether the members of the elites occupying the highest positions in foreign companies do have economic power; second, whether this economic power is translated into social power; third, whether from both the economic power and the social power political power ensues.

From what has been presented so far we know that: a) the great foreign corporations are not personally represented on the boards of the GEC, of the Industrial Union, or of the Chamber of Commerce by members of those corporations; b) 45 percent of the entrepreneurs included in the sample and rated as prestigious, are non-Argentine; c) none of those high-level executives who move from country to country appear on the list of prestigious entrepreneurs.

It is evident that the vanguard of Argentine entrepreneurship is made up in large proportion of non-Argentines. Some foreign entre-

153

preneurs are wholly assimilated; consequently, they may be equated with the native-born. This is true of those who have founded industries or have continued the operation of the companies established by their national group; it is true of a majority of the German, French, Belgian, and Italian industries established before the 1940s, and of the new Arab, Polish, and Russian companies.

But the situation is different in the case of temporary managers of foreign economic and financial groups. Since they have settled in Argentina at the dictate of a distant board of directors, coming to Buenos Aires implies a promotion as compared to their earlier stay at the Guayaquil, Ciudad del Cabo, or Belo Horizonte office. They come to live in a country where they know that they will spend at most five years. They move into one of the residential quarters of the suburbs (Acassuso, Beccar, or Olivos), they register their children at their native-language school, then the executive settles into an intense, fast-paced routine devoted to his business role.

Since communication within the company is conducted in the original language (English, German, Italian), and the directors are all from the same country, and the department heads, if Argentine, are Italo-Argentines, Anglo-Argentines, or German-Argentines, or former Argentines now living in the United States, the executive has no reason to learn the local language. If some technical problem arises at the factory, at the plant, on the production line, or about quality, precise instructions are sent from central headquarters, located abroad. If important contracts are to be signed, the drafts, except for some matters of form, come already prepared from abroad, and if unforeseen questions of a legal nature arise, local lawyers take charge.

When personnel problems arise, those in charge of industrial and internal relations proceed in accordance with previously issued directives. If any problems arise with the government or if some interest has to be articulated with state institutions, the Central Bank, other governmental financial institutions, or the ministries, the Argentine lawyer takes care of the matter. He also deals with provincial administrations on tax questions and with community authorities on rates and levies. This lawyer, a member of the board, keeps up his high school and university connections and uses them to advantage. He also knows the ministers and how to deal with the bureau chiefs and stimulate the interest of bank managers; in short, he becomes indispensable.

The foreign manager is thus freed from some problems, those that can be solved only by someone who knows the environment and the country. The executive can devote himself fully to his technical vocation, to improving, increasing, and, if possible, surpassing the production line following the directives and limits set, and in harmony with a market whose needs and requirements he knows from the memoranda the technical experts prepare for him.

If the foreign executive is a Rotarian, he will become a member of the local Rotary Club; he will not fail to join the American Club, if he is American, and will also join a golf club, either the Hindú, the San Isidro, or the San Andrés. His daughter will lead her social life within the colony, and his wife, who also has failed to learn Spanish, will live within the circle of her fellow nationals of the same status who are her neighbors. The executive will spend his vacations in the country of origin, and if he is American, instead of the fifteen days he is entitled to, he will be granted a month because of the distance.

Once his term is over, the executive will be promoted to another agency or branch office in another country and his standing will be appreciably improved if the factory has met its assigned production quota. Like him, all the other great executives of foreign corporations spend years in a country as marginals, withdrawn from its problems, unless there is some catastrophe that affects aspects of manufacturing, the exchange rate, or the export of capital, as has happened in recent years.

The first factor that militates against his economic power being converted into another type of power is apparent: The great foreign corporations, those which constitute the entrepreneurial vanguard, are in the hands of managers who do not identify with the country where they live, partly because their powers are limited. Clearly, they are under specific directives, and any measure they may adopt, beyond those related to the production line, will necessarily have to be ratified by the board of directors. However, this is not the most important impediment; of greater significance is that the psychological mechanisms of the manager are conditioned to operate negatively. In order to transfer economic power to other fields, it is essential not only to have the necessary authority, but also to have established roots and to be personally convinced that one's own fate is closely intertwined with that of the country where the branch office is located.

Thus the managers themselves are not in a position to transform the economic power they have, and thus this power remains unused, though of course in some cases the company may decide to make use of it. This will only be done at the administrative level and only in connection with matters which directly affect the company. In very exceptional cases such intervention may even be conducted through more or less discreet steps taken by the embassy. However, this is never done except to defend the concrete interest of a specific enterprise or entrepreneurial group.

Sources for Financing

When the Argentine Industrial Union was founded in 1887 as the result of a merger of two other entities, 877 persons signed the charter; the overwhelming majority were foreign born. While there were two Estrada brothers, an Escalada, Norberto Quirno Costa, Luis Sáenz Peña, Santa Coloma, Silveyra, Sastre, Unzué, Urien, and an Uriburu who owned vineyards in Salta, all the other founders were Italians, Frenchmen, and Germans who had resided in Argentina only a few years.[3]

Seven years later the second national census was taken. In 1895 there were 23,000 industrial establishments, but the majority were artisans' shops scattered throughout the country. Eighty-five percent of the owners were foreign, and along the coast the percentage rose to more than 90 percent. However, the officers of the Argentine Industrial Union were native-born Argentines. The organization's first board, headed by Antonio Cambaceres (of French parentage, and the local president of the Western Railroad, later congressman and senator), was composed wholly of native-born Argentines, who were actually a minority in the organization they had just founded. These native-born Argentines fulfilled an important function: they were members of the governing class, they were the only ones who spoke the language of the country fluently, who had connections, contacts with the banks, could represent foreign interests, and were knowledgeable about the political situation.

This minority-majority relation lasted a long time. The second president of the Industrial Union was Augustín Silveyra, the third, Joselín Huergo, followed by Francisco Uriburu. Not until well into this century, when the eighth president of the Industrial Union, Casimiro Gómez, was elected, did a non-Argentine for the first time preside over an organization of non-Argentines.

While Joselín Huergo was president, the board of directors established a bank intended exclusively for financing manufacturing activi-

156

ties. Silveyra, Santa Coloma, and other men of the new entrepreneurial organization went on to direct this Industrial Union Bank, although the bank had a short life. These founders, men of vision who understood that they could promote industrialization from their own specific financial angle, were not marginal to the governing class. On the contrary, they were part of it and had numerous connections, through kinship and through business, clubs, and common interests.[4]

An examination of the yearly reports of the Industrial Union from the end of the last century and the beginning of the present one reveals a recurrent concern about banking. From these documents, notes, and petitions presented by the organization it is evident that the governmental banking system took care of agricultural and cattle-raising activities, of the new financial and importing activities, and of the needs of foreign enterprises, but did not take an interest in the activities of the industrialists. Even though in its regulations and by-laws the Argentine National Bank was required to devote part of its portfolio to financing industrial activities, the Industrial Union maintained that the requests of the entrepreneurs did not receive proper consideration.

As time passed, an independent entrepreneurial class slowly emerged, and it gradually occupied the leadership posts of its sector as it acquired economic influence. Therefore, around the first decade of this century those members of the "ruling class" who had become the financial spokesmen for the new and distinct industrial sector had given way to the "natural leaders of the industry."[5] But the latter, though having great personal drive, did not have the indispensable connections. While the cattle-raising aristocracy continued to be intimately connected with the financing centers, which they owned or which belonged to the government, the new industrialists did not know how to meet their credit needs.

The distortion of the private banking and credit allocation systems in Argentina dates from this period. An industry with urgent needs, because it had severed its connection with the ruling class and, thus, with the financial apparatus, was forced to create its own credit sources. But industry was not unified; it was a conglomerate of various groups of different nationalities, united only by their common economic activities. Fortunately for the industrialists, however, starting in the 1920s, new banking groups grew up around ethnic communities; the industrialists, forming various aggregations according to their foreign background, set the financial capacity of their fellow nationals in motion in order to be able to finance their own economic growth.

157

The financing source thus created differed according to the type of foreign community involved, the entrepreneurial characteristics of each, and the background of the various leaders. In some cases the funds for the new banks came exclusively from accumulated savings and in others, through arrangements made with financial groups in their countries of origin. In this way, either new banks were created or branch offices of European and American banks were opened, basically to take care of the financial needs of their fellow nationals in Argentina.

This is how the distortion originated. While the traditional aristocracy had its own banking system, intended for the financing of the activities of the group or of certain established foreign interests and of all the insurance companies established during the first quarter of this century, the rest of the private banking system was created on the basis of ethnic groups. Thus, the Germans created the German Transatlantic Bank; the French, the French Bank of the River Plate and the French and Italian Bank (though the French community in Argentina had enjoyed preferential treatment); and the Dutch established a branch office of the United Dutch Bank.

Spanish immigrants of humble origin, but with sufficient savings, started to deposit them in what would later become the powerful Bank of Galicia and in the Spanish Bank of the River Plate. The Italians established banks which had originated in Italy, such as the Bank of Naples, the Bank of Italy, the New Italian Bank, and the consortium of the Italo-Belgian Bank, and local branch offices of English and American credit institutions were established in Argentina.

Two remaining communities which in the 1930s still had difficulties in relating to the holders of political power finally established their own banks—the Jewish banks (the Israelite Bank and the Commercial Bank of Buenos Aires) and the Syrian-Lebanese Bank.

Although these banks eventually broadened their sphere of action and overstepped the strict boundaries of their own communities, (the number of foreigners was slowly decreasing, a native generation was emerging, and the nation was becoming more integrated), the existence of such diversified financial sources has contributed both to the strengthening of loyalties within the respective communities and to the fragmentation of the entrepreneurial groups in Argentina. The subsequent nationalization of the banking system made credit policies more impersonal, but the division of the entrepreneurial groups according to ethnic bases continued.

The Entrepreneurs and the Modernization Process[6]

It would be difficult to prove that during the 1930s the industrialists constituted a "subordinated group."[7] They could have been considered subordinated only from the psychological point of view. Since economically it is obvious that they were successful, they could have been subordinated only if the ruling sectors had denigrated them. Had this been the case, what sociologists have demonstrated happens in similar situations would have resulted: the industrialists would have closed ranks and, rejecting the value system of the dominant class, would eventually have set up their own. But as it has been indicated, this did not happen. At least as a block the entrepreneurs enjoyed the recognition of their peers and of almost all the emerging social sectors, even though they may have been ignored by the traditional upper class. As will be seen later, only some industrial groups were subordinated, not as industrialists, but for other reasons.

Neither can it be said that in Argentina the entrepreneurs have rejected the values of the dominant group. They simply did not have these values, or, at least, the entrepreneurs belonging to the original generation of European immigrants did not have them. However, as they moved up on the economic scale, and as their place was taken by the following generation, the status mentality of the family group changed, and in the process their mores and values changed also. This was especially true in the case of the children. As the latter became accepted and began to feel secure and to adopt the gestures, the usages, the vocabulary and manners of the ruling sectors, and as they joined the latter's clubs and frequented the same amusement and resort centers, they tried to imitate the elite in all its aspects, and to be guided by its value system. For this reason, most of the European industrialists and businessmen did not become subordinated groups. What barriers could there be against the Italian and Spanish entrepreneurs since the Buenos Aires upper class, with very rare exceptions, came from the same rather recent Italo-Spanish immigrant stock? For entrepreneurs of Anglo-Saxon origin the situation was even more favorable. In this case there was no question of subordination. The most distinguished social group of Buenos Aires would never have looked upon an Anglo-Saxon, or a German, or a Belgian, or a Swiss, and much less a Frenchman, as subordinate. Whatever their origin and background, these Europeans were presumed to be identified with the highest strata, as

159

long as there was no proof to the contrary. If later on many of these European entrepreneurs became marginal it was a voluntary process. If they were not fully integrated into an intrinsically open society, if they were not actively incorporated into the ruling elites of the nation, if, on the contrary, they withdrew within the recesses of their own communities, it was through voluntary segregation.

The reasons why these Anglo-Saxon, French, German, and Belgian "entrepreneurial bourgeoisies" did not become part of the ruling sectors of society merit an analytical study in themselves. It would be logical to expect these foreign groups to find economic success the normal channel to their upward mobility. But other doors were not closed to their children. In other chapters of this work it has been shown that leaders in other fields of activity came from families of German descent. Three ministers of the armed services[8] and three Argentine bishops were sons of Germans, but not of important entrepreneurs. If these and their Anglo-Saxon and French counterparts withdrew into their specific entrepreneurial world it was through a voluntary and deliberate withdrawal. Since other available channels were not closed to them, it is fair to assume that, if the generations born in Argentina followed the route chosen for them by their parents, it was because family influence was extremely strong and because family socialization took place around and as a function of bourgeois economic values. Furthermore, they were driven by their own economic ambitions to continue the work started by their foreign predecessors. When the paternal enterprise was transformed into a corporation, the total block of shares remained in the hands of relatives or fellow nationals or of Argentines born within the respective foreign community.

Under these circumstances, prestige, recognition, and social, as distinct from economic, power would be sought not within the context of the total society, which would not be aware of these people, but within their own restricted social group. Then their greatest weight, their greatest power would be brought into play within their own community in connection with the problems, values, and topics related to their country of origin. Whatever economic and social status was achieved was shown at the club located in Belgrano, Acassuso, or Villa Ballester to which fellow nationals of the British, American, or German cultural associations belonged, at the school cooperatives, and, in some cases, at the church where those coming from the same country and region (Scotch, German-Swiss, or Swedes) worshipped together.

160

There have been, however, two subordinated groups with a high level of aspiration: the Jews and the Arabs (mainly from Syria). Since they came from the lowest rungs of the social ladder, the route to be followed was longer because of their lower origin, and the barriers to be overcome were more numerous and difficult. The Jews, with greater internal cohesion than the other groups, added to their marginality on the basis of origin that of a strict religious community closed to others. Something similar happened to the Moslem sector of the Arab immigrants.

In the case of the Jews, since they had no access to the armed forces or to ranching, and were excluded from the Church, the entrepreneurial world was the only one open to them. Feeling discriminated against, they thought of themselves as "looked down upon" by a group which appeared to ignore them. Knowing that the struggle for status, and for obtaining prestige would be more difficult for them than for the other groups, their determination to take advantage of all opportunities was all the greater. Their capacity to save had been developed to a point unknown by the other social sectors and subsequent massive re-investment placed them in control of resources vital for the economy of the nation.

In this way the Jewish entrepreneurial group internalized the norms for "ascetic bourgeoisies." They did not invent their own value framework; they adopted the value system which European bourgeoisies displayed during the most difficult formative stages of capitalism. This value system was known to the other emerging immigrant groups, but was not adopted by them. It was respected by Spanish and Italian immigrants, but it was never "lived" as it was by Syrians and Jews.

Because in the beginning a "social blockade" operated against Jewish businessmen, they, on the one hand, clung desperately to "bourgeois asceticism" and, on the other, became innovators and modernizers. The Jewish entrepreneurial group, when it realized it had become successful, was compelled, since it was marginal to society as a whole, to set up its own specific gathering places where the new status might be evaluated and the new prestige might be approved and recognized. Unlike the Anglo-Saxon case, however, their "blockade" lasted only as long as the immigrant generation. For all practical purposes, the "blockade" disappeared for those born in Argentina, but the sons of Anglo-Saxons "blockaded" themselves.

The Jewish immigrant generation, like all the other foreign ones, practiced economic leadership, especially in industry and commerce,

161

and since only some of their group were subject to the traditional ruling sector's blockade, the Jewish entrepreneurs were able to impose their own prestige norms and some of their values. The norms and values of modernization and economic development based on bourgeois criteria were imposed by all immigrant entrepreneurs; but while Syrians and Jews were their best exponents, these values became acceptable as a result of the efforts of the Italians and the Spaniards.

The process subsequently culminated in a curious value symbiosis. The traditional ruling groups at last recognized that economic success in both commerce and industry might become a source of prestige. On the other hand, the emerging groups, as soon as they moved up in society, started to assimilate the norms of the old prestige groups, which they took for their model. Thus, emerging groups, and especially the generation sprung from Italian, Spanish, Russian, Polish, Jewish, and Syrian ancestors, internalized the frame of reference of the socially established, while the latter came to accept the values of the economically successful newcomers, though the traditional upper class did not identify with the newcomers publicly.

The problem of economic achievement had been solved for the first native-born Jewish generation by their parents in an open and mobile society. The children's problem now was to enter other careers. Outside the entrepreneurial field they continued to feel subordinated, and they attacked this resistance as earnestly as their parents had attacked the economic one, though now their attack was directed toward other objectives. The first Argentine-born generation of Jewish entrepreneurial background devoted itself to intellectual creativity and to scientific and artistic endeavors. When the Perón regime fell, the opportunity to overcome the barriers in the intellectual field arrived, and the doors of university faculties, research centers, laboratories, professorships and scientific institutes opened to this Judeo-Argentine generation with a high level of aspiration.

The Industrialists as a Bankrupt Power Factor

When the economic crash of 1890 came, the entrepreneurs of the very new Industrial Union (it was two years old) undertook a publicity campaign to persuade the public to restrict importation of those articles that could be produced within the country and petitioned the government to adopt protectionist measures in order to bring about full employment.

During the first few years of this century the exhibitions put on by the Argentine Industrial Union contributed to promote the idea that the incipient manufacturing production should receive the support of both the domestic consumer market and the government. In 1933 a large meeting of industrial men took place at a boxing stadium located in downtown Buenos Aires. They were not only entrepreneurs but also employees and laborers, that is, all who at that difficult moment in the life of the nation were facing an uncertain future. This was the time of the Great Depression when unemployment was widespread, the domestic market was restricted, and financial difficulties were serious.

Bringing together behind a petition all those who, whatever their position within industry, were in the same situation was not entirely new; an earlier generation had done the same thirty years before, gathering at Lorea Square and petitioning the government for protectionist measures.

The great assembly of 1933 took place, as the president of the Industrial Union explained from the rostrum, because industrial men should demand that the executive branch adopt measures for the protection of manufactures. This demand was kept up by the industrialists during most of Luis Colombo's term of office as president of the Industrial Union. When the Roca commission left for Great Britain to sign a meat quota agreement, Colombo, in view of the possibility that a reduction of import duties might mean the ruin of the entrepreneurs, addressed a note to President Augustín P. Justo, in which he made some demands.[9]

Throughout the last three decades the entrepreneurs never again have acted together or have taken concrete stands in accordance with this precedent of mobilization of the whole industry. This change in attitude coincided with two events. On the one hand, manufacturing replaced agriculture as the largest source of the GNP and, on the other, political groups interested in industrial development started to come into power. Never again were the entrepreneurs to mobilize, and the tone of their demands and the manner of presenting them became much more discreet. This change of attitude leads to several questions: Why is it that industrialists seem to have become incapable of articulating their interests with the ability and vigor with which they had done so before? Why do the various enterprises not agree to take great

163

collective decisions? Why do they, despite their economic weight, their role in modernization, and the fact that they have been technological innovators, not have more weight within the life of the nation? What keeps the entrepreneurs from becoming a power factor similar to the armed forces? What inhibits them from articulating their interests with the same ability that the cattle-raisers of the Rural Society have shown? It is evident that there are many points demanding clarification.

First, the entrepreneurial sector may lack unity because it is relatively new. Even assuming that the entrepreneurs might really be a cohesive group, with group consciousness and norms, the organization of new groups is usually deficient, and their understanding of their own real interests is unclear and diffuse. In this sense the industrial sector is newer than the other groups constituted as power factors. But this does not explain everything. Its emergence antedates the emergence of labor union activity, yet the consciousness of unity which the labor unions display is incomparably more developed than that of the industrialists. Apparently, the labor unionists understand that numbers, unity of purpose and objectives, and organization give them strength, while their employers do not. The entrepreneurs continue to believe that each has his own strength, that each has his own objective, that each one should look out for his own personal profit and benefit, which do not precisely coincide with the interests of other entrepreneurs.

The second factor that seems to have had a negative influence on the adequate articulation of the entrepreneurs' interests is the diversity of the groups making up this sector. There are two different blocs of enterprises: the branch offices of international companies and the native entrepreneurs. As has been indicated, the former do not participate directly at the highest level of industrial organizations, partly because national production requirements do not always run parallel with their own. Thus, these large enterprises feel that their interests are relatively well represented within the managerial organizations, and they go along with decisions, especially when the organizations present petitions on financial matters, on restrictions on imports, or on some government intervention to change the "free-play rules" of enterprises.

There is also the difference in size of industries. There are two industrial strata, almost without any intermediate levels: the large and economically powerful enterprises which employ a large labor force, and the 90 percent of the industrialists at the shop level which employ

164

a permanent labor force of less than ten people. Because Argentina is still a pre-capitalist society, or, more properly, since capitalist development has not been harmonious, there are two entrepreneurial levels. The larger enterprises do not necessarily exert the greater influence on the control of common interests and business; sometimes quite the reverse is the case. It is generally the spokesmen for the intermediate or not-so-large enterprises who direct the enterpreneurial movement.

Third, unity is adversely affected because of personal and group conflicts and the different national origins among the entrepreneurs. It has already been pointed out that one of the many dividing lines that cuts through this enterpreneurial sector originates in the fact that different groups are structured around common values, norms, and social circles, and especially around common financial sources. All these groups are not aggregated; they are opposed to each other or, at best, suspicious of each other, usually because of ethnic differences and because of problems related to events outside Argentina. The situation does not create tension lines, but it does erect barriers to communication, which in this case are dysfunctional.[10]

Thus, though objectively entrepreneurs would seem to have common interests, such interests are not clearly perceived because the differences in form among the entrepreneurial groups are the first to be noticed.

There are old entrepreneurs, heirs of the founders, and there are also new entrepreneurs whose rapidly acquired fortunes are looked upon with suspicion by the old sectors because the latter consider the acquisition of these fortunes to be connected with politics. Besides the very large American, British, and German enterprises, there are national capital enterprises established around old English, German, and Italian national groups. There are traditional Belgian and French export enterprises, and there are also very new enterprises established by until recently unknown Arabs and Jews. Within the hypothetical bloc of the entrepeneurs, are traditional owners whose ways have not been brought up to date, new captains of industry motivated by a desire for instant profits, and the brand-new "corporate entrepreneurs" to whom the development of the enterprise means more than large short-term profits.

The potential causes for conflict are numerous: the different size of the enterprises, the length of time since they were established, the fact that they belong to different national groups, and the differences in behavior and motivation. These make the creation of group norms,

165

cohesion, interests, objectives, and leadership difficult. No elements that could act as catalysts have yet appeared, and the differences still count far more than the similarities.

One of the clearest pieces of evidence that shows the lines of discord are stronger than those of agreement is that there are two entrepeneurial organizations, but what is even more significant is that it is precisely in the political arena that the final motivation for discord is found. Instead of the social factor of entrepreneurial economic power influencing the political field, it is the latter—traditional politization understood in its most simplistic terms—that is the framework for the former. The logical order is subverted and the political dichotomy of friend-enemy is institutionalized over and above common interests.

In politics, power is not held, but exercised. If it is not exercised, there is no political power despite all the economic and social power that may be possessed. Argentine entrepreneurs have not exhibited objective consciousness that power could be exercised or the desire to do so.[11] Entrepreneurs have been absorbed by the preoccupation of reaching the highest status possible, for the sole, exclusive, and personal benefit of themselves, their families, their group, their enterprise, but not for any entity, corps, institution, or social sector outside their own domain.

The former president of an entrepreneurial organization confidentially maintains that "entrepreneurs have never ceased to rule in Argentina," and he points out in favor of his thesis that "many decrees are drawn up in private offices and bureaus. . . . The entrepreneurs who, because of their political relations and contacts, impose their points of view on the others are to be found within a radius of fifteen blocks around the Presidential office." The writer feels that this is not true, that the entrepreneurs obtain benefits exclusively for their own enterprises, whether these benefits pertain to customs, tariffs, credit, or taxes. They negotiate, petition, and bring influence to bear until they get the favorable decision for themselves and their business, but not for the industry as a whole. The entrepreneurs do not rule as a unified sector vis-à-vis other sectors, even though hundreds of entrepreneurs individually and for their own exclusive benefit may obtain that favorable decision which interests them alone.[12] The entrepreneurs do not rule because, lacking solidarity, they have no other motivation than the manufacture of their own status. Since they are prestige seekers, their time is absorbed by the enterprise and then by the accumulation of all possible external trappings of prestige.

166

Economic power does not necesarily bring parallel political power.[13] What economic power does bring is the potential for political power if there is the intent, the understanding, and the vocation to exercise it. But if the largest enterprises are not interested in the exercise of leadership; if the entrepreneurs fear involvements which will take them away from their enterprises; if they are only motivated by concrete and obvious results (new status, more external symbols of prestige); if the group lacks maturity, if there is no objective group consciousness; if as a result of their experiences they believe that political activity is more likely to result in loss of prestige than in anything else, all this will lead to a vacuum between the economic power held and the political power which they do not wish to exercise.

Since they lack cohesion and have no frame of reference of their own, the members of the entrepreneurial bourgeoisie, as they have gone up the social scale, have been co-opted by the old upper class. They have lost a certain dynamic power, and, since they do not have the capacity to generate ideologies, they accept the prestige scale, the value system, and the stratification of the preceding social structure. Without even realizing it, they have adopted as their own the value framework of the traditional rural sector.

These entrepreneurs who moved up bought ranches once they had acquired enough capital, not only for economic diversification, but also to qualify under the old prestige norms. They had achieved wealth by a route other than ranching, traditional financing, or the practice of law. After having bought land, some entrepreneurs took a further step and became dairy ranchers, a complementing luxury. Instead of steadfastly defending their own interests, as they had done when their prestige was still marginal, they tried to identify with the ideas, points of view, and arguments of the rural sector. Even within entrepreneurial organizations, they sometimes disregarded their own interests in favor of the ones developed by the traditional rural elite.

There was also a leadership crisis among the entrepreneurs. From 1925 to 1946 Luis Colombo, the classical example of the self-made man, the perfect expression of his era, and the sort of personality then common among the entrepreneurs, exercised undisputed leadership. He was a leader who embodied the group's aspirations. His personal decline entailed that of the group. In 1946 he committed the great mistake of having the Industrial Union contribute heavily to the coffers of the candidate who eventually lost. As a result, the organization was placed under governmental control; and even though it con-

167

tinued to have a sort of latent life, it took many years to rebuild its leadership team.

The Argentine entrepreneur distinguished himself as long as he was led by an old fashioned *patrón*, and the group was composed of men who were themselves old-fashioned *patrones:* the leader embodied group reality. At the present time, the entrepreneurial group is partly made up of new corporate executives who are just part of a corporate hierarchy made up of impersonal managers. This impersonality is also present among the leadership of the entrepreneurial organizations.

The bureaucratization of the system precludes the possibility of personal leadership on the Colombo pattern and checks the impetus of strong personalities. This type of leadership is possible today only in party politics and in labor union activities, though it is not even possible in all the unions, but only in those with certain characteristics. It is no longer possible among the entrepreneurs where the existence of a ruling elite would not in itself be sufficient for the entrepreneurs to play a significant role. For them to do so, it is essential that the sector be boosted up as a whole, or at least that this be done to a whole set of innovating entrepreneurs who, because they head important enterprises, may be able to lead the way.

It is possible to ascertain the absence of a cohesive entrepreneurial elite, one authentically creative, since the leading industrial sectors[14] have been notorious for being behind the times, opposing governmental projects as well as those proposed by other groups. In such cases, these entrepreneurs have reacted by offering solutions which were based on orthodox principles of economic dogma, rather than on the facts. This is a strange attitude for entrepreneurs to take since the personality type which is preponderant in these sectors is usually that of the executive accustomed to making decisions on the basis of facts, not abstract considerations. This is the type of personality that makes decisions on the basis of the events he himself sets in motion and not simply as a response to the stimuli presented by other groups.[15]

It is possible to be a "power factor" only to the extent that the power possessed is made effective in a coherent manner; that is, first it must be possible to do so, and then it must be done intelligently. The armed forces have no problem; when they want to act as a power factor what they must make effective is the direct exercise of force, or the threat of the use of force. Since this force comes from the state and resides in the use of a state instrument, there is no problem or complication.

But both the industrial forces and the large rural producers can only

168

make effective the power that comes from money, from the amount they are ready to throw into the political arena, the direction they give the use of these funds, and where they concentrate them. The large rural landowners have no problem in donating money for political purposes since they are free to dispose of their own private funds, but it is a complicated matter for industrialists who manage the funds of others, of enterprises that are corporately owned. Besides, once the decision to do so is made, it must be done intelligently. As one of the top level leaders says, "on election eve, all the entrepreneurs play all the colors, just in case." This has been one of the two routes followed in the attempt to gain a number of momentary friends at election time.

The other route was that followed by some large entrepreneurs who on each occasion have consulted together and decided to support only one of the candidates, but unfortunately in the last fifteen years every time they have done so they have bet on the losing candidates. In the 1946 and 1951 elections they supported the presidential candidates who lost. In 1946 the Industrial Union went so far as to solicit financial support by a circular letter addressed to entrepreneurs and member organizations. In the 1957 elections for delegates to the constitutional convention, the entrepreneurs of the city of Buenos Aires supported a party which won only one delegate. In 1958 they were divided. In 1962, entrepreneurial groups in the province of Buenos Aires contributed to paying for the very costly propaganda campaign of the government candidate who lost, and the same thing happened in July, 1963, when in the new presidential elections "strong groups" backed a candidate who came in third.[16]

Notes

1. The analysis of the composition of the Boards of Directors has been made by correlating the names as they appear in the *Guía de las sociedades anónimas* (Buenos Aires: Editorial El Accionista) with the biographical documentary sources set forth in the preceding chapter.

2. One general, two colonels, and one navy captain are on the board of Atanor (a mixed capital corporation). On that of Siderurgia Argentina (also a mixed capital corporation), there are two generals, one colonel, and one navy captain; on the Kaiser board there are three Air Force generals, and on that of Fiat Someca two Air Force generals, all retired.

3. The complete list of founders may be found in *Revista de la unión industrial argentina*, Vol. 75, second series, No. 14, January–February, 1962.

4. For the history of the beginnings of the industry, see A. R. Guerrero, *La industria argentina* (Buenos Aires: n.p., 1944) and A. Dorfman, *Historia de la industria argentina* (Buenos Aires: Escuela de Estudios Argentinos, 1942).

5. From the yearly reports of the Argentine Industrial Union for the first years of the century.

6. See among others, M. F. Millikan and Donald L. M. Blackner (eds.), *The Emerging Nations: Their Growth and United States Policy* (Boston: Little Brown, 1961). Also B. F. Hoselitz, "El desarrollo económico en América Latina," *Desarrollo económico*, Vol. 2, No. 3, Buenos Aires, October–December, 1962, and E. E. Hagen, "Como comienza el crecimiento económico. Una teoría general aplicada al Japón," *Desarrollo económico*, Vol. 2, No. 2, Buenos Aires, July–September, 1962. To place the process in the Argentine context, see Guido Di Tella and M. Zymelman, "Etapas del desarrollo económico argentino," paper delivered at the Jornadas Argentinas y Latinoamericanas de Sociología, held in Buenos Aires, in 1961 (mimeo.).

7. When writing of "subordinated groups with a high level of aspiration" reference is made to Hagen's theory. This author has elaborated a series of hypotheses on the possible cases in which a "subordinated group" may become the principal agent for social change. One of these valid hypotheses would apply in those cases in which a "socially subordinated" group, because all its opportunities for upward mobility are blocked, has to reject the old values, elaborate new prestige norms, and create its own channels for upward mobility. For the application of Hagen's hypothesis to Argentina, see Torcuato S. Di Tella, "Los procesos políticos y sociales de la industrialización," *Desarrollo económico*, Vol. 2, No. 3, Buenos Aires, October–December, 1962.

8. Admiral Hartung, Air Force General Krausse, Lt. General Rattenbach.

9. He demanded the continuation of protectionism. C.A.A. See the collection of notes, speeches, and articles by Luis Colombo in the Industrial Union Library.

10. Perhaps the case closest to that of Argentina is that of Brazil. Fernando Enrique Cardoso "O empresário industrial e o desenvolvimento econômico do Brasil" (São Paulo, 1963, mimeo.) sets forth some of the characteristics of the Brazilian sector as an independent stratum, which is more similar than different from the Argentine entrepreneurial group. For one thing, because of the speed with which that stratum was built up, as a result of the superimposing of groups whose industrial tradition is very recent, the "traditional industrialists" (the extreme cases) are those who can point to two generations in the business. Hence, according to the author, the "preindustrial" and recent origin of the group inhibits its acting as a class. In Brazil, together with an overwhelming majority of industrialists of immigrant background, a minority of "segments of the old seigneurial strata" are active, but the latter possess much more political influence than the former, as is the case in Argentina. In Cardoso's opinion, the

170

Brazilian industrialists constitute a recent and heterogeneous social stratum, which makes it difficult to obtain the necessary maturity for elaborating uniform modes of thought, feeling, and action, and inhibits them from constructing an industrial ideology.

11. See the conclusions reached by Zalduendo, *op. cit.*, who, after analyzing the results of his survey, maintains that the Argentine entrepreneur does not visualize the role he plays within society, and even less does he seem ready to face the dangers of command or power.

12. Cardoso reaches the same conclusions about the Brazilian entrepreneurs: "Lacking the necessary socialization to play the roles they should accept, the entrepreneurs only respond as an electoral 'maneuvering mass,' polarizing their interests around 'abstract vindications', such as 'high cost of living,' or 'against inflation' and 'against the Government.' " The author maintains that the entrepreneurs seem to associate the government with all the evils that befall the country through a rationalization which is typical of the behavior of the middle classes. This is the reason why the isolated participation of industrialists and industrial groups in politics tends to be characterized by its individualism and, very often, by opportunism: "they act in order to achieve some degree of influence which will allow direct benefits for themselves or for their enterprises." (p. 205), *op. cit.*

13. In Argentina, the transfer of economic power from the agricultural to the industrial sectors begins to become discernible in 1945. At five-year intervals the figures show that, starting after World War II, the industrialists contributed more on a percentage basis to the gross national product than did the rural sectors. Nevertheless, the "political power" relation is exactly the opposite.

Contribution to the Gross National Product by the

Economic Sectors

Five-Year Intervals	Percentage of GNP	
	Industrial	Rural
1935–1939	20.4	24.3
1940–1944	21.0	24.7
1945–1949	23.5	18.5
1950–1954	22.7	16.6

14. Not all of them, but the very ones belonging to the most important organizations.

15. See the Round Table of *Clarín* (special meeting of August 28, 1960) on the subject of "Argentine Industry. Its improvement and expansion," especially the contribution by Jorge A. Sábato.

16. Hugo Berlatzky and Silvia Novick of the Department of Sociology of the School of Philosophy and Letters, University of Buenos Aires, have carried out a study on a theme on which nothing has previously been pub-

lished in Argentina and which has been an important source for Chapters 7 and 8: "Delimitación y análisis de los grupos económicos en la Argentina" (unpublished monograph). Using the lists of directors of corporations and using the interlocking technique, they have classified eight groups to which they have given arbitrary names taken from some of the corporations included in the group. The results were as follows:

1) The *Tornquist* group, 38 industrial, banking, and insurance companies.

2) The *La Papelera* group, an Italian group.

3) *Bunge y Born*, import, export, and oils.

4) The *Dálmine* group, also Italian, metallurgy.

5) The *Siam* group.

6) *Braun Menéndez*, a Patagonian agricultural, commercial, industrial, and shipping group.

7) The *Italo* group, electrical and diversified.

8) The *Williams* group, Swedish and British capital.

The existence of these "groups" breaks the pattern of industrial concentration in Argentina, since the majority in Argentina are shops employing up to 10 workers (85 percent of enterprises in the 1946 census). In the 1954 census this percentage rose to 90 percent. These figures, which imply a reversal of the world-wide trend toward economic concentration, have, with reference to what is of interest here, an adverse effect, the existence of two levels of stratification: (a) The great corporations as the entrepreneurial minority; (b) The overwhelming majority at the shop level. This greatly hampers the creation of a homogeneous entrepreneurial elite and also the leadership of the large enterprises. The intermediate stratum, which would be the next following, is very small. Yet, it is from that entrepreneurial intermediate stratum that the leaders of the two management organizations emerge.

172

9. THE CHURCH

THE RELIGIOUS conduct of the individual has given rise to an extensive literature written from the specific viewpoint of the social scientist. The social scientist views religion as one more social phenomenon and has found it possible to measure, catalogue, and study its manifestations in society, while ignoring its intrinsically supernatural aspects.

The religious phenomenon, viewed as one of the many manifestations of personality, has been considered by social scientists from the point of view of the cultural environment within which the individual lives, as have organized religion and ecclesiastical structure. Both the professional sociologist and those priests who are anxious to acquaint themselves with the structure of the group within which they serve have employed the same techniques, which are the product of an identical methodological attitude.

Religious authorities within a given society can also be studied by using this methodology. The resulting study will not provide *the* explanation of the essence of religious authority, nor will the study of the socioeconomic structures and their relation to religion give the key to acceptance or rejection of a given faith.[1] Aspects of both these phenomena, however, are subject to proof insofar as they can be perceived by use of a scientific method. Thus, while an analysis of the religious group as a means of achieving holiness is beyond the limited possibilities of the sociologist, its bureaucratic organization and temporal structure may be understood and analyzed by means of the techniques of the social sciences in the same way as any other institution which comprises the elements of a bureaucratic organization and an authoritarian administration.

In analyzing the hierarchy of the Catholic Church, the achievement of the supreme value prized by every religious group—holiness—cannot be determined, but the type of career followed by religious authorities is subject to determination.

173

These studies accept a limitation which is found in all fields of knowledge, but which is more specific in this case. Those "individuals who occupy the highest positions" in the ecclesiastical structure may be those who most perfectly exemplify holiness, but this is irrelevant to the sociologist. In analyzing ecclesiastical hierarchies, the sociologist is interested in them only in their administrative aspect. Pastors within the spiritual order are also administrators at a bureaucratic and earthly level. This temporal aspect is the only one that interests the sociologist for several reasons, among them that it is the only aspect that he can readily perceive.[2] The analysis will be confined to the hierarchical authorities of the Roman Catholic Church in Argentina. Various reasons support its inclusion in this study.

First, relations between the Church and the state are institutionalized. By a constitutional provision of 1853, Argentina has recognized the Roman Catholic faith and has given it financial support. This recognition is such that it even requires a minimum religious observance by the president. This is a unilateral declaration on the part of the state. The state exercises patronage and by virtue of this appoints the highest authorities of the recognized faith. It thus turns into public officials those who hold the highest religious positions and requires previous legal approval for official Vatican communications to enter the country. This twofold influence, based on constitutional provisions, implies an official recognition of a specific faith and at the same time subordinates this recognized form of worship (and it alone) to the authority of the temporal order.

The majority of Argentines are, at least nominally, Roman Catholics, but the actual extent of religious observance could be ascertained only by adequate sociological surveys. Such surveys would make it possible to determine what percentage of the population practices its faith regularly, how many do so only occasionally and desultorily, how many have fallen away or have stopped practicing their faith, and also the figures for other religious faiths.[3]

Without scientific data, an impressionistic overview indicates that religious sentiment is widespread throughout all strata of the population. Apparently, there are no appreciable differences in practice in the urban centers as compared to rural environments. How that sentiment is expressed is another matter, since this may be done through distorted manifestations of faith and may indeed be characterized by substantial ignorance of dogma even among practicing Catholics. It may also be

174

that the adjustment of that sentiment to the norms and prescriptions of organized religion may be weak and desultory.

The authority of the Church extends, as does the authority of all ideologies with world views, to levels other than the specifically spiritual. The religious phenomenon, when it creates group feeling, group norms, group behavior, and a specific system of loyalties, becomes temporal power.

The spiritual authority of the Church (aside from its intrinsic value) is exercised within the temporal world, which in this case is Argentine society. Within this society it may meet with varying responses which may be considered from two different points of view. First, the attitude of the State when it accepts the directives of the Church or confines itself to "not innovating" would have to be studied. Second, acceptance of those directives by society and its various groups (practicing, baptized but not practicing, members of other faiths, and unbelievers) would have to be analyzed. The situation would vary according to the intent of the directive in question, to its degree of complexity, and to the publicity given it. Evaluation of these various responses could be made only by the use of data from surveys, which do not exist.

A fourth reason for inclusion of the Catholic hierarchy in this study is that during the twenty-five years covered by the study, the Church has played an important role. The various "situations," classified in accordance with the attitude of the Church and the objectively observable degree of participation of its highest authorities, are as follows:

The Church acts publicly and expresses itself through its hierarchical authorities on three doctrinal points: relations of Church and state, the magisterium of the Church, and family legislation, especially concerning matrimony. This intervention may take the form of a declaration directed to the religious group on the eve of elections, which reminds the faithful of the Church's program. This type of declaration has two effects: it acts as a "veto" on the dissident groups (albeit the veto is valid only for voters who are influenced by the Church); and it serves as a form of interaction with the parties by providing tacit support of those who publicly proclaim the doctrine of the Church and accord with those who accept its *modus vivendi*.

This type of intervention was significant during the 1946 presidential election and again in the 1951 elections when both candidates expressly adjusted their campaigns to the requirements of the Church. In the main, the same thing happened in 1958. In the 1963 presidential elec-

175

tions these doctrinal aspects were not relevant in view of the terms of the electoral conflict.

A second type of direct intervention operates on the plane of actual events rather than on that of abstract ideas. Within the quarter of a century covered by this study, two of the problems have not come up or, at least, one came up only incidentally as part of a much more complex institutional situation. During these twenty-five years the issue of the Church's role in education has come up five times. It was first raised at the time of the decree approving religious education in the public schools of December, 1943; the second time was in 1946 when that decree was ratified by Congress; the third, in 1955 when the same provision was repealed; the fourth, in 1955, after Perón was overthrown, when the Catholic university by-laws were approved by decree; and the fifth, in 1958 when congressional approval was again given the above-mentioned university decree.[4] On four of these five occasions religious expectations were satisfied. In these cases the religious group, through its hierarchy, made its opinion known and backed its stand by marshalling and mobilizing the support of the faithful on a national scale.

On a second degree of the scale, the religious institution may more or less directly, or more or less indirectly, foster and inspire certain events, but without thereby implying formal participation by the Church. The religious persecution that began around the middle of November, 1954, gave rise to responses which could generally be classified as direct intervention, but the religious groups played a decisive role in the outcome of that situation (the September 1955 revolution) without formal participation by the Church as an institution.

A third degree within the scale is represented by the cases in which the Church interacts with the formal state authorities and with other temporal powers. This happens every time the authorities of the nation adapt their behavior or their statements in accordance with the expectations of the Church. It may be a unilateral attitude assumed by the authorities and in some cases it may even be of doubtful authenticity. The interaction may take place between the Church and other power groups, or with the Church acting as mediator. In these cases it is always the highest hierarchical authority that intervenes at the request of the groups concerned or as a result of the needs of the moment. The occasions on which the Church through its hierarchical authorities has acted as mediator between the striking laborers and the state and when it intervened at the request of the railroad union and during the

176

great metallurgical strike are recent examples of this. The Church has also acted as mediator on other occasions on its own initiative, as it did during the armed confrontations of September, 1962, and April, 1963.

On a fourth level there are those situations in which Christian groups, not the Church itself, allege or state that they are inspired by the Church's program, as is the case in some political parties and groups. In these cases there is a wide range of possibilities: the party or group may be directly inspired by religious doctrine, it may explicitly state that it is not against any of the basic points of doctrine, or it may establish a tacit *modus vivendi* with ecclesiastical authorities, postponing the consideration of controversial points. In all these cases, "formal groups" are being considered, whether they have direct contacts, or institutionalized or simply tangential and occasional relations with the religious hierarchy. Religious organizations, especially the lay ones, which form part of the Church itself, are not included.

Finally, on a fifth level, one would be dealing not with groups, but with individuals who, without using the name of the Church, act either through the latter or as though they were connected with it. It is also necessary to discriminate among them according to the system and the degree of loyalty they have toward the institution: whether they are members expressly subject to canon regulations or simply lay people.

The first category includes members of the clergy who in one way or another participate in national political processes, either covertly or publicly. In this case, they participate as mere private individuals, and the obligation they assume falls upon them alone, and not on their religious group. But, if they do not explicitly claim that they do not speak for the Church, and if they are high in the hierarchy, outsiders attribute the attitudes they express to the Church also. In the second category are the private individuals who share in the system of religious loyalties and exercise functions of great institutional significance for the Church.

Throughout the twenty-five year period of institutional life only two key functions appear clearly defined in the relations between the Church and the state, but this does not mean that during this period they have been controlled by people directly connected with the Church. The undersecretariat for worship has been filled by militant Catholics only for a third of that time, and Catholic ministers of education, as well as Catholic undersecretaries of education, have regularly alternated with ministers who were not Catholics.

177

Church Hierarchies in Argentina

Bishops are appointed through very special machinery in Argentina. Since the right of *Patronato*, inherited from the Spanish Crown, is still in effect, the appointment is made through state organs. In accordance with Article 86, paragraph 8, of the National Constitution, the executive branch exercises the right of *Patronato*, and the appointment of the future bishop is made on the basis of a triple nomination by the Senate. In practice (aside from the strict provisions of the Constitution) the appointment of bishops is not an arbitrary act on the part of state authorities, since ecclesiastical authorities are consulted beforehand. What is more, in recent years it has become the custom— though there is no legal rule to this effect—to have the original nomination come from the Vatican mission accredited in Argentina. If the candidate suggested by the Apostolic Nunciature is not rejected by the authorities of the nation, his candidacy follows a somewhat informal procedure. Since the Vatican does not recognize the right of *Patronato* claimed by Argentina, a *modus vivendi* has been established by virtue of which, through preliminary conversations, an attempt is made to avoid a confrontation.

This appointment method (it may be that *de facto* the original appointment is decided by the Roman Curia and the state confirms it *a posteriori*) is the result of a modern attitude and, not being legally binding, is a custom which may be abandoned. Since the presidency of Alvear (1922–1928), during which an incident occurred between the Church and the state about the appointment of a bishop, this manner of appointing has never occasioned any friction.

Bishops and archbishops have three special characteristics which set them apart from the other members of the ruling elite studied in this work. First, they are invested with a double role: they are religious authorities and also state officials. Second, their appointments are for life. This is, of course, not true in any of the other sectors analyzed. Third, though they are at the head of national districts, the universality of the Church and religious ecumenicism makes them transcend frontiers, and their status is universal.

Previous chapters have presented analyses of leaders' careers, but some modification of the notion of "career" is necessary in this chapter. While from the viewpoint of the bureaucratic role played, becoming a bishop is a distinction which might imply a sort of culmination of the career, the latter, that is, the career, does not exist in the ecclesiastical order. If, in the armed forces the culmination of the career of an officer is becoming a general, or, at least, that is the objective of the cadet who enters the Military College, an equivalent does not exist in the Church. In Argentina, bishops and archbishops together represent one percent of all the clergy. In earlier times, when there were only twenty dioceses, the figure was only 0.5 percent. Even much lower percentages are recorded in societies where the proportion of the faithful to each member of the clergy is very different from that existing in Argentina (for example, in Belgium).[5]

Although it may be said that there is no such thing as an ecclesiastical career, those who reach the top positions in the Church are indeed the product of a career. The fortunate culmination of a career in this case does not imply compliance with the greatest value, that is, the most faithful practice of religious virtues, but, rather, being a pastor of souls in the spiritual order, a good administrator of an ecclesiastical district in the temporal, and a proper functionary from the point of view of the state.

The average age of an Argentine bishop at the time of consecration is 46. Generally speaking, the bishops are young, but one finds that there are two different levels of average age. The incumbents of arch-bishoprics, that is, those who are at the head of the more central or important jurisdictions, usually are older when consecrated. On the other hand, the bishops of some smaller dioceses are comparatively younger, and so the range in age on assuming the post is between 36 and 64. Only 6 of a sample of 50 have been consecrated while in their thirties, and 7 were consecrated past the age of 55.

In 1934, when new dioceses were created in Argentina, young bishops were consecrated. As an immediate consequence of the International Eucharistic Congress, that date has been very important in the life of the Church. At that time it implied a rejuvenation at the top.

Twenty years later, at the beginning of the conflict with the Perón regime in 1954, 7 of the 20 bishops were over 65, the majority was between 55 and 65, and only 3 were less than 55. Table 9.1 shows the age breakdown of diocesian bishops in 1954 and in 1961.

It seems apparent that a rejuvenation took place in 1961; table 9.2 indicates the ratio of titular bishops of sees who were incumbents in 1936 and 1946 and were still in office in 1961. The data show that one-fourth of those who were members of the Episcopal College of Argentina in 1961 had been appointed shortly after the Eucharistic Congress of 1934; this ratio reflects the moderating element in almost every

179

TABLE 9.1

Age of the Bishops in 1954 and 1961

Age of Bishops	1954	1961
Over 65 years old	35%	28%
Between 55 and 65	50%	26%
Less than 55	15%	46%
Total	100%	100%

TABLE 9.2

Continuity of the Church Hierarchy

			Percentage Still in Office	
Bishops	Total	Still in Office in 1961	of 1936 or 1946 total	of 1961 total
Incumbents in 1936	21	9	42	25
Incumbents in 1946	22	14	63	40

social body—continuity in spite of change. Furthermore, 40 percent of the 1961 incumbents were already in office in 1946. At the same time, it should be emphasized that more than 60 percent of the bishops who were at the head of dioceses in 1946 were still in office in 1961.

According to these percentages, the Church, since its pastors exercise their functions *ad vitam*, is the institution where the renewal of hierarchies is slowest. There is no other group in which a comparable percentage of the 1946 leaders continues in office in 1961. There are none among holders of formal power, none among the senior officers of the armed forces, none among the entrepreneurial leaders. As it will be seen later, it is only among the leaders of some political parties that anything resembling this situation is to be found.

In 1962 and 1963 new dioceses were created. Again, the creation of dioceses by dividing the existing ones has become an instrument for renewal at the top, a "functional palliative" applied to the life tenure of the role.[6]

In 1961, bearing in mind the "continuity of the function," the following groups may be identified:

(a) a group at the head of its dioceses uninterruptedly since 1934 or 1935;

180

(b) a younger group, consecrated in 1957. That was precisely the year when twelve dioceses were created. In 1961 there were 35; then in that year they were increased by a third and filled by new bishops;

(c) A group in an intermediate situation. They are bishops who at various times have replaced those who have died.

The typical Argentine bishop[7] was born between 1890 and 1910, in a rural environment, either in the country or in very small towns or in a provincial city with a moderate number of inhabitants. A third of them was born within the province of Buenos Aires, particularly in places where there have been colonization plans and settlements of immigrants. An analysis of the universal sample shows that the Argentine bishops were born in:

The Buenos Aires Metropolitan Area	8
Towns in the province of Buenos Aires	16
Santa Fe (rural communities in the south)	7
Córdoba (half in the city and half in the Sierra)	8
Entre Ríos	3
Other provinces	3
Abroad	4

The sample employed, although universal, is very small. Table 9.3 compares the place of birth of Church authorities with that of senior army officers. While "the rest of the country" accounts for the greatest number of bishops, this is due to the high percentages of the rural regions of the provinces of Buenos Aires and Santa Fe, which are not significant as birthplaces of army officers.

TABLE 9.3

Bishops and Senior Officers of the Army by
Place of Birth (Percentages)

Region	Army Generals	Bishops
Buenos Aires Metropolitan Area	42	18
Entre Ríos-Corrientes	13	8
Córdoba	6	16
Traditional Northwest	10	2
Rest of the country	29	58
Total	100	100

The norm, as it appears from the statistical sample analyzed, is for the Argentine bishop to come from a rural background, or at least from what are now small towns, but at the time of their birth were mere hamlets. They are sons of immigrants. The Argentine bishops are first-generation sons of the groups that settled in Argentina during the period between 1880 and the first years of the century, mostly Italians from Piamonte.

While in many cases concrete data on the occupations of the bishops' parents in their new land is not available, there are indications that they came as sharecroppers, hoping to acquire ownership of the land they worked. This is confirmed by the fact that a large proportion of the future bishops was born in the *pampa gringa* of Santa Fe and in similar regions of the province of Buenos Aires. Of 39 bishops, 19 were sons of Italians, 12 were sons of Spaniards (7 of them Basques), 5 were sons of Germans, 2 of Irishmen, and 1 was the son of Arabs.

Only seven bishops are of Creole origin, and these were born in the provinces and in traditional environments. Five are from Córdoba. The sons of Irishmen were born in the northwestern part of the province of Buenos Aires, in the rural settlements of the Irish colony there. It is not strange that the future Argentine bishops come from families of some of the regions of Europe identified with religious devotion: Ireland, the Basque provinces, and Piamonte. What is curious is that 3 of the bishops who held office in 1963 came from an immigrant group marginal in Argentina, the Germans from the Volga region—Russo-Germans settled in the south of the province of Buenos Aires, around the city of Coronel Suárez. The percentages are as follow:

Bishops of Creole origin 15%
Bishops sons of immigrants 77%
Bishops born abroad 8%

The foreign bishops are regular rather than secular priests (that is, they belong to orders) who have been named bishops in order to care for the spiritual needs of the more marginal dioceses, Patagonia, Misiones, Formosa, and Jujuy.

As for social background, information was obtained on only 41 of the bishops and archbishops out of a total sample of 49.[8] Having submitted the list to qualified judges, and checked the information evaluated against the data on place of birth, immigrant status of the parents,

182

and their occupation at the time of birth of the future bishops, the
results are as follows:

Traditional families of the interior 5
Dependent or well-to-do middle class 18
Lower class 18

The five in the traditional families group were born in Córdoba
within the Córdoba upper class.[9] The Córdoba upper class includes
rural landowners in the Sierra who follow traditional norms, are of
ancient lineage, and have long been residents of the province, regardless of their actual economic situation.

The group of bishops from the middle classes includes, among
others, those born in Buenos Aires and those from Irish families. Of
the 18 bishops from the lower class 13 were born in rural surround-
ings, from which the relation between the type of occupation and
the immigrant sharecropper condition of the parents may be assumed.
The data cover the situation at the time the son entered the seminary,
since there are several cases where subsequent changes occurred in the
status of the parents, who experienced some upward social mobility.

In 1934, when the number of dioceses doubled, a change came about
in the composition of the leading groups of the Church. All the bishops
then appointed were first-generation sons of immigrants. Obviously,
the earlier bishops came from Creole families. The first incumbents of
dioceses from immigrant families were the bishops appointed for
Buenos Aires in 1926, the one for the La Plata diocese in 1928, that
for the Santa Fe diocese in 1932, and the one for Catamarca in the
same year.

The Buenos Aires traditional families have not given sons to the
Church, with the sole exception of Bishop Terrero, the only Bishop
with that background within this century. Before 1934 the traditional
families of Córdoba had not done so either at the highest level. Only
in the Northwest have there been cases of bishops from upper class
families, who later became incumbents of the dioceses of Jujuy, Salta,
and Tucumán.

The "great change" which occurred in the 1930s, when the sons
of immigrants replaced the Creoles as bishops, was the result of structural changes in the population base. The bishop appointed in the
1930s had been born to rural sharecropping families before the end
of the century and had entered the seminary during the first decade

183

of this century. Thus, recruitment of individuals of the most humble background took place in the Church earlier than in the other basic institutions of the country. What could not have been foreseen at the time was that this very broad recruitment would eventually prove a channel for upward social mobility to the highest hierarchical levels. In view of the small number of dioceses (there were 11 until 1934), the seminarian during the early years of the century could not imagine what would happen thirty years later. At that time entering the seminary represented (aside from his vocation) access to higher education, something that would not have been available by any other means.

The Socialization Process

The Argentine bishop had entered ecclesiastical life at a very early age. After primary school he entered the Colegio Apostólico where he went through a course of studies equivalent to high school and prepared for eventual admission to the seminary. Several contemporary bishops entered the seminary before they were 12 years old,[10] with the average age being about 15. There are only two who entered as adults, the incumbent of the San Isidro diocese, who entered the seminary at 30 (a "widower" in ecclesiastical jargon) and the bishop of Reconquista who practiced law before entering the Seminary.

There are no statistical studies which would make possible evaluating the scope of recruitment of future priests during the years when the bishops analyzed here entered the Seminary. All the available figures are for a later period and they show two opposing trends. On the one hand, starting in 1955, the number of seminarians decreased, at least in relation to the total population; taking an index of 100 for 1955, the figures for 1960 are as follows:

	1955	1960
Population of Argentina	100	110
Major Seminarians	100	54
Minor Seminarians	100	67

Table 9.4 compares the ratio of inhabitants per seminarian and the number of seminarians in two different periods. The first covers the period when the bishops included in the sample were studying at the major seminary, the second the period when they were incumbents of dioceses.[11]

184

TABLE 9.4

Total Number of Seminarians and Their Ratio to Population

Year	Total Major Seminarians	Inhabitants Per Seminarian
1912	197	35,000
1960	425	49,000

On the other hand, there seems to have been a trend toward qualitative improvement. In the absence of specific analyses, reference should be made to authoritative testimony which indicates a change in the background of the clergy.[12] It would seem that it is now higher than before, especially as to education, as in this respect it now reaches university or equivalent levels in many cases.

After graduating from the seminary, some of the Argentine bishops have gone to study in Rome, and many of them were ordained there. Taking 1950 and 1961 as cut-off dates, it is found that a majority of the bishops consecrated up to 1950 had studied in Rome; starting with the 1961 appointments the same is again true. During the interim period, however, the majority had only studied within the country; during this period the ratio was 3 to 1 in favor of those who had studied locally. After 1958, when ecclesiastical jurisdiction was regularized in Argentina, as a rule bishops have studied in Rome, since it became materially impossible to obtain proper training within the country.

The appointment of the bishops in 1934 and 1936 followed this pattern, as did several later appointments. Regular students in the local seminaries who showed aptitude for study were sent away to improve their education. The course of studies in Rome was equivalent to a high school course in ecclesiastical studies, mainly in theology and canon law. The bishops appointed in the 1950–1961 interregum came from a period during which the level of Argentine seminaries had been improved, and, besides, at the time they had wanted to obtain further training, World War II had made it impossible to study abroad.

The new bishops who have been appointed to newly created dioceses are younger and are again graduates of Rome, the great majority of them having followed courses of study at the Gregorian University after the war. In this respect, too, the level of education of the most recent Argentine bishops differs from that of previous graduating classes. Aside from theological and dogmatic studies, old bishops had

185

TABLE 9.5

Bishops Who Studied in Rome

Bishops	Total	Studied in Rome	% of Total
1936 Incumbents	21	12	57
Sample used	49	20	40

concentrated exclusively on matters which pertained to the internal life of the Church, while the recently appointed ones, whose degrees are on a university level, specialized in disciplines which required a different methodological attitude.

Once he had finished his studies, the young priest started his specific work. Eleven of the 49 bishops in the sample belong to religious orders. This does not mean that their activities have been confined within the walls of a monastery; on the contrary, these 11 were "missionaries" who had always worked in marginal zones. Five Salesians worked in the Patagonia region, the one Franciscan had been in Formosa Province, and the rest in the provinces of Misiones and Jujuy. The spiritual care of these dioceses is *de facto* exclusively in the hands of religious orders, which means that in practice they constitute apostolic vicarages. The remaining 38 bishops come from the secular clergy. Analyzing their type of career the following groups can be identified:

—— There are 5 bishops who previously had had experience only in parish work.

—— At the opposite extreme, there are 6 bishops who seem to have come from predominantly bureaucratic backgrounds, that is, they have spent very little time in parish work, and most of their priestly life has been spent in the Curia. In these cases the time spent in the Curia varies from 10, 13, or 16 consecutive years for the younger men to 26 for the oldest.

—— However, the rule is ambivalence of roles. This means that the future bishop has spent time in parish work and has had also specific duties within the Church bureaucracy, either simultaneosly, alternatingly, or successively. In the cases of ambivalent functions or of exclusively parish experience the most pronounced ecclesiastical socialization process is affected by the daily encounter with the problems of a diversified body of parishioners.

186

Since 1961 new bishops have been consecrated to occupy new sees. The general impression is that they differ from the stereotype. These new bishops come from higher social strata and from an urban environment; they were consecrated at an earlier age. They entered the seminary later than the others, after being involved in lay Church groups (such as Catholic Action), and studied in Rome.

Society in Transition, Church in Transition

The temporal face of the Church reflects each of the societies on which it rests: that is, without impairing its universality, "organized religion" in each region bears the hallmark of that particular society, although the causal relationship between society and Church is very far from being absolute.

There are cases where the cultural mores of a given society influence those of the Church in such a manner that the two seem to be in accord. This may be due to the society having internalized certain historical patterns set by the Church. At the other extreme, it may be that certain patterns of behavior (as is the case in many African societies) may be openly and absolutely at variance with those of the organized religion, but may coincide with local rites. In this case, the temporal face of the Church does not reflect the substance of that society. If there is any such reflection it is purely accidental.

The same is true when an attempt is made to relate organized religion to the degree of development and historical maturity of a people. As has been very well said elsewhere, organized religion acts in diverse ways in countries with different degrees of development.[13] In some cases, organized religion may act as a brake when it resists change within its own system. This may be true within certain religious communities (such as strict Jewish Orthodoxy) which are opposed to any change or in the case of the distortions of religious practices institutionalized in southern Italy.

In other cases organized religion may become a factor for development. In already developed countries it provides meaning and it contributes to social integration together with other sectors. In this way, organized religion offers objective normative frames of reference of indisputable value, as it does in France, Belgium, and Holland.

There may be a third possibility. This occurs in some underdevel-

187

oped countries where it is precisely organized religion that takes on the role of promoting development and accepts and institutionalizes change within its own system. This would seem to be the role played by ecclesiastical institutions in the Congo, in Uganda, and in India, among the underdeveloped countries of Asia and Africa; closer to Argentina's experience is the role they play in societies in full transition, such as Chile.

Those who have studied this matter point out that in general terms the external forms which organized worship may take may be reduced to three basic categories:

—— The Church may adopt a dynamic form, creating new values, renewing practices, and being sustained by the prestige which flows from its acts.

—— At the other extreme, the Church may still be clothed in traditional forms, may concentrate on the preservation of appearances, may insist on the unconditional acceptance of tradition, and may emphasize the negative aspect. In this traditional form the faithful become an amorphous mass because of the lack of high-level scholars and theologians. The traditional religious milieu and the traditional political system become amalgamated, and the Church limits itself exclusively to seeking governmental support.

—— Intermediate situations are possible, where both components are found, either because in the life of the Church the exterior and the interior attitudes may differ, or because in different areas of the same nation both antithetical situations are to be found, or because the actual situation is more fluid and embodies elements of both "models." At the elite level, a dynamic group coexists with a traditional one; that is, both developmental and conservative elites may be found.

It is to be presumed (and the analysis can only be continued at this grossly estimative level) that a correlation may be established between the length of time a bishop has occupied the episcopal office, his age, and the adoption of one or the other attitude. In other words, the first correlation would seem to be that more traditional and "conservative" attitudes are found in the older episcopal sees than in the newer, and conversely, that "dynamic religious attitudes" are preponderant in the newer sees.

The second correlation is that more traditional and conservative attitudes are found in bishops who have been at the head of the diocese longer, and conversely, that "dynamic attitudes" are preponderant

188

among newly appointed incumbents. Whether the attitude in the final analysis turns out to be of one type or the other is important in order to determine the role the Church plays in the institutional processes of Argentina. The intrinsically supernatural sense of that attitude is not being considered precisely because it is not perceptible to the social scientist.

When societies are living through a process of social disintegration, organized religion offers to official groups (if not to all, at least to those who appear identified with it) objective and firm normative frames of reference. If the religious elite is also dynamic, it is much easier to give contingent form to that which is essentially immutable.

Interpreters of contemporary Argentine life agree that the country has undergone one of its most profound moral crises precisely during the period covered by this study. During this period there has been "anomie" both at the top and bottom of the social structure; the "normative frames of reference" have been broken at both levels. During such periods, the role of the religious institution is functionally indispensable, since it is the only one in Argentine society capable of setting such frames of reference and giving a transcendental meaning to human actions.

In Argentina, as in the rest of Latin America, the Catholic Church expresses and interprets the sentiments of a large portion of the population. As such, the religious element, organized and framed in a temporal institution, is one of the basic components of the country's social body. But when the social body abandons traditional forms and is still searching for new forms, the roles of organized religion are more essential than ever. In fact, it can be said that:

—— To carry out a basic process of change, the assistance of organized religion is essential. In its temporal form, organized religion may either restrain or give impetus to change. If a modification is sought in the attitudes of the population and mobilization of vast social sectors is needed to bring about favorable changes, it is indispensable, both in Argentina and elsewhere in Latin America, to have the Catholic Church play a dynamic role in the process.

—— The religious element embodies a world of values which during processes of change (especially if the processes are acute) must be present. Transition to a more advanced stage of development brings with it an outlook of increasing materialism and overvaluation of material goods to the detriment of other values. Only organized religion may at

189

such times insist didactically on the primacy of the spiritual and offer firm value frameworks.

—— Organized religion offers a teleological sense of change. That is, it is the only group that can present the idea of change for the *better* as opposed to an attitude of change for the sake of change. The fact that its ideas about a "change for the better" may not be shared by many or by some is another matter.

Notes

1. The sociology of religion may well be one of the special fields that have awakened the greatest interest among sociologists from the sociological classics (Compte, Durkheim, Wach, Max Weber, *et al.*) to the more detailed modern studies (Le Bras and his French school) and the contemporaries (E. Pin, S.J., Jean Labbens, F.A. Isambert in France and J. M. Fitcher in the United States). Groups specializing in the sociology of religion hold annual meetings, and, in addition to some publications partially devoted to the subject, a specific one, *Social Compass*, summarizes the studies done in different areas. In order to gain a full understanding of the current thinking on the sociology of religion and of the subjects studied and techniques used by specialists in this field, the following works can be consulted: J. Labbens, *La sociología religiosa* (Andorra: Editorial Casal y Vall, 1961) and Antonio Donini, *Sociología y religión* (Buenos Aires: Editorial Sudamericana, n.d.).

2. A. Birou, *Sociologie et religion, economie et humanisme,* (Paris: Les Editions Ouvrières, 1959) states: "We can say that those that will observe it only 'phenomenologically' as philosophers of religion or as sociologists, will perceive nothing more than the appearances, and will miss the total and final explanation. . . . Nevertheless, the Church, a supernatural reality, the Mystical Body of Christ, became incarnate in the same manner as Christ, who, not belonging to the world, yet became incarnate in the world. Making herself visible, committing herself temporally and terrestially, it has a history and it is a society. . . . If the Church takes on a visible social form, it does not do so temporarily nor accidentally, since its members are corporal and spiritual beings at the same time, and the divine intent is to adapt the Mystery of Salvation to our human condition" (p. 32).

3. Various surveys on religious behavior have not been made public (Tucumán, 9 de Julio, the Sagrado Corazón Parish in Córdoba, and others).

4. The issue in 1943, 1946, and 1955 was the teaching of the Catholic religion in the public schools; the issue in 1955 and 1958 was the possibility of authorizing private universities, which many people took to mean Catholic universities. C.A.A.

5. The clergy-faithful ratio in Argentina in 1960 was 1 priest per 4,355 inhabitants. Compared with other Latin American countries:

Inhabitants per Priest

Chile	2,980
Ecuador	3,180
Colombia	3,490
Uruguay	4,110
Argentina	4,355

Source: A. Donini: "Situación estadística de la Iglesia Argentina en 1960," *Estudios* (Buenos Aires), December, 1961.

6. When 11 new bishoprics were created in 1962 the total number of sees rose to 46. This is why the 9 bishops who had been continuously in office since 1936 represented a slightly lower percentage of the new total, that is, 20 percent. And the 1946 bishops now represent 30 percent. In this way the rejuvenation becomes clearer.

7. For the analysis of the bishops a sample made up of all the incumbents of apostolic sees in the years 1936, 1941, 1946, 1951, 1956, and 1961 has been used. The information was gathered from the *Anuario eclesiástico de la República Argentina* (Buenos Aires: Instituto Bibliotecológico del Arzobispado de Buenos Aires, 1961). The basic work was a paper by Jorge Balán presented to the Seminar on the Sociology of Power of the Department of Sociology of the University of Buenos Aires, used extensively in this chapter.

8. Profound appreciation is expressed to the *Centro de Investigación y Acción Social de la Compañía de Jesús* which made available information on background and social origin which made it possible to elaborate impressionistic categories.

9. Two Bishops Castellano, 2 Bishops Buteler, and Bishop Ferreira Reynafé.

10. Bishops Vicentin, Kemmerer, Scozzina, Tórtolo, Buteler, and S. Martínez.

11. A. Donini: "Situación estadística de la Iglesia Argentina . . ." *op. cit.* To establish a correlation between dioceses-parrishes-clergy and faithful, see Enrique L. Amato, "Apuntes para una sociología religiosa argentina," *Criterio*, (Buenos Aires), Christmas, 1963.

12. F. Joaquín Adúriz, S.J. says: "The social and psychological conditions which the country experienced affect the lack of candidates for the seminary. Until 1940 the majority of the candidates were of humble background. Becoming priests represented for many of them an opportunity to rise from their class. They were generally boys who would not have been able to attend the University because of their economic situation. After the 'Perón process' there was a collective social promotion, at least as a feeling. The lower classes had access to places they could not have frequented before . . . the seminary ceased to be a way out for the lower

191

classes (besides, it had never been attractive as a way out of the economic problem). Today it is the previous cultural training that opens up horizons for the candidate, who arrives at the seminary with intellectual culture, is a university graduate, or normally could be so." *Primera plana*, (Buenos Aires), November 20, 1962.

13. See the paper by FF Justino M. O'Farrell and Antonio Donini, "Tipología de la religión organizada en países subdesarrollados, en transición y desarrollados," submitted to the Twentieth International Sociology Congress of the International Institute of Sociology, (Rio Tercero, Córdoba, 1963) and published in *La sociologia y las sociedades en desarrollo industrial* (Córdoba: Vol. 3, National University of Córdoba, 1963). Extensive use has been made of this work, of some of its premises, the categories it employs, and of its evaluation of organized religion in Argentina.

10. THE PROFESSIONAL POLITICIANS

WHEN THE LATE President John F. Kennedy was Senator from Massachusetts, he once filled out a personal data form by writing that his occupation was "professional politician." Are there many professional politicians in Argentina? Whatever their number, to what extent are they at the center of power or related to the centers where power is generated? This study assumes that there is a differentiated professional group which makes politics its particular goal and way of life, and whose motivations (desire for the common good, ambition for power, ideological beliefs, or love of the political game) jointly or singly are the same ones which motivate public men everywhere. The question, then, is to what extent this group or part of this group is involved with power.

On the universal level "men who are in politics" have changed in accordance with historical changes. Max Weber's analysis is a classic which indicates how throughout the centuries different professional categories have monopolized power: medicine men, priests, warriors, courtiers, the nobility, and lawyers. Then, around the turn of the century, "party politicians" appeared. This term includes the conglomerate of men who live by and for politics and whose professional activity takes place within parties and elective posts.[1]

The problem is to ascertain whether these two terms "to live by" and "to live for" apply to the same persons, to determine empirically whether it is accurate to say that one is the goal, the vocational objective, and the other the means of livelihood.

Reference to a fairly recent case in Argentine history may help. The Radical Party started to reorganize itself under the Uriburu administration (1930–32). Members of the "anti-personalist" faction led the way; these were men in the public eye who bore well-known names and who, in accordance with the fashionable preoccupations of the time, wanted to offer the country acceptable choices. In that 1932 Na-

193

tional Committee all the members lived for politics, with the sole exception of Martín Noel, an architect. However, it is quite possible that none of them made his living *by* politics, although Julio C. Borda and Enrique Mosca had just occupied high provincial positions. The other members of that National Committee not only did not earn their living by politics, but, on the contrary, their political activities reduced their personal fortunes. This was true in the case of Adolfo Güemes, Julio Simón Avellaneda, Raúl Rodríguez de la Torre and Marcelo T. de Alvear. This is an example, though perhaps an extreme one, of the exclusion of one of the terms. On the other hand, up to 1943 many politicians were able to live from their public posts as congressmen, governors, and in other public offices. Those in the opposition did so, too, as provincial legislators, councilmen, or ministers. In 1943 there was a considerable stock of professional politicians, but the revolution that followed constituted a rejection of them.

During the Perón era, one could not continue to live by politics if one was not a Peronist, unless one could do so as an opposition congressman, but these opportunities were very limited. However, there were many professional politicians who continued to live for politics to such an extent that their activities had to take place in exile because of Perón's intolerance and because of their involvement in activities against the regime.

After Perón fell, the previous political structure was reestablished, and experienced people who had been able to retain part of their electoral following continued to find politics a way of making a living, or, at least, a way of gaining access to the sources of power or to those close to the sources of power which represented a means of obtaining income.

Be that as it may, politicians had to have a separate profession. No longer were there rich people who lost their estates or sold their lands at bargain prices in order to pay the debts of the political party. The parties were led by men of more humble background, and they had to struggle for their daily bread. In view of the precariousness of their tenure of public office, they could not completely abandon their original profession. Therefore, one cannot accept the classical definition of a politician without many reservations. First, because in Argentina there has been a complete change in the situation. During the conservative period and during the Alvear administration, the highest party levels were the private preserve of well-known men, of the wealthy who financed the party apparatus from their own funds. When these people arrived in power they made up for their expenditures and reimbursed themselves by means of discreet participation in any new private activity for economic expansion. This period of well-known party figures, of patrons who reimbursed themselves, ended with the 1943 revolution.

Consequently, only those who consistently operate within the party framework in fulfilling their public vocation will be considered "professional politicians" for the purpose of this study, although through this activity they may not solve their pecuniary problems.

This chapter will deal only with high-level professional politicians, ignoring the low-level politicians. Those excluded are known in the Spanish-speaking world as *caudillos* (or "bosses"), the local and precinct leaders. They are not relevant to this study because they work within limited areas to the advantage of a fraction of the party, and they spend most of their energies in internal politics, in the party "kitchen." In that way they become what are called *punteros* in political jargon, or support men for the men higher up. When victory comes, these local *caudillos* set their sights on getting an "intendency," a political *jefatura*, a post as councilman or as community suppliers. This type of politician is as true a professional as can be found, since he lives from his office and from the perquisites of that office; nevertheless, he is not included in the discussion for the above mentioned reason.

This study is limited to consideration of the most important politicians, whatever their personal merits. They are the most important politicians because they direct the party machinery from national headquarters, executive boards, or higher councils of the party. Holding these positions, however, does not in itself indicate anything about their actual influence in the adoption of important decisions. In other words, being part of the leadership of even a great party does not in itself indicate that these leaders actually rule.

Since Argentina has had a presidential and not a parliamentary system, those who are in power at the moment, that is, the highest officials of the party in power, are the ones who rule. The ones in the opposition do not rule. But if the party is solid and well organized (which is unusual in Argentina) opposition leaders do rule within their respective groups. Their relation to power will depend upon a conjunction of variables. Some of these variables, such as organization, size, ideology,

195

internal discipline, and electoral support, make possible the following provisional typology.

There are large majority political parties and small political parties in Argentina. In the large political parties, the organization is usually quite weak, the ideology lax, and they in fact operate only as instruments for reaching power, despite the declarations they issue and the values they proclaim.[2] Basically, these large parties are machines, and the internal divisions, the schisms, the factions separated from the common trunk and differentiated by additions bear witness to factional struggles for control of power. The factions contend first for control of the party, then of the nation. Professional politicians who are active in these large parties have opportunities to reach power, but to do so they must depend upon the *punteros* or local *caudillos* to support their faction.

In the small parties, on the other hand, there are two possibilities. There are "hinge minority parties" and "strictly ideological parties." Since the latter will be discussed below, reference will be made here to the former. When the opportunity arises, these small hinge parties, which are strictly controlled by a small group, strike political bargains in order to secure a share of power, acting as hinges between the large parties. These are the parties Maurice Duverger at one time called "parties with a minority vocation." There are no factions within these; small groups control them and their political life is intermittent and so is the activity of the professional politicians who direct them, who alternate political functions with the exercise of a profession. Since the directing group is compact and is conscious of its own smallness, there is no chance for factions or ideological struggles to develop.

The second variable to be considered is the ideological one, that is, the influence of party ideology on the type of behavior and the degree of internal organization. The strictly ideological parties, for example, become an end in themselves; their organization is minutely detailed, their activity is constant, and they are the most militant. Their internal party life, unlike that of large parties, absorbs a great proportion of the energies of the leaders. Their ideologies are a transposition of the great currents of European thought with the addition of certain specific local norms. Except in the case of the Communist Party, the opportunity to become professionals is much less within these parties than within the hinge parties, and it may even be nil. This is not true of the Communists because the leaders are paid by the party.

196

The relationship of all the component elements, that is, the size of the party, the internal organization, the possibility of divisions, and the professionalism of the leaders would seem to depend upon the importance which ideology assumes within the internal life of the party. This relationship may be established on the basis of a scale.

1. When ideology is elevated to the dignity of dogma, splinter groups will exist in proportion to the deviations or hetorodox interpretations which may occur. The interpretations will be heterodox at least in relation to the exegesis of the group which controls the party, though in these cases one cannot properly speak of parties, since they are more like sects, such as the Trotskyites. Professionalism is nil, just as participation in power is nil.

2. On the next level there is absolute ideological cohesion with specific professionalism, no visible splinter groups, and zero participation in power. In this case party leaders "rule" only within the party; the Communist Party is an example of this type.

3. On a third level are the somewhat more lax ideological parties, where personal rivalries very often are camouflaged as ideological differences. As a group their members are not usually professional politicians, but individually some of the luckier ones may become so by holding elective office.

4. The small hinge parties could be placed on the fourth level, since they have occasional opportunities for co-participation in power and for professionalization.

5. The large traditional parties appear on the fifth level. They are generally divided into many splinter groups, with added differentiated labels; political professionalization of some of their leaders is very possible, and both the Radical and Conservative Parties have on various occasions had the responsibility of ruling the country.

From 1930 to 1943 the Conservative Party was in power; that is, it was the operative channel. Its leaders were classical examples of professional politicians. A splinter group from the Radical Party carried some party members to power in 1945 until its permanent absorption into the Peronist movement. From 1958 on, one of the two branches of the Radical Party has controlled almost all power, and at the end of its term the other branch has taken its place. This means that these large traditional parties have operated as access channels to power through their own machine for less than half the period analyzed. One of them has again become an instrument for the replacement of formal political leaders beginning in 1963.

197

TABLE 10.1

Districts Represented by Party Leaders
1936–1961

Party	Federal District and Buenos Aires Province	Córdoba Province	Santa Fe Province	North-east Region	North-west Region	Cuyo Region	Others	Total
Conservative	9	6	1	4	8	11	—	39
Socialist	75	—	1	1	1	1	—	79
Progressive Democrats	7	—	13	3	—	—	—	23
Christian Democrats	10	3	2	1	2	1	3	22
Peronist	41	1	4	1	3	2	—	52
Radical	19	5	4	6	10	6	3	53

6. Lastly, there are the parties of a "personalist" type, or essentially a party organization identified with the success or failure of a personalist leader. Peronism was this type of movement. The party founded by Álvaro Alsogaray and some provincial parties are other examples. In these cases the opportunities of the party officials are dependent on what the leader has done, or on whether or not he holds power or has amassed so much wealth that some of the activities of the officials of the party may be financed by him.

The Argentine Political Staff

What follows is an attempt to study a group of men who, for a quarter of a century, have made up the party leadership teams. This group includes the members of the national committees, executive boards, or higher party councils in the sample years chosen for this study: 1936, 1941, 1946, 1951, 1956, and 1961.[3]

The specific situations of the parties must be taken into account in considering the place of origin of party leaders. For example, Radicals seek balanced representation of all regions on their national committee, Socialism has been virtually a metropolitan party, and the Progressive Democratic Party is basically a Santa Fe Province organization. Tables 10.1 and 10.2 provide a breakdown of the geographic representation found at the highest levels of party leadership.

TABLE 10.2

Regional Distribution of Party Leaders

Region	% of Total Leaders
Capital and Buenos Aires Province	60
Province of Santa Fe	9
Province of Córdoba	6
Entre Ríos, Corrientes, and Misiones	6
Northwestern Provinces	9
Cuyo	8
Remainder	2

Table 10.3 analyzes the profession of the leaders included in the sample party by party.

199

TABLE 10.3
Profession of Party Leaders

Party	Profes-sionals & Military	Ranchers, Business-men, Indus-trialists	Newspaper-men, White Collar Workers	Working Class	No Data	Total
Conserva-tive	34	2	1	–	2	39
Socialist	41	–	24	1	13	79
Progressive Democrats	39	4	–	–	–	43
Christian Democrats	18	1	1	–	2	22
Peronist	21	5	2	13	11	52
Radical	35	5	4	–	9	53

On the basis of these occupational data, and considering only those leaders for whom this type of information is available, it becomes possible to place them in social categories; the results are summarized in Table 10.4. This table has been drawn up on the basis of a gross estimate arrived at by adding only the occupational data while disregarding such factors as family background, auto-identification, social mobility, and other values. Table 10.4 shows that the political team in most cases is recruited from the middle class, especially the well-to-do bourgeoisie, with the exception of a third of the Socialist leaders who come from the dependent sectors of the middle class and a third of the Peronist leaders who have a working-class background.[4]

TABLE 10.4
Social Background of Party Leaders (Percentages)

Party	Well-to-do Bourgeoisie	Dependent Middle Class	Working Class
Conservatives	97	3	—
Socialists	62	36	2
Progressive Democrats	100	—	—
Christian Democrats	95	5	—
Peronists	63	5	32
Radicals	90	10	—

200

There are many cases of leaders who defy neat categorization. The Conservative leaders were both professional men and important rural landowners.[5] Up to 1943 the leaders of the Conservative Party were also professional politicians in the strictest sense of the word. Their status was determined by occupational prestige, the basic source of income, and the almost continuous occupation of public office. The following members of the Conservative directing bodies who held office as congressmen, senators, governors, ministers, high officials, or provincial legislators may serve as examples:

Adrián C. Escobar	1904–1946
Robustiano Patrón Costas	1902–1943
Gilberto Suárez Lago	1922–1943
Reynaldo Pastor	1922–1951 (except for the interval of the 1943 revolution until 1946. Then he was elected deputy by the opposition.)
José Aguirre Cámara	1922–1943
Antonio Santamarina	1908–1941
Alberto Arancibia Rodríguez	1915–1943

It is therefore impossible to determine their background exclusively on the basis of type of occupation.

The percentage of lawyers recorded in Table 10.5, as well as in other studies, comes as no surprise.[6] Physicians are active mainly at the provincial level; many governors and former governors held medical degrees. This fact, which is common in Argentina, is anomalous on a

TABLE 10.5

Party Leaders According to their University or Military Profession

| Party | University Professionals | | | Military | Total | % Lawyers of Total |
	Lawyers	Physicians	Others			
Conservative	34	—	—	—	34	100
Socialist	21	15	5	—	41	51
Democ. Prog.	33	2	4	—	39	84
Christian Dem.	13	1	4	—	18	72
Radical	27	6	2	—	35	77
Peronist	10	3	2	6	21	48

world scale, for physicians do not participate in politics on a large scale outside Latin America. The presence of physicians on European and American political staffs is unthinkable, though there has been a single great exception: when socialist parties started to form in Europe (around the end of last century, and the beginning of this) many scientific men were active in them from humanitarian motives. Something similar happened in Argentina and in other Latin American socialist parties.

In Argentina, the political success of physicians is especially notable in rural and traditional areas. There the contact the physician has with his patients often transforms the latter into a political clientele. In a rural milieu, when there are no lawyers, the physician represents the university intelligentsia.

It is interesting that no teachers or professors form part of the leading groups except among the Socialists. In African countries, this professional group seems to exercise political leadership or at least has become part of it. The reason is obvious: they embody the local intelligentsia.

In looking over the roster of Conservative Party leaders, it becomes evident that during the early years of the sample almost all of them came from traditional families of the interior, the rural landowning families.[7] It is not until the 1961 group of leaders that those of different background appear; the newcomers include those with Italian surnames, some of whom represent families that had recently become wealthy, and even one Jew.

The change came earlier among the Radicals. Once Marcelo T. de Alvear disappeared, so did the group with a more patrician background which had accompanied him. After the 1940s in the sample years, there is not one national committeeman of the Radical Party who is not a first-generation Argentine. There are some exceptions, however, outside the national committee.[8]

Among the Socialist leaders, half are sons of Italian immigrants; there is not a single French or German surname. Jews account for 14 percent. Three of the leaders come from the Buenos Aires traditional families and so, together with the only Creole leader (from Santiago del Estero), are marginal from this point of view.

The typical Progressive Democratic leader was born in Rosario or Santa Fe from a well-to-do bourgeois family which had made its fortune around the 1920s by taking advantage of the commercial expansion in Rosario.

202

Among the Christian Democrats in the sample 1956 and 1961 leadership groups, leaders from Buenos Aires and Córdoba traditional families represent one-third of the total. It is interesting that the grandparents of these leaders in their day had been outstandingly active in the liberal camp. The remaining two thirds were first-generation Argentines, the sons of Italians and Spaniards, only one of them being the son of an Englishman. They are identified with the middle and upper middle class. There are no ranchers nor professional politicians within the ranks of the Christian Democrat leaders.

Of 52 Peronist leaders, 7, that is, 13 percent, come from traditional families from Corrientes, Jujuy, and Salta. But the "average" leader is typically of immigrant ancestry. There is a minority group (some former labor leaders) of undeniable Creole extraction, a group which is not found in the leadership of other political movements.

If this analysis were to end with a summary table, it would show that the political teams come, in general, from the great wave of immigration. Most of these leaders are first-generation Argentines. Their families originally belonged to the middle class, but changes of status eventually identified the leaders with the well-to-do sectors of the bourgeoisie. Whether this identification was mainly due to the type of prestige obtained in party activities is something that will be discussed later. In any case, it is still true that whatever their backgrounds, the political roles of these party men eventually united them to the well-to-do buorgeois sector.

The percentage of women in national leadership posts is very small. There are no women in the Conservative leadership nor in the Radical or Progressive Democrat national committees. Women represent 9 percent of the leadership sector of the Christian Democrats and 6 percent of that of the Socialists. One of the top leaders of the Peronist movement was a woman, and there was at one time a Women's Peronist Party. The new organization of the *Justicialista* High Council (which is not included in the sample because it was formed after 1961) reserves 25 percent of its posts for women.

Recruitment Techniques and the Politician's "Career"

In Argentine society there are no uniform criteria for recruitment of the parties' ruling teams. Criteria vary according to the type of party, since ideologies determine the difference in criteria employed. Each

203

type of party has different criteria for selection of its upper echelons. Thus differences in social origin, background, and place of birth become of secondary importance.

The existence of these different and opposing criteria is one example of the nonconsensual nature of Argentine society. In other countries where consensus is greater or very strong, selection criteria for leadership personnel of all parties is the same. The extreme case is the similarity of recruitment criteria among Republicans and Democrats in the United States, a country where there is a broad consensus.

In some Latin American countries where nonconsensus is not as extreme as in Argentina, selection criteria are uniform, even in the case of groups whose differences seem insurmountable. In Chile and in Uruguay, to take two neighboring countries as examples, parties use, with only minor differences, the same selection criteria whether in the case of *Blancos* or *Colorados* (Uruguay), Socialists or Liberals (Chile), because in those countries the institutionalized political norms are stronger than ideological differences.

This is not true in Argentina as indicated in Table 10.6. This study is focused on the informal criteria employed in selection. Formal criteria are not emphasized because those provided in the parties' by-laws are rather similar; informal criteria are those which become evident from the statistical approach to a certain number of cases. It is assumed that the reader already knows the importance of the makeup of the "inner circle"[9] of political parties, and that, on a world-wide scale, there are different models for selecting that inner circle or the party ruling bodies. The "fully democratic" type of selection is widely employed; in this type the party rank and file elect their rulers by direct vote. Another type is the "restricted democratic" in which party members vote on certain options presented by the group which controls the party. A third is "co-optation by the endogroup," or the situation that arises when the ruling group itself calls, draws, or co-opts others to form part of the ruling bodies without intervention of the rank and file. This is true in the more traditional and less evolved parties, controlled by "notables" and financed by the rulers themselves. A fourth system is the "paternalistic," with such other variants as "personalism." The fifth, "authoritarian vertical" selection, occurs in totalitarian parties where the officers are named by successive delegations from top to bottom, or in parties controlled by a strong leader.

TABLE 10.6

Essential Characteristics of Argentine Party Staffs

Selection Criteria for Leaders and Party Career Types	Nature of Prestige and Professionalism
Conservative 1) Up to 1943 the criterion for selection was co-optation. The large landowners of the party determined and "called" those who were to have a career within the party, their equals in social rank or those who were functionally promoted because of the special nature of their political contribution (for instance, Barceló). 2) Selection on relative democratic base since its reorganization in 1956. Coexistence of free internal elections with paternalism in traditional provinces (Corrientes, San Luis). Since 1956 the "career" has been institutionalized within the party; before that it existed in a relative sense, in view of the limitations imposed by paternalism.	Coexistence of those having ascriptive and political prestige up to 1943. Only political prestige since 1956. But no professionalism, in view of the few electoral victories since 1956, only localized ones in the provincial area. Until 1943, complete professionalism at the highest party level.
Socialist Democratic selection until the division of the party. The career always confined to the Federal Capital locale despite a certain amount of blocking which limited the opportunities of a given group of leaders. For electoral reasons, the career offered only two alternatives in the Capital: congressman or councilman; very rarely a senatorship.	Exclusively endogenous prestige conferred by party activity. Complete political professionalism of about twenty leaders up to 1943; occasional and relative after that date.
Progressive Democrats Co-optation, that is, the group co-opts, invites, attracts or calls equals or presumed equals to fill the posts. A very strong solidly constituted endogroup which also uses intermediate types of democratic selection (by internal elections) but always on the basis of the basic endogroup. Career only for those who are active within the Santa Fe local council, provincial legislator, national candidacy, and so forth.	Exogenous prestige. Derived from social (Thedy-Noble), professional or commercial position in the city of Rosario (Lagos, Muniagurria), from social position in city of Santa Fe. No electoral opportunities for professionalism.

205

Christian Democrat

Democratic selection by successive elections from the bottom. New party, has not had time to institutionalize a political career, as may have happened in other parties with a similar formal structure (Democratic Socialism or Democratic Progressive Party of the Federal Capital). One third of the leaders come from lay institutions of the Church (Catholic Action, and so forth) in which they had been officers. This fact seems in some cases to have been the determining factor in the *curriculum* as is also the establishing of ideological pre-party movements or having been active in them.

Founded in 1956, there has been no time nor electoral opportunity for political professionalism to develop.

Peronista

According to three periods: (1) self-appointment and co-optation for and among leaders of the Labor Party and the Renewal Radical Board. (2) vertical authoritarian appointment by the Leader of the Movement beginning in 1957 (Sole Party of the National Revolution and Peronist Party) (3) authoritarian appointment exclusively for political sectors. Authoritarian appointment from choices presented by the labor union sector beginning in 1958. All appointments made on the part of the Leader of the Movement. There were no careers. By reason of various cases of falling into disgrace, expulsions, excommunications, and so forth, there was not a single leader that at one time or another did not have his career cut short.[10]

The only autonomous source of prestige has been and continues to be success in the labor union field. It is valuable therefore for the party leaders to represent the labor union sector. In view of the labor union-Peronist movement relation, it is an endogenous and exogenous source at the same time. Rarely, prestige is acquired by some political figure because of his activity during the regime. There was administrative professionalism during the regime.

Radical

Democratic appointment, within the limitations imposed by paternalism in some regions and the relative strength of *caudillismo* in all. This is especially true at local headquarters, but in successive stages more formal steps are observed. The "career" is basic in Radicalism, before and after its divisions, to an extent that it is not in any other party. The *cursus honorum* is followed from the local units through various internal stages, up to the presidency of the National Committee (whether the People's Radical or the Intransigent Radical).

Endogenous prestige derived from party activity (posts obtained in the party), political activity in the opposition, and the functions performed. There are no Radical leaders with prestige exogenous to the party, such as social or intellectual activity or success in the economic field. Professionalism includes a sizable number of leaders on the highest level and local urban leaders.

In the 25-year period under study, the case of Radicalism shows most clearly the correlation between (1) the fact that the leader goes through all the stages of the "career," or, to put it another way, that Radical leaders go through a true political *cursus honorum;* (2) endogenous prestige, or the prestige of these leaders, derives solely and exclusively from their party activities and from their public activities in representing the party; and (3) the resulting political professionalism of a considerable number of leaders. Radical leaders represent, therefore, the classic situation in which a unilineal type of relationship may be established between the high level reached within the party, the resulting prestige, and the power which is determined exclusively by the situation of the party at the time.

Politicians and Party Oligarchies

It is a universally observed phenomenon that the inner circles of parties attempt to perpetuate themselves in control and sometimes consciously and others subconsciously build up a framework that will guarantee their continuity in office. The phenomenon has been adequately studied in political science in various areas and with different types of parties and labor organizations. The same phenomenon has been found everywhere.

Table 10.7 indicates the percentage of members of national committees, boards, and high councils that appear repeatedly in the Argentine parties whenever the names are compared. In that table, the

TABLE 10.7

Frequency of Repetition of Argentine Party Leaders
At Five-Year Intervals[11]

Party	Leaders in: In Relation to:	1941 1936	1946 1941	1951 1946	1956 1951	1961 1956
Conservative		–*	–	–	37.5	11.0
Socialist		63.6	100.0	58.3	40.0	80.0
Progressive Democrats		–	–	37.5	50.0	100.0
Christian Democrats		–	–	–	–	11.0
Peronist		–	–	11.0	0.0	0.0
Radical		–	–	11.0	11.0	5.0

* The dashes indicate lack of informative data. "0" indicates absence of repetition.

207

leaders in office in 1941 are compared with those of 1936, those of 1946 with those of 1941, those of 1951 with those of 1946, and so on, until in each case the percentage of repetition is established.

The greatest evidence of oligarchization was found in the Socialist Party prior to its division in 1956. The percentage of repetition is very significant in the Progressive Democratic Party, especially in recent years. Before that the data could not be compared since only provincial boards existed.

Aside from the above, the process reaches its maximum expression in the Communist Party: the basic team has been the same since the 1930s and its two top leaders have been at the head of the Party since it was founded in 1922. The female leader has been active in her post since 1935, and at that level there has been only one important replacement, that occasioned by the expulsion of Real in 1953.

Even though in the Radical Party (both branches) a basic group of thirty top echelon leaders has held control since 1946, at the highest party level there is no repetition of names. The Radicals seek broad representation of the various regions of the country on the national committee, an informal criterion not used by the other parties. This seems to be a party constant at both the highest and intermediate levels. In looking through the list of provincial delegates to the National Committee of the Radical Party from 1922 to 1945,[12] the margin of repetition always seems to be less than a third. The same happened when the Party split. If the list of delegates to the national committee of the People's Radical Party for 1959–1961 is compared with the one for 1957–1959, it will be found that only 38 of the 132 delegates had occupied that position two years before.

All possibility of continuity should be discarded in Peronism, since only the leader is permanent, and almost all the officers at one time or another have been expelled from the party, and appointments are made from the top. The remaining party, the Christian Democratic Party, is too new a party to have been able to bring to maturity a process of this nature. Thus party oligarchization is reduced to the cases already indicated.

According to the sample, the basic Socialist team was made up of 11 persons up to 1961. Bearing in mind that in the sample only 6 different boards are represented, it is found that 3 Socialist officers belonged to the 6 boards, 3 belonged to 5, 3 belonged to 4, and 2 officers to only

2. One of these officers has been in the party leadership without interruption since 1914, one since 1925, and two since 1929.

For the Progressive Democratic Party it is possible to analyze only the four national boards; the earlier ones were provincial. Here the basic team is made up of 8 persons: 2 officers belonged to the 4 boards analyzed, 2 appeared on 3 boards, and 4 officers appeared on 2 of these boards.

Oligarchization is therefore confined to three parties, but it is not possible to say that even in these cases Michels' iron rule of oligarchy applies.[13] For this rule to be valid (as it has proved to be in the case of Socialist Party leadership in Italy, France, Holland, and Germany), certain factors would have to be present—effective control of the rank-and-file and an elaborate internal organization—which do not seem to be present in the Argentine case. Perhaps the Socialist Party of Argentina meets both conditions; this does not explain everything, however, since the two factors—effective control and organization—ceased to exist as soon as the party split, while the process of oligarchization still continued.

It has been indicated that oligarchization has taken place in Argentina within two parties which range from the liberal left to the extreme left. Only in a negative sense and to the extent that one may wish to question why the same thing has not happened to the center and right parties, can the problem be reconsidered.

Party structure and its degree of internal complexity decreases from left to right; the maximum level is encountered in the political movements of the left; greater flexibility, less internal structuring, greater paternalism is found in the conservative right, the liberal groups, and the center parties. These features are not typical of parties on the extreme right whose goal, like that of the extreme left, is to take over power by nonelectoral means. Both extremes require strictly authoritarian procedures and organization.

In the case of Argentina, many liberal and right-wing conservative groups have considered the party an instrument for reaching power, a means and not an end. For many conservatives the party itself does not matter, as long as it is an operational instrument. In some circumstances, and especially if there is insistence on achieving power by the electoral route, the party may be useless. Thus conservatives may see the armed forces or other pressure groups as channels for achieving power, or as groups on whose back it is possible to ride to power. These

209

groups, therefore, are functionally more useful than the party. Conservatives thus may think it unnecessary to waste energy or bother much about the party, which can be useful only on a limited number of occasions.

Summary: Party Politicians, Either Marginal or at the Center of Power

It seems apparent that the possibility of Argentine politicians constituting a differentiated socio-professional sector, a sector to which specific roles have been attributed and which enjoys an especially recognized status, is quite doubtful. At the present time it can be said to exist only among the Radicals, though at an earlier period it had also existed among the Socialists. However, the party leaders play different nonpolitical roles, and while many enjoy some type of recognized prestige, it is due to factors apart from their party activity. They lend this prestige gained in nonpolitical roles to the party machine within which they are active. Thus, for example, some labor leaders lent their personal prestige to the Peronist leadership. Some economically successful men lend their prestige to Conservatism, and others bring to that party traditional ascriptive prestige, especially in the provinces. The fact that they contribute prestige allows some leaders to manage the party machinery and even to use it for their own benefit instead of being exclusively dependent upon the machinery as is the case among the Radicals.

Regarding the role of the professional politician, however, some questions remain unanswered.

We might ask whether full-time involvement in politics does not detract from other types of functions or from the development of some capacities, for example, the intellectual. The answer could only be analyzed within a broader context. It would be interesting to test the hypothesis that professional politicians everywhere have a low intellectual level as a group. This hypothesis maintains that constant activity detracts from the intellectual concentration and introspection necessary to guide future action. In truth, there are no notable intellectuals in the political and party movements in Argentina, at least not among the high-level leaders included in the samples employed. Perhaps some individuals who combine a political and an intellectual vocation were not included in the samples, but they would be a very

210

small minority. In Argentina there seem to be no intellectuals, scientists, or philosophers with responsibility for party leadership; if there have been any occasionally, they have soon retired.

The only way of studying the problem would be to go through the fullest list of party leaders and the most restricted list of professional politicians and evaluate their intellectual capacity to find out whether they "keep up with the times." Since this is not feasible, only an impressionistic opinion can be presented here. This opinion suggests a negative answer.

Objective evidence—that is, parliamentary participation, public activities, televised round tables, and press conference replies of the party leaders—indicate very few of them give evidence of being even moderately well-informed on economics, administration, social sciences, technical and international problems, and so forth.

In no other sector as much as in party leadership is there evidence of so much ossification. This ossification (regardless of the personal qualities which those continuing leaders may have displayed in the past) operates as a block against rejuvenation and necessary ideological and informational updating.

In all the other orders of society, whether military, religious, bureaucratic, or entrepreneurial, there are formal or informal norms for regulating promotion. Those norms require at least fitness for the function. In party politics there is also an informal norm for promotion: success in an election, victory at the polls. But this is the sort of success that may be due to factors completely foreign to the intellectual capacity of the person and even, at times, as in the electoral victories of local *caudillos* or *punteros*, may be the result of the most reprehensible forms of "politicking." Hence, if the highest value on the party scale is attained by repeated electoral victories, this requires techniques and continues practices that are not exactly the most favorable for the development of intellectual qualities.

The second question we might ask is why the collective prestige of politicians, the generic prestige attached to them as a body, is so low. Contrary to what happens in other countries, this type of recognition does not seem to exist in Argentina, partly because of the inadequate, intermittent, and rather inefficient working of the country's institutional machinery, and partly because public opinion identifies professional politicians as the beneficiaries of sinecures, deals, and misappropriation of public funds.

It is quite possible that this widespread opinion may not be war-

211

ranted. In fact, it is likely that with the exception of a few cases, professional politicians are not guilty of the charges public opinion brings against them, for it is true that those identified as having benefited from exactions and sinecures have been not so much the politicians as the administrators, the negotiators, and the influence-peddlers found in all regimes. But what counts for prestige is not the reality, but rather the image held by public opinion.

Professional politicians enjoy good reputations only in functional regimes and in societies which enjoy consensus—in countries where, as in the case of those with a parliamentary system, the political legislator is honored. But such is not the case in Argentina.

The third question concerns the relation of the party politician to power. It must be remembered that in Argentina political debates are stated in terms of mutually exclusive alternatives; consequently, there is no stable political team in power, as happens in countries with parliamentary regimes. In Argentina there are only opportunists in politics, in power one day and out the next, subject to quickly changing circumstances.

It is, therefore, impossible to analyze Argentine professional politicians as a unit. Each case and each situation must be looked at separately. At the time of writing these lines the clearest political situation of the whole quarter century is emerging. The whole People's Radical Party—through its machinery, the professionalism of its leaders, the full-time political career of its men, their exclusively political prestige—has come to power and has taken charge of the whole responsibility for leading. With the Peronist party leaders, who also enjoyed a monopoly of power, the situation was somewhat different; below Perón, their powers were not very specific, being delegated from the top. The rise of Radicalism in 1963 implied that the two levels of power, the central one and the channels for transmission of orders, were covered exclusively by professional party politicians, something that had not happened since 1943.

Notes

1. Max Weber, Le savant et le politique (Paris: Ed. Plon, 1959).
2. In this sense the Radical attitude is typical. Many men in that movement seem to make the party an end in itself, in part precisely because they explicitly attribute a special charisma to it. Irigoyen's thought, which placed the Radical Party above men, is typical in this respect. The same is

212

true of the party historians, writers, and apologists. It is explicitly shown in Gabriel del Mazo, *El radicalismo: Notas sobre su historia y doctrina* (Buenos Aires: Editorial Raigal, 1955).

3. Reference to the 1961 Socialists includes the two Socialist parties in existence at the time. The ruling committee of the Democratic Progressive Party for Santa Fe Province was considered the national ruling body in the early years, since it had been given national jurisdiction. The Christian Democrats, the newest party, appear only in the 1956 and 1961 samples. The analysis of Peronism includes the members of the Labor and Renewal Radical Board of 1945, those of the Sole Party of the National Revolution in 1946, and those of the male branch of the Peronist party and of its High Council reorganized after the events of June, 1955; Peronism did not have a recognized national organization in 1961. Until 1956, the Radical Party was essentially one; the 1961 data includes both the People's Radical Party and the Intransigent Radical Party. The computation has taken into account the number of positions filled, even though the same person may have filled more than one position. Data on Radical Party leaders is incomplete in some cases and is not available in others. Data for this chapter has been sought by the students participating in the Seminars on "Sociology of Power" (1961), and on "Political Parties (1962) held at the Institute of Sociology of the School of Philosophy and Letters of the University of Buenos Aires. They included Silvia Sigal, Julio Tapia, Martha Callejo, Ana María La Guidara, and Graciela Biagini. The author also wishes to express his appreciation to Félix Luna, who made available information on Radical party leaders.

4. The most important work done up to now on social background, family environment, and status elements of the professional politicians is Darío Cantón, *El Parlamento Argentino en épocas de cambio: 1890, 1916 y 1946* (Buenos Aires: Editorial del Instituto, 1966). The author analyzes the legislators in the years 1890, 1916, and 1946 and takes into account their social background. After dividing them into five categories, he notes that all the 1889 senators and representatives came from the upper and middle classes, while only two percent of the 1916 congressmen belonged to the third category. On the other hand, in 1946, 16 percent of the congressmen would belong to the third social category, 3 percent to the fourth and 8 percent to the fifth (laborer). Of the 1946 senators, 11 percent came from a working-class background. That is, the coming of Peronism permitted people with a working-class background to move up to the highest political positions. The 1889 Congress was dominated by Julio A. Roca, with only the Liberal and Conservative parties represented. That of 1916 had Conservative and Radical Party legislators, with a Socialist majority representation from the Federal Capital. But as regards social extraction there were no appreciable differences between the 1916 lawmakers and those at the end of the century.

5. Such as Antonio Santamarina and Robustiano Patrón Costas before 1943 and Laureano Landaburu, Justo Díaz Colodrero, and Eduardo Paz throughout this period.

213

6. The massive presence of lawyers in all political bodies is a universal phenomenon. As Max Weber indicated, "If we review the profession of the members of the Convention during the (French) Revolution, only one proletarian will be found (he was elected under the same electoral law which governed his colleagues) and very few bourgeois entrepreneurs. However, a mass of jurists of all types is found, without whom it would be absolutely impossible to understand the radical mentality of these intellectuals and their proposals. Since then, the modern lawyer and democracy have advanced together." (*op. cit.*). The above mentioned study by Cantón verified the fact that in 1899, 84 percent of the federal congressmen having a university degree were lawyers. The corresponding figures were 74 percent in 1916 and 67 percent in 1946. This seems logical when one remembers the Argentine penchant for the study of law. Sergio Bagú has shown in his *Evolución histórica de la estratificación social en la Argentina* (Buenos Aires: Department of Sociology, University of Buenos Aires, 1961), that, according to the 1895 national census, 57 percent of Argentine university graduates were lawyers; in 1914, the figure was 45 percent.

7. Rodríguez Sáa, Patrón Costas, Landaburu, Díaz Colodrero, Paz, and others.

8. For an analysis on the incongruence of status of the Radicals who accompanied Yrigoyen in 1916, see Silvia Sigal and Ezequiel Gallo, Jr.: "La formación de los partidos contemporáneos. La Unión Cívica Radical 1890–1916," in *Desarrollo económico*, Vol. III, Nos. 1 and 2, Buenos Aires, April–September, 1963.

9. Maurice Duverger, *Political Parties, Their Organization and Activity in the Modern State*, 2nd ed. (New York: Wiley, 1962).

10. Thirty-three of the 52 Peronist leaders included in the sample ceased their political activities after September, 1955; 5 died, 4 were expressly expelled, 8 acted again in "neo-Peronist" parties, and only 2 of the 52 returned to party executive posts after 1955.

11. The data on the Conservative party are incomplete. In the cases of the already divided Socialist and Radical parties of 1961, all factions have been included; thus, there were twice as many leadership positions in these parties in 1961, when compared with 1956.

12. From a comparison of the lists of delegates to the convention published by Gabriel del Mazo, *op. cit.*

13. Robert Michels, *Political Parties; A Sociological Study of the Tendencies of Modern Democracies* (Glencoe, Ill.: Free Press, 1949), formulates his "iron rule of oligarchy," by means of a series of syllogisms. The greater the party membership, Michels maintains, the greater the need for organization. The latter brings on bureaucratization, and in this way the permanence of the leaders in the bureaucratized function is established. This brings about a change in the status mentality of the leaders and ambivalence of behavior. If they act within revolutionary parties they must uphold the need for substantive changes, but basically they deplore jeopardizing the bureaucratic calm attained. Thus, without changing the verbal expressions, they adopt a basically conservative attitude.

214

11. THE UNION LEADERS

IN EVALUATING the role of union leaders in Argentina and in trying to find out to what extent they are part of the ruling sectors, a number of factors should be considered. First is the changing pattern of the union sector both while it was outside the political system and when it later came to operate from inside that system. Next, it must be ascertained how the ideologies held by the unions have determined whether the union sectors have been excluded or have participated in the institutional order, and whether the ideologies served as an aggregating factor or have disrupted the unity of the labor movement. The third factor that must be considered is that of the position of the unions in the political structure, that is, the significance of the working class and its quantitative weight in influencing national decisions; this will require a look at the position taken by the unions in times of crises and of relative prosperity, which may have led to intensification or relaxation of social tensions.

Relations of many different types have existed between the unions and the state during the past sixty years. These different relations might be explained in the light of a concurrence of variables: the ideology that inspired the union at the time, the course the union followed as a result of that ideology, and the type of response by the state to labor demands. In Argentina these variables have produced five stages in the evolution of the labor movement.[1]

1. *The revolutionary stage which culminated in the disorders and repression of the so-called "tragic week" of 1919.* This stage was characterized by the prevalence of anarchist labor unions. The small labor movements of the period did not conceive any other way of enforcing their points of view except by forcible seizure of power. It was assumed that success would allow them, after some preliminary stages, to liquidate the machinery of the state. The state was always regarded as the oppressor. When the situation was conceived in these terms, the

215

response to violence was violence. Except for some proposals for a labor code which were presented at the beginning of the century, there was no legal order that could satisfy the expectations of the workers. The labor leaders would naturally be left outside the prevailing system, since their coming to power through anarchist activities obviously implied the exclusion of all other sectors. In response to this revolutionary period the labor movement was outlawed. The predominance of newly arrived foreign elements (Catalonian, German, Russian, and so on) in the leadership resulted in the exacerbation of nationalistic feeling among the holders of power and in an increase of repressive activity. Repressing the labor movement became an inescapable patriotic duty, subjectively valid for those who undertook it.[2]

2. *The reform stage, during which either Socialist unions or non-political labor leaders prevailed.* This period lasted until the revolution of 1943. During this stage the proponents of reform ideology found ways of interacting to some extent with those holding political power, trusting that by constitutional means legislation could be obtained that would gradually change the condition of the working sector. The Socialist Party became the channel for these aspirations and Congress, their forum. As will be seen later, the change from the preceding stage took place as a result of the leadership exercised by the Railroad Workers Union (RWU) in 1922; many unions slowly brought themselves around to the same attitude. The unions acquired status and were recognized as nongovernmental associations. Although the process was very slow, some of their demands were eventually incorporated into the legislation in force. Labor leaders still had no standing in the institutional life of the nation, however, and the members of the Secretariat of the General Confederation of Labor (GCL) were not part of the ruling elite of the nation, but they did gradually acquire some recognition. In the 1930s the executive branch began to appoint union leaders to represent the labor sectors at the meetings of the International Labor Organization in Geneva.

Labor interests were articulated primarily through the Socialist Party, but its opportunities were limited since it was confined to the federal capital and did not participate in power (though it interacted with other parties).

3. *The "statist" stage with close connection between the unions and formal power.* This stage lasted a decade from 1945 to September, 1955. There was identification on both the ideological and leadership levels. The ruler of the state was at the same time the top leader of the

216

workers, and there was identification at all levels. The labor movement became one of the three bases on which the governing group rested, and the unions became public institutions. Specific legislation for professional associations was enacted, and *de facto* labor unity was obtained by nationwide trade or industry associations that were granted specific recognition by a government agency. This meant that the state, in granting legal representation to only one union for each activity, in practice imposed a single union for that activity.

Participation of all the workers within the union was guaranteed by legal regulations and by a provision included in all collective bargaining agreements. When the employers became the wage withholding agent for union dues, the problem of union financing was solved, and the workers were *de facto* compelled to belong to the union.

The labor movement was in power, but it enjoyed only a share of power. Its leaders were part of the ruling group, but the predominant political leadership, despite its identification with the unions, was alien to them. The political leadership can be said to have imposed norms and selection criteria that penetrated even the labor movement itself and weakened its leadership.

4. *The unions become political tools.* On the one hand they were placed under government control, but nominally continued their institutional life, though in reality many of their leaders had to operate semi-clandestinely. This period began around the middle of November, 1955, and lasted until the return of the GCL to the unions in 1961.

The strikes that took place during that period were almost all motivated by a genuine desire for economic improvement, but most of them should also be charged to partisan agitation. The principle of functional alternatives, which govern relationships within the political field, determined a broadening of the functions of almost all the unions. Since Peronism was disqualified as a party and forbidden to organize its cadres, it channeled its institutional activities through the only means relatively open to it, the unions identified with the *Justicialista* ideology. The unions thus undertook *de facto* representation of this movement, and the Peronist leaders who controlled the unions became political leaders.

5. *The institutional stage* (it might be called that provisionally, in view of the short period which has elapsed since its beginning). This stage can be defined only on the basis of its first public manifestations and in relation to the situation existing before.

When the GCL was returned to the unions, the legal order, which

217

had been suspended temporarily, came into effect again. Financial reorganization was begun, and all unions, whatever their ideological affiliation, joined together in a single organization. This time they joined voluntarily, not under compulsion. Their unity became functional; it was the result of experience rather than of abstract deliberations and was based on minimum consensus. For the first time the central labor organization figured as a power factor, to such an extent that it is the only sector of the nation that is expressly recognized as such.[3] And this is important because it shows a collective decision to become an instrument in the life of the community capable of formulating a concrete program for change.

While the entrepreneurs, the armed forces, and the other sectors tried to justify their intervention with hesitant and shamefaced arguments, labor leaders spelled out their plans. The leaders are part of the system, and since they work with each other on a plane above their ideological differences, the highest officers of the GCL have become part of the ruling sectors of the nation. This time the leaders act on their own, not on delegated, authority. The state recognizes this role, and, though it may view these leaders as part of the political opposition, it institutionalizes and legitimizes union organization.

The addition of these leaders to the spectrum of national leadership, however, depends on two factors: (1) the ideologies and the values they champion being an extension of and in tune with the values and norms which society accepts, and (2) their leadership giving faithful expression to the reality of the sector they represent.

The mechanisms for social upward mobility have operated effectively in Argentina. For this reason its social classes and the class consciousness of its lower class have very specific characteristics. If the attitude which the GCL assumes in this last stage of mature experience disregards this operative mobility and the changes in status mentality brought about by the expectation of this mobility, it would be out of step in relation to the workers' interests it actually articulates.[4] But it does seem that in the stage that is just beginning the leaders have overcome their differences and grasped this reality intuitively rather than scientifically. Attention is no longer focused on ideology as the substance and the determining factor of their behavior; it is now focused on reality. That much of the labor sector is made up of "would-be bourgeois" and aspirants to upward mobility distorts class consciousness and makes impossible the use of classical schemes. Under these circumstances, the distinguishing mark of the new stage, judging by

218

its first manifestations, seems to be recognition of the country's basic realities.

Throughout union history the ideological element appears on the one hand as a stimulus to action and on the other as a distorting factor. As a stimulus, it has stamped its peculiar character on every period, it has variously favored or made difficult the relations with the political system, and it has adapted to the great changes which have been experienced not only in Argentina but also in the rest of the world. Ideology has also operated as a distorting factor by drawing the organizations into bitter conflicts and has damaged labor unity by decreasing the effectiveness and influence of its leaders. The old struggles between anarchists and socialists, which at bottom were only struggles between leaders, precluded the possibility of unity. What should have been debates on methods—whether inflexible or reformist attitudes should be adopted—became sources of hate and insurmountable bitterness. In 1922 the Communists appeared on the scene as a third discordant ideological group.

Central labor organizations in Argentina were based without exception on an ideological factor. The General Union of Workers (Socialist, 1903), the Argentine Regional Workers Federation (anarchist, 1904), the Argentine Labor Union (with communist elements, 1921), the Argentine Workers Confederation (reformist, 1926), and the General Confederation of Labor (socialist, 1929; it later split in two sections, one established in 1935 and the other in 1943), were all consequences of distorting and mutually exclusive ideologies.

When the Extraordinary Congress of the GCL, which modified the by-laws of this organization, took place in 1950, the delegates were mindful of past experiences. Labor organizations had always had an ideological content and, therefore, had always excluded those who did not share their views. Peronism did not contribute anything new in this sense; rather it found a favorable climate. In 1950, the identification of the GCL with the ideology then in power was much more explicit than before, and even the appearance of separatism was lost. The preamble of the new by-laws declared explicitly that the labor organization identified itself with the *Justicialista* doctrine and gave its allegiance to the leader of this movement.

The divisions within the labor movement which occurred between 1955 and 1961 were due to ideological differences.[5] It was only after the thorough institutional reorganization of the GCL in 1961 and the approval of the new by-laws by its 1963 Extraordinary Congress that

219

the problem of conflicts over politics lost a considerable portion of its former bitterness. At least, ideological differences ceased to be strong enough to mar labor unity because for the first time in Argentine labor history functional criteria prevailed over ideological passions, and for the first time men who represented different ideological currents shared the leadership of a central labor organization.

A third factor to be considered in analyzing labor's position in the national leadership is how changes in the nation's structure affect the union membership that eventually may articulate the views of the labor movement and how the behavior of the unions is determined by given economic situations. It is a well-known fact that in Argentina there have been two periods of great industrial expansion, those of 1925–29 and 1945–49. All economists seem to agree on this point. It is public knowledge that, especially during the second period, there was a massive migration of the labor force from the rural to the urban areas. That part of that labor force did not go to the manufacturing sector but rather to increase the tertiary sector is irrelevant to the aspects considered here. The urban migration did increase that portion of the population potentially capable of being unionized. Individuals moved from the rural world where they worked in isolation to urban milieus where conditions were created that made it possible for them to articulate their interests by means of union membership. Needless to say, actual incorporation into the manufacturing sector increased the likelihood of their joining the organized labor movement. This did happen, though when comparative figures are reviewed it is evident that the process did not reach the proportions that might have been originally expected. While the population employed in manufacturing represented 20.8 percent of those economically active in 1925–1929, this percentage rose to 23.9 percent during the Perón era. While the manufacturing and tertiary sectors together represented 64 percent during the earlier period, they increased to 74 percent in 1945–1949.[6]

However, these percentages do not explain why there were 200,000 unionized workers in 1925–29 and 4 million in 1945–49. These figures indicate that structural changes had occurred in the labor base. Such changes create the "raw materials," but these quantitative changes are not enough because the numerical increase in the working class is not sufficient to explain this increase in labor union membership. It is essential for other factors to come into play: the massive incorporation of the individuals within the organic structure on the one hand, and

220

the appearance of a qualitatively operative instrument on the other. The structural changes which had occurred in the composition of the economic factors are not sufficient in themselves to explain unionization. The economic process defines a framework within which the various phenomena occur. But there is no such thing as a "spontaneous movement of the masses"; people must be mobilized and organized in order to achieve a minimum degree of power.

Changes do not usually occur in a synchronized manner. In 1943 a working mass already existed whose interests were not articulated by unions, though unions existed and groups of leaders quarreled among themselves, divorced from the base. However, after 1945 several changes occurred in a synchronized manner: migration to the urban centers, gradual increase in wage-earners in the secondary and tertiary sectors, emergence of working masses and immediate mobilization of these masses in newly created unions under the protection of favorable legislation, and dominance of a political group identified with the process which it had itself begun. This concurrence of the processes of change is exceptional in the labor union field, and because these processes took place so rapidly, with so little opportunity for deliberation, a price eventually had to be paid.

On the other hand, economic changes, whether favorable or unfavorable, do not affect union membership as much as they do the opportunities for action and organized labor's types of behavior. In other words, while the economic structure influences the number of union members, economic cycles influence union behavior. One example from a recent unfavorable economic situation should suffice.

Economists have pointed out that the transfer of income from the industrial to the rural sectors began in 1955. It is generally known that at the same time the workers' share of the net national income began to decrease: while in 1956 it was on the order of 56.9 percent, eight years later it had decreased to 45.9 percent. And though new studies of the gross national product have made the above figures questionable, the moderate overall growth together with uneven income distribution produced a situation in the 1960s that was decidedly unfavorable to the wage-earners. This adverse situation influenced unionists' behavior, for adversity strengthened the sense of unity and allowed the leaders to come to an agreement. Having to face a task together under unfavorable conditions facilitated functional conduct and led to the adoption of rational criteria, to the formulation of general policies and

221

plans, and to their subsequent implementation. The policies and plans thus became a "battle plan" and determined the type of sacrifice required from the unions.

When tensions are increased during an unfavorable economic situation, they tend to make the role of the union more relevant and to increase its influence over its members. Union leaders, under the pressure of circumstances and sometimes carried along by them, come to play roles of primary importance. The roles they play make them an intrinsic part of the country's ruling sector, even though they may act in the opposition or as countervailing forces.

In an opposite situation, in times of great prosperity, the roles change. While the role of the union leader remains institutionalized, his capacity to make decisions and his social weight and prestige are diminished. When the lower class is moving closer to the economic level of the bourgeoisie the credit for increased prosperity tends to go to the entrepreneurs, who are the managers of wealth.

From Growing Membership to Internal Organization

In order to evaluate the role of the labor organizations (and of their leaders), it is necessary to analyze their growing membership. Changes such as increasing industrialization, new services, and migration to urban centers created the necessary conditions; however, they are not sufficient in themselves to explain the phenomena.

Before the great increase, the total number of workers and employees belonging to unions was low. The figures of Table 11.1 do not show a high degree of union membership, nor do they reflect, comparatively speaking, a significant increase. Taking 1936 as the base year, the 1941 index would be 127. One labor union historian maintains that around 1943 the internal divisions and struggles among leaders had caused the number of members to decrease to such an extent that the two labor confederations together did not number 80,000 dues-paying members. The same historian estimates that after the Secretariat of Labor and Welfare had carried on its proselytizing activities and as a result of the creation of new unions, the GCL had a half million members in October, 1945. Statistical deficiencies prevent the confirmation of these figures. But from that time on official statistics should be considered unreliable. The GCL claimed two million members in 1948 and said it had brought together four million workers for the 1950 Ex-

222

traordinary Congress. These figures, whether correct or not, are quantitative expressions. What is important is that the growth in membership has been accompanied by an efficient organization, by a true and harmonious growth of the union body, and by the presence of capable leaders.

TABLE 11.1

Union Membership by Organization and Period

Organization	1936	1941
General Confederation of Labor	262,630	311,076
United Argentine Syndicates	25,095	23,039
Catholic Federation of Female Clerks	8,012	18,675
Autonomous	72,834	120,038
Undefined	1,398	—
Total	369,969	472,828

SOURCE: Reports of the National Department of Labor

The first "model" labor organization in Argentina was the Railroad Workers Union, organized in 1922. It created welfare and social security services and an efficient organization, and it could count on ample resources. The RWU was the first union to have juridical personality and also the first which succeeded in having a special railroad retirement law passed.[7]

The RWU, which had 15,000 members in 1922, started the "collaboration" policy and, serving as a standard for other new unions, encouraged them to lay aside their revolutionary stance and to follow legal channels. It was thus the leading union in the change from using illegitimate means to legitimate means of change, and it was the first to attempt to obtain recognition from the political system in power. Because of the degree of organization, the importance of the services rendered, and the training ground for leaders it offered, it became a model union and achieved de facto control of the governing body of the then new GCL, which it retained uninterruptedly until 1943.

In 1936 the RWU had 75,000 members, or one-third of the total GCL enrollment, and it was in all respects the leading union in Argentina. In the makeup of the Conederation's Central Committee, 18 of the 45 delegates represented the RWU, 5 the Railroad Engineers Union, 3 the trolley operators, 3 the municipal employees, 3 the com-

223

mercial employees and 1 each the minor unions. The balance of power between the Railroad Workers and other unions was markedly unequal. It is not surprising, therefore, that since 1926 the RWU has been the basis of all union organizations, that it lent its quarters for the headquarters of the GCL and its leadership school, and that it became the union financier and sponsor of new unions. Nor is it surprising that from 1930 to 1943 the secretary of the RWU was at the same time secretary general of the GCL.

At five-year intervals the membership of the RWU grew as follows:

1941	65,000
1946	102,000
1951	161,000
1956	210,000
1961	218,000

After 1946, however, this increase in the membership was not accompanied by corresponding influence within the Confederation. Since 1943, no RWU man has been secretary general of the Confederation. Though normally there have been RWU representatives on the Confederation's Secretariat, their share of power decreased substantially. This decrease reflects the changed ratio between RWU membership and total Confederation enrollment; the difference from the situation which existed in 1936 is evident, as indicated in Table 11.2.

TABLE 11.2

Labor Union Membership—1963

		Delegates to GCL	
Organization	Membership	Congress	Central Committee
Railroad Workers Union	222,978	74	28
Central Confederation of Labor	2,334,380	851	505

Consequently, the relation in relative figures between the RWU and the workers' organization is as follows: 9.5 percent of the GCL members (it was 33 percent in 1936), 8.7 percent of the delegates to the Congress, and 5.5 percent of the Confederation's Central Committee (as compared with 40 percent earlier). This change is due to the emer-

224

gence of other unions with the growth of industrial development that did not exist in 1936 and that lessened the influence of the RWU. However, according to the membership indicated for the 1963 Congress, the RWU continued to be the largest union.

TABLE 11.3

Largest Labor Unions and Their Representation[8]

		Delegates	
Union	Members	Congress	Central Committee
Railroad Workers	222,978	74	28
Metal Workers	219,000	73	28
Commercial White Collar Workers	200,789	67	26
Federal Government Workers	190,000	66	25
Textile Workers	150,000	50	17
State Workers	150,000	50	21

Table 11.3 includes only unions that have more than 100,000 members. The commercial employees were already unionized in 1936, but they sent three delegates to the Congress as compared to 18 from the railroad workers; at that time the textile and the metallurgical workers sent 1 delegate each.

The textile and metallurgical unions were for all practical purposes organized during the Perón era. They bear, as will be seen later, the characteristic imprint of the unions developed during that period, which coincided with the growth of textiles and light industry. But what is important, from the 1950s on, is not only that the RWU lost its leadership position, but also that it ceased to be regarded as the model union. With the passing of time, the Electric Power Workers Union became the undisputed model due to its high degree of institutionalization, administrative efficiency, the services it provided for its members, and the ability of its leaders.

The Members of the Secretariat

In accordance with the technique employed throughout this research, the status elements of the individuals who made up the Secretariat of

225

the GCL in the key years from 1936 to 1961, at regular five-year intervals, will be analyzed. Before the amendment of the by-laws, the Secretariat of the GCL had five members; it now has eight.

The 1941 governing team was basically the same as that of 1936. Three of the members of the 1941 Secretariat had appeared on the 1936 one; they were all Socialists and reformists. The president of the RWU (Domenech) was the secretary-general.[9] Two of the members of the 1936 Secretariat represented the Municipal Workers Union, and one of them, Pérez Leirós, was also a member of the 1941 Secretariat. One of the 1936 members belonged to the Streetcar Workers Union then under the *de facto* trusteeship of the RWU. Beside the secretary-general, one of the five members of the 1941 Secretariat also represented the RWU. The fifth member of the Secretariat in both sample years was the representative of the Commercial White Collar Workers Union, Angel Borlenghi, who later on became a key man in the Perón regime.

All the leaders of that period had had full union careers. Their "case histories" showed that they had successively filled the various positions until they had arrived at the highest institutional level of the GCL.[10] Since many of them were active members of the Socialist Party, their political and union histories are sometimes confused. The most characteristic example is found in Francisco Pérez Leirós, who before the 1943 revolution had been reelected congressman four times.[11]

The rest of the top leaders not included within the sample (because they did not form part of the 1936 and 1941 Secretariats) were railroad workers (among them Luis Cerruti who had been secretary general of the GCL since 1930, Melani, Reynals, and others) and Sebastián Marotta of the linotypists union.

In both 1946 and 1951 the leaders were Peronists, but the difference between them lies in the degree of their adherence to the newly organized movement.

In 1946 Luis F. Gay was Secretary-General of the GCL. He had a long history of union activity. Carrero, who had been an agricultural worker in Buenos Aires Province, had entered the telephone company as an assistant cable splicer. In 1928 he took part in the founding of the Telephone Workers Union and almost immediately was named secretary general. When Gay entered the Confederation's Central Committee in 1931 he was the youngest active leader at that level. He founded the Labor Party in 1945 and was its first president. He was removed in 1947 from the General Secretariat of the GCL on the

226

charge of disloyalty toward Peronism, but he continued to represent the Telephone Workers Union.

Aurelio Hernández succeeded Gay in 1947, and he also had a long career in unions. He had been secretary of the lumber union and later had been active within the sanitation union and the United Argentine Syndicates, of which he became secretary. When Hernández was named secretary general of the Confederation, a post which he soon resigned because he did not wish to accept the political supervision which was imposed on him, his appointment was backed by thirty years of continuous front line union activity.

In 1948 José Espejo of the foodstuffs union was named secretary-general of the GCL in an election in which Eva Perón intervened personally. The new secretary, a former truck driver, had started his union activities in 1943, by acting as press secretary of the Truck Drivers Union five years before he was appointed to the top post.

Valerga and Diskin are the only two leaders found in both the 1946 and 1951 Secretariats; both later became congressmen. The former belonged to the Garment Workers Union and the latter to the Commercial White Collar Workers Union. Both had a background of socialist activity and had been active during the reformist period. Valerga's union activity dated from 1926, and Diskin had become known for his loyalty to Angel Borlenghi, with whom he had worked on the front lines of union activity since the 1930s.

The fifth member of the 1946 Secretariat represented the Municipal Workers Union. He had been active in that union since 1919 as a delegate and a member of the board. Active in the Confederation since its inception, he had been a member of its Central Committee in 1933.

Besides those already named, a representative of the Telephone Workers Union and one of the Shoe Workers Union were on the GCL Secretariat in 1951. These leaders did not have union backgrounds comparable to those of the others.

During the years between the key dates here considered, a representative of the government employees (a Peronist congressman) was also part of the Secretariat. He had a long history of activity in the union and in the socialist ranks. Another leader, a sugar mill worker who had been born in Tucumán Province and who was on the Secretariat, had been a union leader only since 1942. He had been active six years before reaching the top institutional position in 1948, but this is understandable since his union had only recently been established in the northwestern section of the country. The third leader (a naturalized

227

Argentine of Uruguayan birth) came from the RWU and represented the incorporation of the "new situation" into this union's traditional influence in the labor movement in existence prior to the Perón regime. He had not occupied all the positions at various levels as was traditional within this union, but had instead risen to the Secretariat by skipping some of the leadership steps. This leader later became a Peronist congressman. The fourth, a naturalized Argentine of Cuban birth, represented the Metal Workers Union (this union had gradually grown in importance during the Perón era) and, beginning at the level of shop delegate, had filled all the positions in a union career. The fifth top leader was another naturalized Argentine. He had been born in Spain and had been active in the Streetcar Workers Union since 1939, had been a delegate from his union to the GCL, a member of his union's Administrative Committee in 1943, and in 1948 was named executive secretary of the GCL.

In 1955, before the fall of the Perón regime, changes were made in the GCL Secretariat in accord with changes which tended increasingly to bureaucratize the organization, placing at its head men of progressively less significance and of minimal union background. The new secretary belonged to the Pharmaceutical Workers Union, and all his activity had developed under the Perón regime. He had also occupied executive posts before becoming secretary of the GCL. Of the other members of the Secretariat, one represented the Beer Workers Union, which was not very important, and the other the bureaucratized State Workers Union. Both had developed their union careers during the Perón era, and they were not to be active again after Perón's fall.

For obvious reasons, the 1956 and 1961 Secretariats cannot be studied as has been done previously throughout this work. In 1956 the GCL was placed under government control, many of its former leaders were in jail, and all who had been active in any way during the preceeding decade were disqualified. In 1961 a commission had been provisionally appointed to take charge of the GCL. Therefore, only the new eight-member Secretariat chosen by the 1963 GCL Congress can be studied. It should be immediately pointed out that it is the first of mixed membership, both ideologically and in terms of political allegiance, in GCL history. From 1930 to 1943 the labor organization had been socialist; the differences as to the degree of fidelity to or independence from the party brought about the 1935 and 1943 splits. From 1946 to 1955 the GCL Secretariat had been wholly Peronist; all

228

its members had joined the party, and several of them had been Peronist congressmen.

In the makeup of the 1963 Secretariat there are two groups: the majority one is Peronist, made up of individuals from the "62 unions" identified with Peronism, and the rest represent "independent unions"[12] and other unions specifically not Peronist. Table 11.4 outlines the unions that those eight leaders represent, the ideological stance of those unions, and their weight within the labor organization. The Secretariat's makeup leads to the following conclusion: Some leaders effectively combine the great weight of their union with adherence to the ideology favored by the majority (the textile and metal workers); others are representatives of small unions which share the majority ideological position of Peronism (the garment and soft drink unions). There is also a representative of a union with a very high level of internal organization and an intermediate ideological position (the Electrical Workers, a Peronist union, though not publicly acknowledged as such).

TABLE 11.4

Importance of the Unions Represented in the Makeup
Of the GCL Secretariat, 1963

Union Represented	Ideological Position	Total Dues-Paying Members	% of Total GCL	Delegates to Congress Total	%
GCL Total		2,434,280	100.0	851	100.0
Garment	Peronist	80,000	3.0	26	3.0
Soft Drinks	Peronist	6,200	0.2	5	0.5
Metallurgical	Peronist	219,000	9.0	73	8.5
Textiles	Peronist	150,000	6.0	50	5.8
Electrical	Independent Peronist	41,250	1.5	14	1.7
Printing	Independent	32,200	1.3	10	1.1
Locomotive Engineers	Independent	26,500	1.00	9	1.0
Traveling Salesmen	Independent	22,000	0.9	7	0.8

On the other hand, one does not find the leaders of the most important unions which subscribe to the minority, or non-Peronist, ideology representing this line of thought.[13] Rather, this role is played by small independent unions: the Locomotive Engineers, Traveling

229

Salesmen, and Printers. It would seem that the minority seats were not given to the more powerful independent unions in order to minimize direct confrontations, at least in the first Secretariat, which was the result of a compromise.

One of the significant facts about the group now directing the GCL is that the overwhelming majority belong to a new generation, to a generation which did not function as union members during the pre-Peronist period. They began working during the Peronist government at the shop, section, or district level, without figuring in the higher echelons. That generation broke into the activities of the GCL after 1955 under pressure of circumstances; there was a vacuum in the leadership. The earlier leadership was in difficulties because many of the last Peronist union leaders had lost prestige, and the others had been legally disqualified. The government officials in control of the GCL had imposed the old leaders from before 1943. By the mere passage of time those old leaders had become completely divorced from the rank-and-file. Then, when a vacuum in power and leadership occurred, a new generation burst upon the scene.

In the 1963 Secretariat there are six leaders whose ages vary from 35 to 44 and who are typical of those recently promoted. Only two leaders represent a connection with the past: the secretary general, who is 50 years old, and another leader who is 52.

The union career of the present secretary started when he became a delegate at the age of 25. In 1945 he took active part in the organization of the Garment Workers Union, for which he was named secretary for the interior, then assistant secretary in 1947, and finally secretary general in 1949. He has had executive posts in the GCL since 1951, has been a congressman, and twice a political prisoner; when the disqualifications were removed he became a candidate for the post of secretary general of his union. He was elected in 1960, reelected in 1962, and has attended nine conferences of the International Labor Organization in Geneva; in 1963 he was made secretary-general of the GCL.

Riego Ribas, the other union leader connected with the past, started as a leader in 1936 in the printers union, occupying various posts until he became secretary general of his union, a position he filled from 1939 to 1947. Removed from union leadership for political reasons, he reappeared again in 1956 as secretary of his union. He represented the GCL at only one of the International Labor Organization conferences, and he headed the independent sector the the GCL.

230

The other six members of the Secretariat belong to the generation born in the 1920s. They were too young to have been active prior to the Perón era. They began their union activities after 1945, but at the plant or section level. However, one of them at that time was a member of the Confederation's Central Committee. Their breakthrough into the higher echelons dates from 1956, when they took the place of the former leaders and later, after the disqualifications were removed, they defeated the former leaders in the first free union elections, which took place in 1958.

Personal Characteristics of the Leaders and the Bureaucratization Process

It is difficult to evaluate the intellectual level of the leaders in the past. The most that can be attempted is an informed guess of an impressionistic type such as emerges from comparing the documents issued by the GCL and from assessing the public performance of the leaders and the speeches and statements made by them. Placing the analysis within a historical context, it might be pointed out that since the 1920s there has been a cyclical pattern in the general intellectual level of the leaders. In this case, formal educational level means little since, as labor leaders, they are presumed to be self-taught. What counts is the "life lived" and the experiences thus acquired.[14]

TABLE 11.5

Formal Education of Labor Leaders Participating
In the 1964 GCL Leadership Training Course

Level	Assistants	Leadership	Total	% of Total
Incomplete Elementary	6	3	9	5
Complete Elementary	41	47	88	52
Incomplete High School	22	29	51	30
Complete High School	5	9	14	8
University	—	8	8	5
Total	74	96	170	100

If the analysis is confined to objective consideration of collective intellectual levels, four stages may be discerned.

231

Today the high level of the anarchist declarations, acts, and publications of the 1920s would arouse comment because the ideology on the highest leadership level was educationally "functional." International ideological solidarity made it possible for the leader (who was nearly always a foreigner) to receive specialized European publications. This solidarity enabled the anarchist publication *La Protesta* to keep up with the slightest details of the world anarchist labor movement and to devote many columns to the news of what happened in Angola, Rumania, Chicago, and elsewhere.[15]

But this solidarity was precisely what posed a problem for the would-be organizers. It is common knowledge that the early radical press of Argentina was edited in French, Italian, or German, rather than in Spanish. Even in the 1920s the anarchist general staff was foreign, the Communist daily was bilingual (*La Internacional*, the Communist Party organ, had a section in Italian), and the United Argentine Syndicates held meetings at which the speaker might address the audience in Yiddish.[16] The gulf between the level of these European leaders and that of the masses they hoped to organize was notorious, and communication between the two on the level of highly intellectual messages on world affairs was virtually impossible.

The second stage began to be defined around the 1930s and lasted well into the 1940s. The language of the GCL and of its statements and meetings was the same as that employed by the Socialist Party. In this case also the ideological solidarity was "functional." The self-taught railroad or municipal union leader or the commercial white collar worker had been intellectually nourished on socialist literature, which was written in the vernacular or was translated from European authors. At the same time, the problems that preoccupied socialists were also imported; concern about an external event (the Spanish Civil War)[17] and the struggle against fascism[18] absorbed all the energies of the labor organization and monopolized its publications.

During the Perón era the collective intellectual level of the GCL suffered a decline. The bonds with the outside world which had formerly contributed to the socialization of the leadership within great world ideological currents had been broken. All the literature was now in the vernacular and followed the official press and its style. In this sense, as in others, a process of nationalization had come about in the Argentine labor union movement, which has survived the regime that produced it. The replacing of red flags by the national one, the substitution of solidarity with the other social sectors identified with the same

232

political line for the earlier international class solidarity, the abandonment of an ideology which stressed social conflict and the substitution of a different one stressing the integrating forces within the national community had appreciable effects.

Only the literature produced by the head of the movement filled the vacuum along the lines being discussed here, and only a few ideas, rather on the level of slogans than on that of authentic doctrine, made up for the inadequacies of an inevitably deficient intellectual formation. But since the vernacular production was meager, it could not adequately satisfy the requirements for intellectual formation. Only the "revisionist" historical literature filled the vacuum, providing the leaders with an interpretation of events. This functional activity had previously been performed by anarchist and Marxist literary output. However, precisely when the possibility of communication was established so that the leaders might have addressed the masses in comprehensible language, the collective intellectual level of the GCL leadership underwent the same process of decline as that of the rest of the country. A reading of the public papers produced by the GCL during those years, the speeches of the secretaries-general to the large gatherings that took place, and the text of the preamble to the GCL by-laws, approved in 1950, document this assertion. One could even question whether the leadership of the GCL actually was in command of its members during this time, for all the important strikes of the period were conducted outside the GCL and by informal leaders.[19]

Once the GCL had been freed from government control (in 1962), the intellectual level rose again. During this period the new leaders once more came into contact with the outside world and they brought to their posts a relatively higher level of formal education (of the 8 leaders, 4 had had some high school training), more solid ideological preparation, and counseling by technical staffs which were used for the first time as instruments for rationalization at the top.

Another subject which would merit in-depth analysis is that of the moral qualifications of the leaders, meaning by this a generous devotion to rendering service. It would seem that in some cases ideologies may have served as parameters of conduct, determining the adjustment of union behavior to more or less strict codes.

It is to be presumed that among the leaders of the early period the degree of asceticism would have been very high. To be a leader during the period of resistance to government authority necessarily implied a missionary type of personality, that is, a man totally persuaded of the

233

worth of his task. During the 1930s qualification levels were lowered. When a tacit *modus vivendi* with the government developed, the labor leader became professionalized and found himself leading a bureaucracy. If the possibility of a political career is added it is easy to understand that devotion to collective service might have diminished. Yet during these years the RWU had a good training school for leaders.

During the Perón period this gradual decline in the attitude toward service on the part of the labor leaders became more pronounced because the unions, which had become bureaucratized organizations, were part of a system where the prevailing preoccupation was not one of a moral nature, and personal sacrifice for the general welfare was not common. It is difficult to generalize because the moral crisis did not affect all leaders equally. Those of the unions which had a more solid cadre formation withstood the degeneration better, and after Perón fell, their leaders were found blameless. In the newer unions that had been created in a hurry and that were solely and exclusively the product of the regime in power, moral values suffered more.

There were honest men in some unions who left a positive legacy and taught that authentic unionism was identified with the practice of virtues. This was the case with Natalini, a leader of the Electrical Workers Union whose personal influence became decisive in a union which had been founded in 1943 and had not had any organization prior to the advent of Peronism.

The GCL had to pay for its involvement with the Peronist government. The union leader might simultaneously hold a government position such as a post on the organization administering the retirement fund, or perhaps he held elective office. The ambivalence of roles, however, was detrimental to the formation of an efficient union staff devoted to specific tasks. The extreme case was that of the labor attachés in the Argentine embassies; they were removed from their familiar milieu and suddenly forced to exercise conflicting roles concurrently: diplomats on the one hand, union leaders on the other. When they returned from their missions, that is, when those labor attachés theoretically enriched by foreign experiences should have returned to their unions, a massive desertion took place instead. Of 108 labor attachés appointed during the Peronist administration, only two returned to their labor union functions.[20] The exceptions were the secretary of the meat union and a former director of the bakers union. Furthermore, an analysis of the members of the GCL Secretariat for the years 1946,

234

1947, 1951, and 1955 shows that only one of the 18 members returned to his union post after 1958. The defection of these leaders is due to various causes, but perhaps the loss of prestige may be considered among the most decisive. In many cases the union itself, that is, the rank and file, closed off any possibility of return by the electoral route.

In the case of the labor attachés, the factor involved seems to be different; the ambivalence of status they lived through and the final triumph of the diplomatic status ended by modifying the original status mentality. That is, these former leaders had experienced such marked upward social mobility that in the end it alienated them from their unions. This change resulting from upward social mobility appears to be difficult to avoid, particularly at the highest levels of labor union leadership. Defections of the type described above have been happening from the beginning of the reformist period; they were widespread during the Perón era.

The uninterrupted exercise of a union career brings with it the need for its leaders to interact with economic and political leaders. The roles assumed and the responsibilities faced by the labor leaders may lead to a change in status mentality, even when no actual change in status takes place; it would seem to be a permanent characteristic of Argentine unionism on the personal level. It does not necessarily imply a betrayal of the interests of the labor sectors since, despite the changes of which the leader may be conscious, objectively he may act in accord with the interests of the social sectors which have given him their mandate.

A participant-observer, a member of the Secretariat, discussing the degree of devotion and engagement of the leaders, has drawn up the following typology:[21]

a) There are leaders by vocation, who are genuinely devoted to the service of their organization. They are, he says, "those who do not make the union a sinecure nor their office a source of income."

b) There are also the temporary leaders who, when their term of office is finished, retire and do not reappear whether they have been effective or not.

c) Finally, there are the opportunists, those who use the organization as a starting point to further their personal ambitions. These are the ones who hold on to office or the union bureaucrats who never return to their former place of work or to the status they had before. The author points out that this is a valid typology for the leaders at

235

the individual union level, but it may possibly also apply to members and former members of the GCL Secretariat such as those analyzed in this study.

The Participation of the Members in Internal Elections as an Instrument for Renewal

The participation of the members in the election of their own leaders can only be studied from 1958 on. Before that date there were various disturbing factors such as the limited number of union members in many of the elections prior to 1943, political control during the Peronist period, and irregular elections between 1956 and 1958. Thus, the first realistic measurement of union balloting were the elections which occurred in the most important unions between 1958 and 1959, when institutional normalization began.[22]

TABLE 11.6

Participation of Members in Union Elections

Percentage of members voting	Labor unions
Over 80	2
Between 70 and 80	1
Between 60 and 70	3
Between 50 and 60	3
Between 40 and 50	—
Less than 40	8
Total	17

These elections, the first within the reorganization period, were characterized by low participation since the average came to less than 40 percent of those registered. The study of each case shows that:

a) Where the internal organization was high, where the union was more institutionalized, where there were more recognized norms and rules of union behavior, there was greater participation. The Electrical Workers Union is a case in point; 83 percent of the registered membership of this union voted.

b) Where the organization was lax and weak, but there was still a very high rate of participation (85 percent among the textile workers)

236

and where the candidate selected received an absolute majority, the personalist leadership variant was in operation.

c) On the other hand, participation was very low in the largest unions (metal and railroad workers) and also where the social sectors from which members are to be recruited do not favor militancy (commercial and state); in these cases there was a 30 percent participation.

To evaluate the degree of renewal in the leadership rosters which resulted from these elections, it must be borne in mind that in many cases mixed slates were submitted. These slates under neo-Peronist labels (of the "62 organizations") also included old guard Peronist or "authentic GCL" leaders. Table 11.7 includes as "neo-62" the leaders of the Peronist new guard who ended by withdrawing from the original political-labor union group. In the results analyzed there are also cases of unions which, though not Peronist, were not committed; they are the "independents." This label sometimes also includes union leaders with Marxist training and some neo-Communists.

TABLE 11.7

Renewal of 1955 Leadership through 1958–59 Union Elections

Renewal through Peronism, new leaders of the "62" and of the "neo-62" organizations	8
Renewal through victory of the "independents"	5
Renewal through victory of the Communists	1
Renewal through victory of the Socialists or independents	1
Partial renewal through victory of combined Peronist "62" and "authentic GCL" slates	2
No renewal, victories of the "authentic GCL"	3
Total unions analyzed	20

An analysis of the results shows that renewal by electoral means, in reference to the 1955 leadership, occurred in 75 percent of the unions analyzed.

It is undoubtedly symptomatic that where the "old guard" leaders were victorious, they had just been freed from two or three years in jail. In the two cases where combined slates were victorious, those who headed those slates also had been set free recently. And in all five cases personalist leadership was evidently involved.

This type of situation seems to occur more often in some unions than in others, for example, among longshoremen, meat workers, restaurant employees, and to a lesser extent metal and textile workers.

237

Together with the analysis of the personality type of the leader, other characteristics proper to the sector must be taken into account. They include predominance of people from the interior in the longshoremen and meat unions, who are given to charismatic type leaderships; and predominance of anti-Franco Spaniards in the makeup of the Restaurant Workers Union, where the Communist slates were victorious.

Institutionalization, on the contrary, makes leadership more impersonal as is true in the case of the Electrical Workers Union and in the RWU. Only in these two unions could the hypothesis be tested according to which an elaborate internal organization and the perfecting of the bureaucratic apparatus tend to make the leader perpetuate himself in office, and hence tend to consolidate internal oligarchical circles.[23]

Notes

1. Presented by Raúl Puigbó, in "Historia del sindicalismo argentino" (Buenos Aires: Centro de Altos Estudios, 1963.) mimeo.
2. For a history of the early period of labor unions, see Sebastián Marotta, El movimiento sindical argentino; su génesis y desarrollo (Buenos Aires: Ediciones "Lacio," 1960–61).
3. See José Alonso and others, Los trabajadores, la política y la Nación (Buenos Aires: Agrupación Nuevo Rumbo, 1963).
4. As Gino Germani has shown in his appendix to Seymour Martin Lipset and Reinhard Bendix, Movilidad social en la sociedad industrial (Buenos Aires: Eudeba, 1963), Argentine society has been one of those where "upward mobility" has operated in a truly effective way. From 1869 to 1895, a period of full expansion, the middle sectors in the stratification pyramid grew at a rate of 0.56 percent a year, which is extremely satisfactory. From that time up to 1950, the rate was about 0.29 percent a year. In this way a point was reached in which between 65 and 75 percent of the individuals in the middle levels had a manual-labor or lower-class background. The survey on social stratification carried out by the Institute of Sociology under his direction showed that in Greater Buenos Aires 36.5 percent of the original lower class had moved upwards and become incorporated into the middle class. These indices of upward mobility are in some cases equal, and sometimes surpass, those recorded in industrial cities in the United States, Canada, and Australia. See also Gino Germani, La movilidad social en la Argentina (Buenos Aires: Departmento de Sociología, Facultad de Filosofía y Letras, Universidad de Buenos Aires, n.d.)
5. The groups were the Peronist faction, known as the "62 unions," the anti-Peronist faction, identified as the "32 unions," the pro-Communist MUCS, and the "independent" faction. C.A.A.

238

6. Aldo Ferrer, *La economía argentina. Las etapas de su desarrollo y problemas actuales* (Mexico: Fondo de Cultura Económica, 1963). In this connection see also the remarks of the economists who took part in the meetings held by the General Confederation of Labor in Buenos Aires, July 31 to August 6, 1963, reproduced in *Jornadas económicas* (Buenos Aires: Confederación General del Trabajo, 1963).

7. For a detailed history of the Railroad Workers Union, see Manuel Fernández, *La unión ferroviaria a través del tiempo, 1922–1947* (Buenos Aires: Unión Ferroviaria, 1947).

8. From the statistical table on the makeup of the labor union forces on the eve of the meeting of the Congress in 1963, published by *Primera Plana* (Buenos Aires) January 22, 1963.

9. Domenech's career had started in 1922 in one of the railroad shops of the city of Rosario, at first as delegate from his section and then through all the successive stages of a union career: assistant treasurer of the RWU in 1927, member of the board in 1931, President of the RWU from 1934 to 1941, and Secretary General of the GCL from 1936 on.

10. The case histories of the GCL leaders have been reconstructed partly through the invaluable collaboration of Santiago Senén González, who placed his personal files at the disposal of the writer and who interviewed the present leaders to collect data on their union background. The rest of the information was obtained from the GCL library collection of union papers. Unfortunately, the official GCL publication file covers only up to the year 1943. Later editions have disappeared both from the library of the labor union association and from other labor union libraries, and no copies for the 1945–1955 period are available.

11. Francisco Pérez Leirós entered the Municipal Workers Union in 1915. In 1919 he was appointed secretary of the union, a post which he held continuously until 1944. He became a member of the GCL Secretariat in 1941, and twenty years later was again appointed assistant secretary. Pérez Leirós personifies one of the most genuine cases of professional labor unionists. He became a member of the Socialist Party in 1912, was a real estate salesman, and was a congressman in 1924–28, 1932–34, 1934–38, and 1942–43.

The political history of Angel Borlenghi, who until 1943 belonged to the reformist unions and to socialist politics, would later take a very different turn. However, this is too well known to merit further attention here.

12. The term "independent unions" included true independent unions as well as unions which were not Peronist; Peronist unions were known as the "62." C.A.A.

13. Such as the Commercial White Collar Workers Union or the RWU.

14. In 1964 a course on labor union training for leaders was given for the second time at GCL. The course included four different levels: the two higher ones were those on Assistants and Leadership. Recruitment for these courses was from among the members of the secretariats and at the highest level from the secretaries of the unions and zone delegates. The writer has studied the registration entries, separated the data on place of

239

birth, occupational activity, and educational level of the leaders, and on the courses on labor unionism they had previously taken. Almost all the leaders (three-fourths) had been born in the Buenos Aires metropolitan area, that is, in an urban milieu. Very few came from rural localities in the provinces of Buenos Aires and of Córdoba, and the marginal ones were the only ones who came from outside those zones. Sixty percent of those registered as representatives of blue collar and white collar unions performed tasks proper to the latter category at their place of work, and the remaining 40 percent tasks proper to the former group. In accordance with the age pyramid:

62 percent were between 31 and 45 years old
22 percent were younger than 30 years old
16 percent were over 45 years old

Basically, this is a sample which might be representative of the group of leaders in March, 1964. The predominance of white collar over blue collar workers might perhaps be considered a faithful reflection of the labor union situation at the leadership level. That is why the percentages for formal levels of study are to a certain extent important insofar as they can act as indicators to evaluate the degree to which the union leaders are self-educated.

Half of them are at the elementary education level, but 13 percent are at the high school level. There are no academic course graduates, only industrial technicians and teachers. Two of the eight with a university education in the leadership course were professionals: one a physician for the announcers union who had received his degree as a mature person, and one an architect who had finished his studies while working for the state and being leader of that union. The marginal one is the representative of the longshoremen's union, who was a second-year student in agricultural engineering and worked as time-keeper at the docks. Only 4 of the 170 had done prior work in labor union training courses at some school conducted by the workers' organization.

15. Content analysis was applied to the newspapers *Acción Obrera*, the organ for the Lumber Workers Union affiliated with the United Argentine Syndicates, in the 1925–1928 issues, and *La Protesta*, in the 1926, 1928, and 1929 issues.

16. See the collection of *La Internacional*, volumes for 1924 to 1926.

17. See the collection of the GCL newspaper, from July, 1936 to March 1939, inclusive. The first page of this weekly paper was always devoted to the difficulties of the Spanish controversy. All the funds collected publicly by the GCL during that period were intended for the Republican troops. Half of the statements by the GCL secretary published in the newspaper were related to the Civil War that was devastating Spain.

18. See the collection of the GCL newspaper for the year 1941.

19. The 1947 textile strike, the metal workers strike of 1948 (outlawed by the Peronist government), the 1949 strike called by the printers (also outlawed), the banking white collar workers strike of September, 1950

(outlawed), and the 1954 metal workers strike repudiating their union authorities, constitute sufficient evidence.

20. Information provided by the Personnel Office of the Argentine Ministry of Foreign Relations and Worship.

21. In "Dirigentes," an article published in *Luz y Fuerza*, the newspaper for the above mentioned Federation, Vol. III, No. 9, 1962.

22. The labor unions included were: Foodstuffs, Banking, Shoes, Meat, Commerce, Railroads (Engineers and Workers), Printers, Restaurants, Electricity, Metal, Municipal, Oil, Longshoremen, Health, Textiles, State, Trolley, Garment, and Glass. Complete information could be gathered only on 17 of the 20 unions.

23. In this case, the so-called "iron law of oligarchy," formulated by Michel, cannot be applied, since it would be valid only in those very well-structured voluntary associations with very complex internal organizations, such as political parties, labor unions, etc. This is something that, with few exceptions, does not happen in Argentine unions.

12. ARGENTINA WITHOUT A GOVERNING ELITE

IT IS NOT possible to speak of a "ruling elite" in Argentina. This statement will require an explanation, since from the strictly functional viewpoint there must always be an elite; that is, an aggregate of individuals who hold the highest positions and head the basic institutions are functionally an elite.

The term "ruling elite," however, has other connotations. The existence of a real elite (that is, something more than a functional elite), or a group of individuals who act in concert, lead the community, direct it with a view to achieving certain ends and objectives, and accept approximately similar normative frameworks is not evident in the case of Argentina.

In this sense there is no "ruling elite" in Argentina, even though there are always many individuals who "command." The existence of an elite does not depend on its members having a similar origin or being the product of the same socializing process. Their channels for achieving leadership and their degree of spiritual maturity may be very different, but they act as an elite to the extent that they are in agreement either expressly or tacitly about more or less similar objectives. It does not matter, therefore, whether those who make up the elite come from different fields of activity (this is the ideal and it occurs specifically in the more developed societies) or whether they are basically recruited from one or two areas.

The existence of a real elite is determined by what is actually done. Deeds are the indicators that make the existence of a real elite evident. This is not true in Argentina, or rather, in the case of Argentina, the situation of the country at all levels indicates a crisis in leadership. The crisis is structural, and politicians, economists, moral philosophers, and educators have all given their version of it. This does not imply espousal of any theory, but there obviously is a leadership crisis: a whole group and a whole generation of leaders have failed.

242

It must be emphasized that events in their incontrovertible objectivity must provide the basis for judgment. There are sectors of the life of the nation that seem to have come through untouched and there are also leadership groups that have been affected very little. In each case the specific situation must be used in arriving at a judgment. In view of the evidence, it is not the researcher who must prove the failure of leadership. On the contrary, the burden of proof, despite some acknowledged cases of partially successful leadership, must lie with those who attempt to deny the above statement.

In this closing chapter all the loose ends left from the earlier chapters will be brought together, and an attempt will be made to find an explanation for the leadership crisis. It may not be "the" explanation, but it will be an explanation that emerges from the investigations and analyses presented in chapter after chapter. It will not pretend to be the final answer, only the answer produced by sociological analysis. This will be a partial and limited explanation that must necessarily be articulated with others such as the judgments of moral philosophers, economists, the brilliant intuitions of essayists and so forth. For this reason, anything that might fall within these categories is expressly excluded from this analysis, not because the influence of moral factors is disregarded, nor because people and events have been prejudged, but simply because such evaluations are not within the scope of this book.

This explanation is a small contribution by the social scientist toward clarifying the problem, and it is presented just as it emerges from the analyses and from comparing the results of the latter with broader interpretative studies. Since the task of the sociologist is naturally limited, and sociology is not a modern substitute for infused knowledge, the vision which sociology offers must necessarily be articulated with many others, but a sociological vision is what has emerged from this study and this is what is presented.

Through scrupulous adherence to scientific methods and to objective analysis, which must be the strictly observed norms for this type of study, a first explanation of the reasons for the failure of leadership emerges. But the reader must not expect to find a didactic orientation here—that is, a subjective orientation toward how and in what way change should be shaped—because this is not the place for prescription. He will find here only what is evident from the facts, though it is possible that the analysis of the facts may provide him with an overview of the actual relations of power.

This book whiles away the time with bachelors, priests, and barbers, with shepherds, tellers of tales, satisfied dukes, false knights, traveling galley slaves, insular sycophants, and peasants turned squires. What Argentina needs is a grand Quixotic collective gesture, but this cannot be accomplished by a single group; it is a task that requires a whole generation. Studies such as this one, with their attempt at scientific precision, are the antithesis of the books of knight errantry which while away the time of waiting. These studies should at least serve as a "warning to the traveler" such as the ones Don Quixote himself must have received when he was about to start on the most heroic of adventures. Let such warnings advise him of what he will encounter when barely embarked on his journey and of the voices that will attempt to dissuade him in the name of prudence and try to gather all the "neighbors" together so that nothing will disturb the quiet of the siesta.

When Argentine society was relatively simple, a small group governed the country. This group was the guardian of public opinion and performed multiple functions and successively played different roles.

Bartolomé Mitre was an army man, a newspaperman while in exile, and a writer. When he returned he became a legislator, a victorious officer at Pavón, then president, and again supreme commander during the War with Paraguay.[1] He was also a historian, a translator of Dante, a politician who founded a party, the keystone of national conciliation projects, and a newspaperman who organized his own newspaper company.

Julio A. Roca was an army man, the leader of an expedition into the desert, an experienced politician, president of the Republic, rancher, and again president. He organized the army and gave the original impetus to economic development not only by bringing in immigrants and seeking economic expansion by contracts, but also because of the territories he added to the nation by subjecting them to civilized control.

Carlos Pellegrini was a great public speaker, a congressman, and an economist. He founded the Banco de la Nación and the two institutions most characteristic of a whole sector: the Jockey Club and what later became the Conservative Party. In the Federal Lower House, he made one of the most authentically pro-industrial speeches of that time and provided the most serious critical analyses, before passage of the Sáenz Peña Act, of the legitimacy of the bases on which the political power of his group rested. He invited this group to face newly emerging situations realistically.

244

But perhaps Lucio V. Mansilla was most typical of this class, even as to all its contradictions. He was brought up as a federalist to continue the Rosas tradition, but he became a liberal and progressive. He was an army man, a hero of the War with Paraguay, the first governor of the then territory of Chaco, and was in charge of the frontiers. One of the first Argentines (if not the first) to circle the globe, he was a newspaperman, a polyglot, and ambassador to Berlin and St. Petersburg. He was a *grand seigneur*, the idol of his troops, at home in the salons and in the tents, in charge of the Río Cuarto Fort, author of one of the most perfect examples of our national literature, translator of Horace and Vergil, and an interpreter of the Pampas Indians, an oligarch and a promoter of progress, truly Creole and truly universal at the same time.

This ruling class, made up of a relatively small number of men who took turns in playing various roles, did not have an explicit program. However, an implicit program does emerge from the events they precipitated and the measures they adopted. This group of men personifies a stage within the democratization process: that of limited democracy, where only a small group, which identified itself with "public opinion," led a society in which the majority were governed and in which, politically speaking, it did not have a substantial voice. This was possible in a simple society which had not evolved much and whose structure was not complex.[2]

When this governing class, which promoted progress and gave development its first impetus, disappeared, another took its place in which individuals began to intermingle, to change the rules of behavior and the status mentality. Part of the new ruling class lacked experience and had to acquire it suddenly. It started to rule when society was becoming more complex. The remnants of the former ruling class—the highborn heirs—continued to play a part in political functions, as has been shown in the previous chapters, but not always a decisive one. Since they lacked the drive of their elders, they retained only the more incidental and unessential part of their legacy: the belief that they had ascriptive rights to continue to occupy public office.

There were conservative leaders who perpetuated themselves in office and in legislative posts, who held on to the apparatus of the state, to its administrative aspects, even when they had lost all the basic resources of national life: the industrialists were almost all foreigners, many still marginal; the military forces were recruited from the mid-

245

dle strata; the ecclesiastical authorities came from rural backgrounds and were the sons of sharecroppers and small farmers; and the new politicians, who sought the prestige and recognition which their parents lacked, came from European families recently arrived in the country.

In effect, the leadership of the various sectors was in many different hands. At various times, but generally speaking around the 1920s, leaders from different backgrounds gradually appeared in each of the fields of activity.

This change in the leadership presented the first problem. As society became more complex and diversified, new men appeared who were no longer universal men such as Roca, Mitre, Mansilla, or Pellegrini. They were the first wave of the unavoidable "barbarous specialists." Inexperience always has to be paid for, and the direct and immediate cost is paid not only by the inexpert group, but by the whole of society. In all developed countries, when the transition from oligarchic or aristocratic rule to another with a broader democratic base occurs, there is an interval of adjustment and maladjustment. This is inevitable; it happened in Germany in the post-World War I period, in the United States, and in France. In Argentina this interval has been very long and the cost of inexperience has been high. There are some reasons, however, which, without justifying it, explain it and which may give a clue—the clue found by the social scientist—for understanding the roots of the present leadership crisis. The question is, how did it happen?

Throughout this investigation an attempt has been made to show from what sectors the present rulers emerged, and how, as a result of great structural changes such as the assimilation of immigrants, the broadening of the middle sectors, and the diversification of the economy, the ruling groups have come from different backgrounds.

The differences in origin have a bearing on explaining some of the results: there have been no common processes of socialization. During their formative years those who later became leaders had no common points of contact, no common centers or places of reference, and there was no aggregating entity or party or institution. Consequently, their training and formation were extremely diversified. Thus if the present problem of the rulers is their complete and radical lack of communication, such lack is the result of conditions whose roots must be sought in the past.

If there is lack of communication among contemporary leaders, it

246

is because they do not know one another. They are leaders in a pluralistic society who come from the most diverse sectors. When these leaders were young, in the 1920s and 1930s, they might have been able to draw close the bonds between them and could have had personal relations; but they did not have the necessary institutions, the educational centers, or any common meeting ground that might have served as a nucleus to bring all or some of them together. While their early life might not have prevented their becoming victims of egocentric attitudes later, it might at least have made dialogue easier.

The traditional oligarchy did not face this problem because its leaders came from the same families and from the same educational establishments, and belonged to the same clubs. At the time of Mitre, Roca, Pellegrini, and Mansilla, all those who ruled were generally related, almost all graduates of the same schools, all fellow members who met at the Jockey Club, the *Club del Progreso*, and at the *Círculo de Armas*. They were a true ruling class. Their children continued to meet at the *Círculo de Armas* and at the Jockey Club. But since they no longer ruled the country (although occasionally they controlled the national administration) at best all they could do was to distribute posts and embassies among themselves.

On the other hand, when the leaders being considered now were young, they had no places where they could express and interchange ideas and even come to know the values, the points of view, and the arguments of their occasional opponents. When dialogue would have been fruitful, since they were young and at an age favorable for influencing each other, there was no opportunity to do so. The young priest studied in Rome, the new Navy officer settled at a base in the South, the son of the entrepreneur studied in Zurich or at a British school, or took up textile engineering in Belgium or France. The newly arrived Arabian or Polish self-made man who was an apprentice in a factory did not even dream of the part he would eventually play in the 1950s. The would-be politician studied law, and busied himself at party headquarters, and the large rural landowner frequented only the meeting places of his own group.

Thus it is a secondary consideration whether there are cross-overs and relations between some sectors and not between others. It is hardly relevant that later on the necessities of leadership have obliged many to face the opinion of their new opponents. All this came too late. Dialogue could no longer be useful. Conversation, on the contrary, took

247

place, as one leader to another, one status to another, among mature men whose opinions about everything had already hardened and become unchangeable.

This fact must be looked at within a historical context, taking into account what can be learned from more evolved societies. In all of them sooner or later oligarchic rule was disrupted, and a period of transition to a new type of leadership, to a broader democracy resulted. This transition and the transition to the next stage was more or less traumatic in different cases. In both cases oligarchic elites were displaced by new specialized elites. "Specialized" does not in this case mean that the new men were experts in a given technique, but rather that their experience was confined to only one field. Military matters came to be controlled by military professionals rather than by the old military aristocrats; industry came to be guided by entrepreneurs rather than by the old political landholders; and politics became the private preserve of "party men," who should come from the middle sectors in a "broader democracy" regime.

In any case, these new specialized elites paid the price of their immaturity. However, in all modern industrialized societies, the subsequent stage has been that of the appearance of rebuilding elites. This does not necessarily imply that the new leaders must be men of universal vision and knowledge. They may be so, but the rule in developed societies is that the top positions are occupied by the leaders of the diverse sectors and that they become integrated. Such integration will be all the more feasible the more these leaders are aware that they need each other and that convergence is indispensable for the proper progress of the community.

In the case of Argentina the appearance of rebuilding elites has been unduly delayed, but it cannot be delayed much longer. In accordance with the sequence of events in the process shown by the patterns set by other countries the appearance of these elites is due now. This is a problem for future generations, which is not likely to be solved by this generation of leaders. First of all because the generation which now "rules" lacks something important, just as all those who previously succeeded each other did. Everything indicates that this "something" which troubles them is the lack of a previous base. A base is needed for ruling, for leading men, for knowing when to compromise and when to rise to the demands of the situation. A base is needed for the necessary technical knowledge to set a modern nation-state in motion.

The problem would therefore seem to have its roots in the absence of a high level of collective leadership. A high level means here the level required by contemporary needs, such as that for political leadership. This means both controlling the complicated workings of the state and exercising the eternal arts of government. For example, the art of knowing how to compromise is an eternal art, and only those who are politically mature know how to compromise. In Argentina there have been few mature politicians, and these few have been ignored by their own generation, since each of the various sectors found in Argentine society, fully convinced that it is the depository of all truth, has wanted to carry its truth to its ultimate consequences.

Leaving this aside, since political maturity is obtained only by experience, what should be pointed out is that the deficiencies in the previous training of the ruling generations have become evident from the data supplied by experience. This statement is an attempt at a general judgment, since there are undoubtedly very many praiseworthy exceptions to this rule in various fields of activity. But it would seem that, at a collective level and disregarding individual cases, there has been a lowering, an "objective descent," in the general level of the nation's political maturity. What is maintained here is that a whole ruling generation was not sufficiently prepared, did not have or had not had at the proper time the opportunity to prepare itself at the level of the roles it later was to play. This lowering can be proved by the present condition of the country. The fact that it is collective is proved by the many cases of those who did prepare adequately, but despite their very praiseworthy personal efforts they were not able to communicate this preparation to a whole generation which was "on the downturn." And this "collective and generational downturn" is the result of having lowered the requirement levels.

Throughout these chapters it has been seen that a substantial proportion of the rulers had higher education: all the presidents, the governors of provinces, almost all the professional politicians, plus a third of the large entrepreneurs and over a third of the rural leaders. However, the number of men with higher education, which might seem high, does not mean anything in itself and might distort proper evaluation of the facts. Almost all these men were lawyers, a profession which is not very suitable for leadership. Modern leadership requires inductive minds instead of deductive ones, the making of plans on the basis of existential data and not on those of a normative nature, and a variety

249

of highly technical information in order to manage the machinery of the state. Lawyers also master a technique, but it is that of handling legal cases. However, in Argentina, all the ruling bodies have been in the hands of lawyers. It is not that this is wrong; in 1964 it is simply outmoded.

From the data it is evident that the generation that has been ruling and the one that ruled until recently were not prepared to offer society true ruling elites, since elites seldom have a life of their own, but tend to be an expression of their environments. If there were any elite individuals, the environment was not favorable to them. The data show that a whole generation was collectively ill-prepared. Undoubtedly this was because, in the 1920s and 1930s and the beginning of the 1940s, to be adequately prepared did not seem strictly indispensable. Argentina seemed to have an immense future: its progress was unlimited, it was the grain bowl of the world, and it offered limitless wealth and countless opportunities. Collectively there was no reason to demand much of one's self. It was not necessary to do so in Argentina because the future belonged to Argentina, and the country as well as each and every one of its sons had its own dynamics of growth. The future did not require any personal effort, sacrifice, or responsibility on the part of each Argentine.

This optimism soon turned out not to be justified. When the Argentines found out that the future was not a metaphysical category, it was too late. While it is true that the worth of a man or of a group is proved when he faces an obstacle, in Argentina a whole mature society found that it had not even been prepared to imagine the possibility of an obstacle.

Argentina was modern, and that is why its citizens did not realize that it was not sufficiently developed. Argentina was more modern than Spain and Italy in the 1920s, 1930s, and the beginning of the 1940s, and the immigrants who came to her shores were behind the times. If those Spanish or Italian immigrants were brought up to date, they owed it all to Argentina. Everything was solved, Argentina had the best of everything: first, the longest street, then the widest one; some Argentine was always setting a record, and for success in Paris all that was required was to be dark-haired and Argentine.

Argentines were chauvinists because they lacked a real sense of nationhood and strong integrating bonds. On the strength of proclamations, of wanting to affirm something they did not feel vitally, Argen-

250

tines were nationalists without a nation. Ortega y Gasset had already pointed this out (the ruling class which he knew did not descend from its status in order not to make evident its basic vacuity) when in his letter to a young student he congratulated him on "recognizing that you are ignorant of something; recognizing that there is something you do not know is an attitude not usually found among Argentines." The Spanish philosopher indicated the uncertainty of the future in store for Argentines if they did not change course. Since Argentines were nationalists without a nation, Ortega y Gasset's essays aroused unanimous protest, Count Keyserling was accused of being a drunkard because he dared to criticize Argentina, and Waldo Frank was beaten the very night he said what he really thought.

The university studies which many of the leaders may have completed were not very substantial. Substitutes for knowledge seemed to cover up the gaps and to save appearances. When things changed, when the state machinery became more complicated, when Argentines found out that the route to the future lay precisely through what they should "already" have done, when because of the postwar period their self-proclaimed nationalism should have proved that they were self-sufficient, it was already too late. To the increasingly more urgent concrete demands in all fields they responded by resorting to the "general culture" they possessed.

After this came the rude awakening. Almost all the ruling sectors opposed Peronism, yet Peronism won. When everything seemed to indicate that through Peronism and the profound change that it implied new sectors would emerge, when some of Perón's more discerning intellectuals pointed out to their leader the urgent necessity of surrounding himself with the very best people, the opposite happened.[3] Gradually Peronism came to identify loyalty and obsequiousness as the highest value. Intellectual qualities, spiritual values, and capacity for inquiry came to be viewed as indicating an independence of mind which was more than suspect. The selective criteria were modified and a state of mind became prevalent which considered personal effort, success due exclusively to merit, and excellence in any field of activity not very useful. The password of the draftees was applicable: do not arouse attention.

While this situation lowered the collective levels of personal requirements, it did not affect most of the leaders analyzed: around the 1950s their formative period was over and their repertoire of basic ideas would

251

continue to be the same as it already was at that time (with the exception of the few who kept up to date), whether they were in power or in the opposition. If they were in power, there was all the more reason not to change. The propaganda line which convinced them of their self-sufficiency and which presented them as masters in all fields, including nuclear research, tended to keep them away from the great training centers of the world to which they should have flocked.

At that time almost all the leaders of both sides thought only of the political struggle. Politics came to occupy the center of the stage, and other national problems were relegated to the sidelines. The political problem which had dragged on for some years shaped whole generations, both the one that came before and the one that came after. Under the pressure of urgency, and constantly subjected to political events, the leaders became the victims of the inexorable play of dichotomous relations.

When the traditionalists came back to power after Perón, they, like the Bourbons after the restoration, remembered all the grievances and had forgotten none of the grudges. They did not realize that the Perón period had made them lose twelve years in which they had not had time to become acquainted with the technical complexities of the state they were taking over again. While many of the men who then took control in some sectors of the country introduced changes which were consonant with the times, almost all the politicians who came to govern the "legal country" were shaped by the worst of the experiences they had undergone, or internalized, in sociological terms. In effect so much of their time had been devoted exclusively to the political struggle that they looked upon it as their personal quarrel, an integral part of their personality. They had been so shaped by the political experience of exclusion from power that, upon their return, they followed the very practices of those who had formerly been in power. They understood politics as the art of excluding, and their political relations were dichotomous categories: either friend or foe.

Thus has Argentine history come to be a succession of discontinuities. In this work it has not been possible to make a study of the "circulation of the elites" the classics discuss, since through a succession of discontinuities, a few almost complete breaks have taken place. These political discontinuities came to affect the institutional continuity of the nation; the new leaders acted as though what had been done by previous governing teams was not binding on the state, as though

252

previous political leaders had not governed Argentina. For example, there was no hesitation in putting forward internationally the claim of financial bankruptcy for the state, as though by attributing it to others, the successors became free to exhibit it. The administrative personality of the state was ignored and one administration, in order to blame the preceding one, bore witness before the world to what was in reality its own dishonesty.

These factors shaped a whole generation; to those aspects of a political nature—the lack of an effective base for the exercise of the new roles—and to those of a psycho-social nature—the unjustified sense of self-sufficiency—a third one should be added. This is Peronism which, like a new King Midas, caused a reaction in all those it reached, producing three types: those who rejected everything about Peronism without recognizing any merit whatever, those who accepted everything in Peronism without any critical evaluation, and, beside these extreme positions, the few who wished to be objective.

If Peronism were to be omitted as a factor in the leadership crisis with the argument that it eludes scientific analysis, such an argument would imply nothing less than a concealment of the determining factor of the distorting pull to one side or the other experienced by the present governing group. It is the basic factor that has shaped a whole generation which is now and will continue to be tied to the past to the extent that it does not succeed in overcoming the dichotomy in which it has lived. The solution to the crisis in leadership can come only through a "new generation" made up of new and revitalized people, who may have been able to shape their own attitudes and internalize their experiences before assuming power.

The Perspectives for the Immediate Future

Any possibility of change is subordinate to a series of requirements which this is not the time to consider. They imply a policy of change and a strategy that must be left for a future work. In any case, before doing this it is desirable to present the conclusions that emerge from the analyses made as to the "hour of replacement." Change can come only when individuals who are outside the terms that have given rise to conflict appear in the command positions. As the lines are now drawn and as they appear in the light of the power relations studied, there is no reason to assume that any one of the great dissenting groups would be able to impose its point of view on the others, at least not on a long-term basis and in a substantial manner.

The "hour of replacement" will arrive only when a generation emerges whose attitude is new, whose formative bases are better, and which is truly a rebuilding elite. In modern industrialized societies the new elites are formed by rebuilding elites, that is, by the various sectors which functionally converge at the top. Therefore, at the hour of replacement the elites must be not only functionally but also ideologically rebuilding elites, and even historically so. The joining of the loose ends of history and the integrating of the historic continuity of the community in order to embrace the orthodox and the heterodox will be the most difficult accomplishment.

It may be objected that at the end of this investigation personal desires are allowed to intrude on the analysis. But the fact is that what has been pointed out are "functional requisites" characteristic of all free pluralistic and even approximately harmonious societies. The "new ruling elites" may not have any of the characteristics indicated, but then they will hardly be elites ruling within a framework of liberty and within a pluralistic and harmonious society. They will be ruling elites, but in a different type of society, from which one or all of these terms will be excluded. Since it is the writer's hope that change will come about in a free world, he does intrude his desires in this respect.

What the sociologist cannot do is forecast the future. In the light of the development of other industrial countries, he can only judge that one or two of the sectors analyzed will have to take the lead. It has already been said many times throughout these pages that changes are unsynchronized and have different rhythms. This is true in Argentina: one social sector alone cannot take the lead, two or three must start the reconversion. The change will come into operation later, as a "demonstration effect" on other sectors. Those who do not adopt change or who are not capable of interpreting it will be left behind. To say what sector and what groups will be in the lead is beyond the scope of this work and belongs in the field of prophecy. However, something does become evident from these analyses. In some of the institutions new individuals, whose attitudes appear to be different, may be perceived together with the present leadership. This is evident to some extent among labor leaders and among the new Catholic Church authorities. As far as can be gathered from general impressions and from the judgment of experts, young entrepreneurs may also be trying

254

to express, outside the administrative machinery, a different attitude from that assumed by those who preceded them. To pass judgment in other fields, such as the military, becomes more difficult; the armed forces are represented by the high commands, and that makes it difficult to evaluate from available sources whatever attitudes favorable to change there may be. Moreover, in view of the military normative order, such change can only come when those who share the new attitude get to the highest ranks.

From the analyses conducted in these chapters a curious picture emerges. There is a generational gap in political parties; with one possible exception there is no replacement generation. With a view to the future, the parties may become a no man's land. If they were not so malleable, they would be born, grow, and die quickly; and if they were not so irrelevant, the future they offer would be tremendously uncertain.

Whether the change comes about or not in any or all sectors and what group takes the lead will have substantial significance for society. While the structural situation seems to be pointing in the direction of change, to identify how, when, and in what manner it will come about, as well as through what promoting group, is beyond the social scientist's analytical capacity. It is one thing to hypothesize a situation and generational replacement as preconditions for change, and it is another matter to predict which new leadership sectors will rise to the demands of the situation.

When the time comes, the social scientist can offer an element which is indispensable to any modernizing group: a picture of reality as it emerges from his analysis. That is, the social scientist can contribute something the governing generation lacked: studies of reality which are indispensable for and must precede any long-range work. This is a rationalizing element which was not available before, though, of course, a ruling generation formed by ascription would not have been conditioned to receive or assimilate such information.

The social scientist has an operative instrument and a baggage of accumulated knowledge that could be profitably used by political leaders. He can warn the would-be leaders that everything has not been done, nor ever was, nor is everything yet to be done; that the therapy to be applied to Argentina is not the same that would be suitable for Nigeria. Argentina is not a traditionally underdeveloped country, as the defeatists had come to believe; on the contrary, it is, in the light of all the parameters, a modern country, as modern as many European countries.

255

The problem, the terrible problem, lies in that Argentina's basic political development is not sufficient to support its superstructure of modernity.[4]

Social scientists can warn in time that in Argentina adventures are not to be attempted, and that it is good for the would-be leaders to consider more carefully the sectors that they see in their dreams as the liberating catalysts. The lower sectors have very special characteristics due to the high degree of social mobility which relates them to the middle classes.[5] The Argentine middle classes, like those of Chile and Uruguay, have very special characteristics also, which make them differ substantially from those which at one time constituted the bourgeois greatness of France and Germany.[6]

Aside from these facts and this data, there is only one thing that the social scientist can forecast as to the collective level of personal requirements of the future leadership. This forecast is that the level will be much higher than it is at present, both as to personal qualifications and to previous accomplishments, as well as to experience required to arrive at the highest institutionalized positions. This certainty arises from one fact. A whole generation has matured since the crisis. And there is another generation—the one now in its twenties—which came to awareness in the midst of the crisis. The crisis in this respect has been generously functional. It has forced people to demand more of themselves, to multiply their abilities, to perfect themselves, to go abroad, to study at the great world centers. Now the struggle is harder in all fields, there are many competitors, and the desired place in the sun must be pursued.

This is the only serious, responsible, and possible point of departure from which the future can be viewed with optimism. The crisis during which the new generations have come to maturity or during which they have grown up has led to a personal and intimate formation of awareness. It has brought the younger people together, has favored dialogue, has sharpened the critical spirit, and has afforded rational criteria. Moreover, those who are now in their twenties are not affected by what at one time divided their fathers—all that is felt to be somebody else's past.

But above all, in order to envisage the possibility of a replacement generation, it is essential that the erroneous conviction held by the old rulers be eradicated. Luckily everyone has finally come to realize that God is not Argentine.

Notes

1. The War with Paraguay was fought by Argentina, Uruguay, and Brazil on one side, against Paraguay on the other. It lasted five years (1865–1870), and it was savagely fought on both sides. C.A.A.

2. For a collective reevaluation of the role of this type of elite in Latin America, see the study made by José Medina Echavarría, "Consideraciones sociológicas sobre el desarrollo económico de América Latina" (mimeographed publication of the United Nations Economic and Social Council, 1962). Also see on the role of the continuing elites, the study by the same author, "La opinión de un sociólogo" (document presented to the work group on the social aspects of the economic development of Latin America, which met in Mexico, in December, 1960), and UNESCO, *Social Aspects of Economic Development in Latin America*, Vol. II (Paris, 1963).

3. Ernesto Palacio, *La teoría del estado* (Buenos Aires: Editorial Política, 1950) has the great intellectual merit of being the first and only work produced in Argentina that tries to adapt to a new historical and conceptual analysis the hypotheses of Mosca and Pareto. But, in addition, reading carefully between the lines, those who are seeking hidden meanings detect a warning to the personalist leader: in the long run he will not be able to govern without an authentic ruling elite, even though he may persist in the attempt to maintain a pseudo ruling class.

4. On Argentina as a modern society, insufficiently developed, read the analysis, prepared on the basis of the statistical parameters of modernity and development by Gino Germani, "La Argentina, desarrollo económico y modernización," in *200 Millones* (Buenos Aires), No. 10, October, 1963.

5. On the degree of social mobility in the Buenos Aires Metropolitan Area, see Gino Germani, *La movilidad social en la Argentina* (Buenos Aires: Departamento de Sociología, Facultad de Filosofía y Letras, Universidad de Buenos Aires, Publication No. 60). See also an appendix by the same author in Lipset and Bendix, *Movilidad social en la sociedad industrial* (Buenos Aires: Eudeba, 1963).

6. See Secretaría de la CEPAL, *El desarrollo social de América Latina en la postguerra* (Buenos Aires: Solar-Hachette, 1963), where the different types of behavior of the "bourgeois sectors" in southern South America are classified in comparison with what had happened half a century before in the great European centers.

257

13. AN APPENDIX: FROM 1964 TO 1968

THE ORIGINAL version of this book was written in Spanish for the Argentine public, which might be assumed to be aware of the events discussed. For this reason many things were not explained, and the last chapter may have seemed to exceed the bounds of research and to contain a message. All this is true to some extent, as will be seen later. The last chapter was not written for the international academic community, but rather it was composed with the Argentine decision-makers in mind.

This Appendix to the English version now presented attempts to describe and interpret the basic events that have occurred in the 1964–68 period and that lie within the scope of this study. In this new chapter, five points will be discussed: (1) two very significant political events that took place after 1964; (2) the changes that have taken place in the personal status of the leaders; (3) the new power relations across sectors; (4) the most important difficulties arising from the attempt to place the case of Argentina within schemes of political development; and (5) a new analysis based on the original version of this study.

1. A military revolution overthrew the constitutional government at the end of June, 1966. This is the most important political event of the period 1964–68. Thus, in June, 1966, a change occurred in the political elite, in the bases of government support, in the governmental structure and in the criteria for legitimacy. Even though there was much that was new, a phase of the cycle was being repeated.

The commanders-in-chief of the three military services assumed power in June, 1966, and they delegated that power to a former commander-in-chief of the Army, who was then retired. Therefore, from that time the armed forces have held the constituent power, since they invested one of their members with authority to govern. Once in

258

power, the seizure was given a semblance of legality, and, by means of a legal fiction, institutional continuity was assumed to exist.

Formal government became more personalistic with the passing of time; the president used his authority to remove the individuals who had held the constituent power. In other words, the commanders-in-chief of the three military services at the time of the takeover were replaced. These two events were the most important political occurrences during this period that might bring about a new type of relationship among the various elites.

Between 1966 and 1968 one of the cycles pointed out in the book was repeated. The military took over the exercise of political power, and the professional politicians were replaced. Events confirmed the assertion made in one of the chapters that in Argentina professional politicians have only two options: they either occupy the very center of power or they are wholly marginal.

Between October, 1936, and October, 1968, that is, within a period of 32 years, 22 years and 9 months must be assigned to government by political parties. But during this time power was always held exclusively by the party whose "turn" it was. The others did not participate. In a mutually exclusive political system such as that of Argentina, one party has always monopolized all power, and there has been no system of inter-party agreements or coparticipation.

But in the second case (which covers a total of almost ten years of the period studied in the main sections of the book and in this Appendix) when the government resulted from a military revolt, not only was the party formerly in power radically eliminated, but the other political groups did not fill the vacuum.

The coup d'état of 1966 was the result of a series of situations which it is not within the scope of this work to enumerate. As in all previous cases, the move had manifest and latent causes. The government overthrown was charged, among other things, with being inefficient in solving the problems of the country, especially those of an economic nature; in promoting technological development; and in solving the most acute social problems. The government was also charged with having created a power vacuum. The governing People's Radical Party represented 30 percent of the electorate. Since it was unable to bring men from other parties into a coalition with a greater electoral base, party members occupied all the public offices. The basic charge, however, was that the government did not represent any of the various sectors

259

of the country and that, since it was simultaneously opposed by both entrepreneurs and labor union leaders, it failed to offer a viable alternative for promoting development, a process which could no longer be delayed. There seems to be some truth to this charge.

The armed forces saw themselves as more efficient or, at least, as being better able to select men who might be efficient. The military felt that in a political system not based on elections, the men suited for governing functions might better be selected from the technocracy rather than from the party. The problem was the power vacuum. Basically, Argentina has, except for rare intervals, moved within a power vacuum since the fall of Perón. No party has had sufficient electoral strength to be able to govern, and it has not been possible to arrive at effective agreements among the parties. In this respect the situation of Argentina, in terms of electoral mathematics, was rather similar to that of France during the Fourth Republic. One party was very important but still was unable to obtain 51 percent of the votes; its partial and inadequate victories resulted in a reaction on the part of the other forces. Thus the armed forces invoked the "reserve power" doctrine and filled the vacuum, since they were convinced that if they did not do so, in future elections only the Peronists would have been able to do it.

There was another aspect, however. The political "formula" invoked, or, if you will, the rationalization of the coup, was based on the promises of modernization and of the creation of new and authentic channels for community participation. The armed forces promised modernization of the economic structure, public services, technology, and the educational system. At the same time they promised the creation of new machinery for more adequately aggregating the various interests, values, and philosophies within the political system. More important than all these specific promises was the expectation that they would bring the country out of its frustration and restore its lost international prestige by mobilizing all available resources.

To achieve these objectives, it was necessary to carry out a basic substantive transformation. The military thought that this transformation would never take place under the electoral system, much less under a system of precarious electoral minorities, and that it was therefore necessary to start by removing all the obstacles. Professional politicians constituted the first obstacle in the way of such a transformation.

So many promises awakened great institutional expectations. The word "institutional" is used because in one way or another all the

260

groups covered by this analysis have supported the 1966 coup d'état, or at least the hopes it aroused. The entrepreneurs supported the coup d'état explicitly, and the labor union leaders gave the new authorities a "blank check." The military of all the three branches felt that the new incumbent represented their views, and the religious authorities were gratified by the spiritual zeal of many of the members of the new elite. The universities, the party removed from power, other minority parties, the left, and the extreme ideological left went over to the ranks of the opposition.

2. The first question that arises in this Appendix is that of the continuity or change of the elements characteristic of the status and types of careers of Argentine leaders. The first answer, although based exclusively on impressions rather than on an in-depth investigation, would be that no substantial changes are evident. Therefore, in general, all that was stated in the earlier chapters remains valid; the conclusions projected for the last four years and the trends recorded have been confirmed, with exceptions only as here expressly indicated.

As will be recalled, the samples were selected at five-year intervals, and the last one employed was the one for 1961. To follow the same procedure, the 1961 sample would have to be compared with one for 1966 before the coup d'état took place. This will be done, but an equivalent sample for 1968 will also be compared as an up-to-date frame of reference.

a) *The governmental political sector.* The "government elite" of 1966 was wholly of party men. They included the minister of Economics and other highly technical posts. Just as all party men have generally had a middle-class background, these did too, not having changed their social status in the interim. If they had gained prestige, this gain was due solely to their collective electoral victory, but this higher prestige did not attach to their person, but rather was inherent in the position. The personal status of the People's Radical Party leaders had not changed, and social prestige was low even when they occupied public office.

In the government elite of 1966 lawyers again predominated. There were no military men, and the president was a physician who had alternately practiced his profession in a provincial town and occupied elective office.

The men of the 1966 sample were generally born in the interior, and their primary and secondary schooling was obtained partly in public schools, partly in religious schools, but the latter did not have

261

high status. These men entered the Radical Party early in life (with a single exception who had previously occasionally been active in the Socialist Party), and they were almost all the sons of Radicals. Since they had been busy with political affairs, they had not excelled academically, but they had been active in student organizations. They had not traveled abroad in their youth nor as mature men, which means that they may have lacked a general knowledge of developed countries that could have provided them with a frame of reference. Almost all had served their *cursus honorum* wholly within the party. Moreover, in public office they had occupied only the lower municipal and provincial positions. However, the president and the vice president of the nation and the ministers of foreign affairs and economics had previously served in Congress. None of the members of the team had had previous administrative experience at the national level because the People's Radical Party had not been in power before. The locally based group had been the frame of reference for the activities of all these men, and the party (and its various internal factions within which they were active) was the group to which they related.

The background and composition of the 1968 political elite strikes the observer as very different. To begin with, it appears to be socially more prestigious than the 1966 one. As has been stated in a previous chapter, there seems to be a constant characteristic after each military coup d'état: those appointed to high governmental positions belonged to higher social levels. The opposite is true in "party monopoly" regimes: more men of a middle-class background who lack important economic status or social prestige are among those appointed by these regimes. (The Conservatives discussed at the beginning of this study constitute the single exception to this rule.) However, a distinction must be made between the two main 1968 groups: the military and the civilians.

If in the 1968 sample the government team is considered to be made up of the president, the five ministers, the key secretariats of the presidency, the president of the Argentine National Security Council, and the governors of the three most important provinces, the military represent only 25 percent of the total elite in this sample. The analyses made of the armed forces in Chapter 4 are generally applicable to these retired military officers, with only one exception.

These senior officers were in active service with their present grade in 1956 and in 1961, as the case may be; their training had been exclusively military. In the beginning they fulfilled all the requirements and occupied all the successive ranks in the military hierarchy. But the president had not fulfilled the requirements of the Escuela Superior de Guerra. Earlier, two members of the sample had been commanders-in-chief and a third had been secretary of the Army.

The civilians account for 75 percent of the positions analyzed and generally come from a higher social background; this is particularly true of the first civilian subgroup encompassing those who have political, educational, and judicial responsibilities, as well as the governor of Córdoba Province. High social background in this case means being recognized as members of the traditional upper class, but of provincial origin. This means that they do not share to the same extent the prevailingly liberal (in the European sense of the word) orientation of the Buenos Aires upper class. These leaders come from the provincial upper classes, but they reside in Buenos Aires, and all without exception have been educated at prestigious private Catholic schools; all have law degrees. None of these political, educational, and judicial officials had previously taken an important part in party activities. However, they had been active in nonpartisan formal groups traditionally connected with the armed forces. They have all been successful in their legal careers, and they all accept the religious values and the formal structure of the Catholic Church.

A second civilian subgroup includes some, but not all, of the members of the economic staff and some, but not all, of the technical staff. The original social background of this group is not the same as that of the previous one; it is lower in terms of social prestige, but since in Argentina there is no necessary correlation between high economic status and social prestige, this lack of correspondence is evident in the second subgroup, some of its members having high economic status. The leaders of the second subgroup were educated in public schools and in nonreligious private schools. They are economists, engineers, technicians, or planners and have apparently come to office as a result of professional success. Within the sample, the two civilian subgroups are evenly divided; while the members of the first subgroup have personal prestige independent of their positions, among the members of the second their positions seem to determine their prestige. The only exception within the second subgroup is the minister of economics, who comes from a family with a financial and entrepreneurial background. Unlike the 1966 governing staff, all the 1968 civilians have without exception done postgraduate work abroad, several of the ministers as holders of fellowships in the United States. This last factor is new and

263

may be partly explained by the average age of the ministers, which is lower than that of the 1966 staff; but basically the explanation is to be found in that it is only in recent years that the United States has become a basic frame of reference in the eyes of the Argentines.

b) *The military officers.* There is no new data on the senior officers of the armed forces. Although nothing can be affirmed about their origins, nothing warrants assuming that their backgrounds are substantially different from those recorded in Chapters 3 and 4. However, the educational levels of these officers are higher than those of the other samples, or at least they are equal to the highest recorded. These officers entered the Military Academy at a time when completion of high school studies, or at least of a substantial part, was required. Furthermore, almost all were trained during a time when American influence had begun to replace the German. While all without exception experienced during their career the various phases of the military "de-institutionalization" which occurred between 1955 and 1963, they have assumed the highest hierarchical positions in the later period, that is, at the time when the hierarchical order was reestablished and the cadres were restructured exclusively in accordance with professional norms.

c) *The entrepreneurs.* The 1966 and 1968 entrepreneurial leaders are generally the same as in 1961. Some of the names have changed, but the position or positions within the leadership cadres have hardly changed. This is also true of the Rural Society and of the Industrial Union and the General Economic Confederation. In the latter, its founder again became president in 1966 and early in 1968.

d) *The Catholic hierarchy.* In 1966 there were 37 bishops at the head of dioceses, 12 archbishops, and one vacant see. In 1968 there were no changes. Sixteen percent of these religious leaders were over 65 years old (as compared with 28 percent in the 1961 sample) and 55 percent less than 55 years old (as compared with 46 percent in the 1961 sample). There is therefore a very slight rejuvenation. Fifteen of these bishops had been born in large cities, as compared to 22 born in small rural localities in the Pampa region. The group of the new sample is therefore somewhat more urban as compared to the earlier one. There are still more bishops of Italian and Spanish parentage, but the novelty is that 6 bishops consecrated to head new dioceses after 1961 come from the Buenos Aires upper class, and 3 of them are identified publicly with the more progressive bishops. This is logical within a group where generally the most traditional attitudes seem to be found among those coming from the rural areas and who are the first native-born

264

generation. There is a certain coherence in this identification of attitudes. Similar studies in a Latin American context (in Chile) have given the same results. There is a greater openness and a greater social vocation in religious leaders from the highest strata as a result of their seeing themselves as having a greater ideological commitment in favor of change and greater responsibility toward the economically more disadvantaged groups.

Forty percent of the 1966 bishops had studied in Rome at the Gregorian University, the same percentage shown by the total sample. There is another novelty evident among the new bishops occupying new sees; this is that a substantial proportion of them were in other professions before joining the priesthood. Two 1966 and 1968 bishops had previously been physicians, two had been lawyers, one was an agricultural engineer, one was a high school teacher, and another was an advanced medical student.

e) *The political parties.* In 1966 the political parties were factionalized and split by internal quarrels. The 1966 People's Radical leaders, with one notable exception, belonged to the secondary level because the traditional top leaders were in office. Peronism has had a succession of leaders, but all have without exception been dependent on Perón's varying directives, and he has been out of the country for over a decade. Socialism had subdivided into two major factions and one of its factions (the most radical one) had in turn subdivided into two, which again had divided. The other parties were without electoral significance, and only by a fiction could they have been placed on an equal footing with the Radicals and the Peronists.

In general the criteria for the selection of leaders were the same as set forth in Chapter 10, except that in the case of Peronism the changing attitudes of its founder aggravated the situation. His attitudes, though apparently contradictory, all have tended to the same end: not to allow any successor in the political sector of his movement and to prevent by any and all means the appearance of natural leaders in the labor union sector.

In 1968 there were no political parties active in government. Their activities were forbidden, and their headquarters were closed.

3. The Argentine governmental system since 1966 seems to belong to the "Bismarckian" type. This writer has already stated this elsewhere[1] in the course of classifying the situation within the trilogy used by Helio Jaguaribe to place political systems within the total development processes.[2] The Brazilian specialist states that a third or "Bis-

marckian" model may be placed beside the two classic political models within which development processes have taken place, that is, the liberal capitalist and the socialist systems. This Bismarckian model is a correction to development on a capitalist base, but, like the capitalist model, it presupposes an economic system based on the interplay of market relations and the existence of private entrepreneurs. Unlike the classical liberal capitalist model, this model assumes a government that is strong and centralized and that has long-range objectives. The government does not represent the expression of the various interests, but rather it orients these interests. It is not penetrated by the economic system, but rather it imposes its own standard. Government is not strictly based on formal democratic canons, and only those leading the Bismarckian system know what its duration is to be. As Jaguaribe conceives it, it would seem that in Bismarckianism, development is generated from the center and that the agents of development would be the private sectors, supported and sustained by the government. Development becomes an objective of the state, it is identified with security, and its official protection is guaranteed. But the government does not subsume the economic functions nor does it attempt to do so.

The situation in Argentina in 1968 to some extent resembles this model, or at least the governing team publicly has made certain promises which might fit a Bismarckian model. The truth is that both in the model and in the case now being analyzed the governing staff comes from the traditional sectors, but this staff, despite its background, promotes modernization. In the case of Argentina a corresponding staff has promised modernization, and this has been the "formula" invoked to justify the coup d'état. Ultimately, whether the government modernizes fully, or partly, or not at all, or whether it lets the promises remain as such, is all beyond the scope of this analysis. In this case only the strictly formal aspects are considered; that is, identifications are verified and the "formula" chosen is classified. Only specific investigation at the end of this regime could show what has been done and what has remained mere promise.

In the model, the system is authoritarian but not dictatorial. In the German case, while the holder of power who gives his name to this model was not a military man, he was intimately identified with the armed forces to such an extent that he depended on them. Bismarckianism would seem to be similar to modernizing traditionalism. The Argentine system corresponds to the second of these terms and its leaders have promised to carry out the first. But the external forms of

266

expression of the system are conservative, even though its long-range social objectives are liberal. Such a system is in no sense charismatic. On the contrary, it presupposes only authority, hierarchy, and exercise of discipline. It therefore rejects any form of demagogy and populism; that is, it rejects the direct dialogue between the charismatic leader and the masses to which many charismatic Latin American leaders have been prone. In the Bismarckian system the relation between the chief and the masses is a mixture of present "good will" with an expectation that after the unfavorable economic juncture has changed the Bismarckian leader will promote a more redistributive process. But in the Bismarckian model as well as in the actual Argentine case the channels for communication between the chief and the popular sectors are lacking. If the chief enjoys respect it is only because of his image, an image based exclusively on the integrity of his life.

It has been stated before that in 1968 the armed forces are the constituent power through their commanders-in-chief. They are the ones who appointed the holder of political power. But it has also been stated that in time President Juan Carlos Onganía asserted his Bismarckian authority and, without ignoring the supportive base of his regime's legitimacy, removed the persons who had appointed him, all on the basis of the legal order. This constituted power has closed off all the avenues for political party activity, but has not interfered with most of the other formal liberties.

In power relations, therefore, the structure of the elite seems to be defined very clearly. At the top is the Bismarckian leader. The latter appoints his principal assistants strictly on his own; the assistants, in turn, co-opt theirs. In theory the appointment of men to the upper echelons and the co-optation of men for the intermediate levels is made only through selection from technical staffs, but in practice many particularistic aspects come into play which vitiate what might have been selections made solely and exclusively on the basis of universalistic criteria.

Two staffs make up the new elite, one economic and the other politico-institutional. These staffs in turn appoint men to the intermediate levels of power on the basis of both universalistic and particularistic criteria. This is the reason why there is no pure technocracy in this case; obviously, technocracy could exist only on the basis of selection by universalistic criteria.

The formal government has made the constituent power devote it-

267

self to specific functions. The armed forces are in general institutionally excluded from the government. While some retired military men do make up the elite, it is rather because they share old affinities with the president. This is the reason why up to the present time none of the active military chiefs has played the role of informal leader, one of the "constants" of the political system since 1936, already discussed in one of the earlier chapters of this work. But the "reserve power" of the armed forces, although institutionally excluded, is something more than a reserve. The armed forces have assumed a responsibility which has been delegated to one person, whom they tacitly confirm. Therefore, the power of that person also arises from the fact of confirmation. It is as though there were a tacit daily plebiscite of the Army, Navy, and Air Force high commands.

The other elites are either co-opted or carry the weight of their own sector to which reference has already been made throughout this book. However, there are certain changes which modify the trends. Since political parties are banned, the political leaders are without a function. They have also lost prestige to a great degree, since almost without exception all other groups consider them responsible for the breakdown of constitutional order. A recent survey conducted exclusively among entrepreneurial leaders of the Industrial Union and the Industrial Confederation clearly demonstrates how these leaders regard professional politicians: 91 percent of the entrepreneurial leaders questioned maintained that the coup d'état was inevitable in view of the incapacity of the political parties to fulfill the functions which society had delegated to them.[3] There are different shades of opinion within this 91 percent. Fifty-one percent of those questioned charged the politicians with the sole responsibility for the failure of democracy, while 26 percent maintained that the failure was one of the most important factors leading to the revolt. Only 14 percent considered it of only secondary importance.

No other surveys permit visualizing the opinions of the various elites on this subject, but an impressionistic version would indicate that similar answers might be obtained from labor union and Rural Society leaders. There is no way of establishing the truth of this hypothesis. There is only the immediate experience of the isolated opinions of several of these leaders. What is especially interesting is that the attitude seems to be similar in two very dissimilar sectors.

Returning to the industrial leaders, 60 percent of those questioned in the survey mentioned above maintain that political parties should not reappear for at least five years. But 27 percent of the total, or a little less than half of those in this category, would extend the ban to ten years. Professor John William Freels, Jr., maintains that not only are there no appreciable differences between the answers of the leaders of the Industrial Union and those of the Industrial Confederation, but even that their answers are very similar. However, the entrepreneurs—whether industrial or agricultural—are not in power, either, even though they may feel closely identified with the Onganía regime. The entrepreneurs appear to have been co-opted by the current holders of power at a very high level, as in the cases of the ministers of defense and economics, who are genuine representatives of the entrepreneurial sector. But, in the last analysis, they are not holders of power, although some leaders of the financial sectors appear close to the actual holders.

Public opinion polls that have been published confirm the above view. The degree of identification with the government is in direct relation to the position of those questioned on the social stratification scale. The higher the economic positions, the greater the identification; the lower the status, the greater the rejection. Thus it is possible, without fearing to base these opinions on too inadequate a sample, to proclaim the subjective identification of the entrepreneurial elite with the government team. But what is especially interesting is that the entrepreneurial elite identifies with the government because of the similarity of some points of view; the government elite, on the other hand, does not identify with the entrepreneurial elite. This is why the government is classified as Bismarckianism since the government is not a superstructure of the economic powers.

The religious elites have felt the effects of an external change, that is, of the change brought about in the Catholic Church and originating in an external frame of reference; that is, external in relation to Argentina, but internal in relation to the body of the Church. In Argentina ecclesiastical "aggiornamento" has been rather slow and it may be said without ignoring the inevitable exceptions that it has not been characterized by spectacular changes. As a consequence of that transformation in the external frame of reference, the religious elite seems to have reconsidered the nature of its relations with the government and as a result of certain constitutional changes, such as the disappearance of the *Patronato* or right of the political authorities to name the incumbents of dioceses, it seems to have gained greater freedom. Strangely enough, however, its internal change is not evident from its external expression. This is not so much the result of the will of the

269

Church as of the action of some of the members of the political elite. One part of the elite is characterized, among other things, by its religious militancy; however, because of the lack of synchronization of the changes and the lag or delay in the occurrence of certain changes, this part of the elite has not had time to adapt its thought processes to Rome's religious directives. This is the reason why in the beginning the political elite has sought a rapprochment with the religious elite rather than the latter seeking the former.

In 1968 the labor elite is once more divided, in this instance not so much by ideological differences; empirical adaptation vis-à-vis the new government and strategic considerations have determined the present split. There are two labor elites which proclaim their desire to be reunited; but political power has not co-opted one and the other is opposed to the government. The economic system established by the military regime has three stages. In the first stage capitalization and economic stabilization, not redistribution or wage readjustment, have been given priority. In a situation such as this both labor elites are left out of the system, even though the intent may be to invite them at a later stage, which the regime calls the "social period." But until now channels for participation have not been created. If the present division continues, the possibility remains that one of the two labor elites may be co-opted later and that the other will be converted into the standard bearer of the counter-elite.

4. What is maintained in Chapter 12 remains true: Argentina is still without a ruling elite, with only some differences of detail. The first is that the present rulers seem to have overcome the dichotomy between Peronism and anti-Peronism that for so long divided the country into irreconcilable groups. This opinion is only the result of an impressionistic view based on observation during two years. No one can affirm that this situation will continue.

What does exist is a much greater concentration of power. This is clearly the opposite of what has been apparent at other times within the period included in the analysis. The present concentration of power is the opposite of the disassociation of 1966, 1961, and 1956. It does not mean, however, that a great homogenization has taken place and that the decrease in conflicts is necessarily a consequence of that presumed greater homogeneity. There are still difficulties in communication, but these difficulties are of a different nature. Horizontal communication, that is, at a high level among the various sectors and between the latter and the government seems to be more effective. Vertical communica-

270

tion, however, is very inadequate: the degree of communication between the government elite and its presumed corresponding bases, and between the government elite and the non-elite is deficient because there are no channels for articulation. Nor does there seem to be any functional specialization in the government elite as a whole. Many play roles by vertical appointment, that is, because they have been selected or co-opted, but more do so for particularistic reasons than through being chosen on the basis of impersonal and universalistic criteria. Therefore, lacking a popular base, this pseudo-elite or government elite also is pseudo-technocratic. Hardly any of its members may be considered technocrats. However, interpretation of all this could emerge only from a more thorough analysis than the one conducted in these pages.

Argentina continues to be an extreme case of failure of synchronization. To the various failures of synchronization indicated for the period 1936–1961 others could be added or the previous ones may have become intensified. It is a country with a broad middle class, so broad indeed that it exceeds the internal logic of the development processes, and with an educational system which continues to graduate capable technicians who cannot be absorbed by the economic system. As has been stated before and is confirmed now, none of the fashionable interpretative criteria for the countries of Latin America seems to be applicable in the Argentine case. There is no formula that can explain a country where the broadening of the middle sectors complicates the situation by increasing the demands for conspicuous consumption within a regime of retarded economic growth. There is no "recipe" for agrarian reform in a country with low population density, low birth rate, with an unpopulated countryside, which became urbanized much earlier than it should have, and where the shifts within the labor force constantly increase the size of the tertiary sector of the economy.

The increase in education is not a solution in a country where high school graduates or those who expect high school diplomas make up a frustrated sector, and it is very naïve to think that everything depends on the number or quality of students registered in universities.[4] Along general lines, the training of the university graduate is quite adequate in comparison to worldwide standards.

Thus caution must be exercised in attempting to place this government elite within any of the interpretative frameworks on political development, since with the customary indices the result would once more be a notable contradiction. The contradiction does not matter;

271

Argentina is full of contradictions. But these contradictory indices are not significant in themselves, aside from the fact that they bear witness to the failure of synchronization; they must be restudied in a historical context, that is, with the data for this society as the starting point.

For example, Argentina has high indices for political information and communication. It has the proper indices for functional articulation of interests. It has, or would have, contradictory indices for political participation. Formally since 1916, but more particularly since 1951, the vote has been more of a duty assigned to all citizens than a civic right. As a result of the laws and political rules in effect, electoral participation has been total during the democratic periods. But as a counterpoise to this, those who voted had very little faith in the true usefulness of this participatory channel, even though between 80 and 90 percent of those registered did so. In a survey carried out in 1962 in the city of Buenos Aires, a substantial proportion of those interviewed (about a third) declared they were skeptical as to the usefulness of what they regarded more as a duty than as a right.[5] The same contradiction is apparent in institutional participation. An adequate articulation of interests has been counterbalanced by a low aggregation of these interests, values, and philosophies into the political system.

However the greatest contradiction is to be found in political socialization. There has been no real socialization around the same values nor have these values been truly shared. Socialization has been nominal, only skin-deep. The writer has already stated this elsewhere: Democracy has not been part of the world of values of the Argentines.[6] For Argentines democracy in the last forty years has had only the value of an instrument. Aside from mere lip-service, the rules of the democratic game have been followed in accordance with the results of those rules. Thus, a favorable outcome has kindled fervor for democracy, but an unfavorable one has triggered a decline in the acceptance of the mechanics of democracy. This has happened repeatedly in cycles because basically it was not the mechanism that mattered, but only the result. This is the reason why it can be argued that there has been no political socialization into democracy. There has been no real internalization of the rules for democratic life. This is the result of an intrinsic attitude of the Argentine people, an attitude which in no way can be discovered from analyzing its political communication and formal participation indices, because the cyclical nature of military interventions can better be explained by the uncertainty of their attach-

272

ment to democracy and this uncertainty is difficult to measure; it can only become known through a living experience.

There is something else that the indices employed to evaluate political development would be found deficient in measuring, at least when applied to the Argentine case, since such indices are intended to measure what is objective. The sum of the indices considered might at best allow the setting up of a presumably objective index of democratization or of political development. However, such an index would still be false, although it might seem true when viewed from a foreign laboratory, because there is something that cannot be measured: as yet there are no indices which express the frustrations of a people, which cannot be measured except as an existential collective reality. There is no way to measure collective frustration because it is wholly subjective: frustration is the distance between the glimpsed expectations and the realities of the present, between the previous image of the role which the community expected to play and that which it actually does play, between the status and prestige it dreamed of and that which it actually has in the concert of nations, between what the prophets promised and the present loss of prestige within the international community.

When a whole people is in a state of collective frustration any way offered to it for overcoming its situation may seem good, even though it may lie outside the framework of formal democracy. As Jorge Graciarena has indicated, classical analyses of political development are formulated on the basis of systems which are basically ethnocentric, which correspond to the world of values of the more developed countries and which obviously belong to "reconciliation."[7] To these situations centered on pluralism, political compromise, and ideological diffuseness, other systems are counterposed which correspond to other ways of facing development. One of these ways is the classic one of the systems of mobilization characterized by the unification of power, a system of loyalties centered on faithfulness and ideological specificity. A third viable system, opposed to these within the typology, Graciarena calls "modernizing autocracies," which also have unitary centralization in power, exclusive and institutional loyalties, and neo-traditional ideological expression.

In these cases, and specifically in the third, which typifies the Argentine situation in 1968, the criteria for an analysis to evaluate political development ends by expressing half-truths, or subjective truths, at least what seems like truth to those looking in from abroad on the basis

273

of a world of very specific values, a high level of development, and a necessarily ethnocentric position, but which do not also express the subjective truths of developing countries.

There is something more to this difficulty in using indices since even in extreme cases of collective rejection of the use of legal participation forms, as in Argentina, after the new delegation of functions, there would be passive participation which is very difficult to measure and consists of tacit rejection, but only with one objective: that of emerging from frustration.

5. The author believes he has read a substantial number of the reviews published about the Spanish language edition of *Los que mandan*. From a strictly professional sociological or political science point of view, there were not many because there are few valuable publications in the social sciences in the extreme southern part of the Western Hemisphere. On the other hand there were many reviews in nonprofessional publications, and they were written from ideological angles, covering the whole spectrum from extreme right to extreme left.

The writer feels that a summary of the criticisms may improve this first English version. All these comments, together with new experiences and greater maturity, may permit a reexamination of the original study.

It is this writer's opinion that in the 1964 version, despite the precautions adopted, some value judgments were included. A writer is not a neutral being, nor must he be so simply because he works in the social sciences. The writer admits that two value judgments slipped by in the chapter on the religious hierarchies which are based on his own beliefs.

It is true that at the end of the second chapter on the armed forces the writer departed from strict analysis with didactic intent. At the time it seemed necessary to do so, and today the writer feels the validity of that attitude has been confirmed. Given the nature of the theme, it could not just be left without an explanation for a nonspecialized public.

It is also true that the conclusions in the final chapter transcend the empirical material accumulated. The fact is that the writer believes that the sociologist should incorporate in his work the living experience he has of his own society, even though such experience may go beyond the conclusions derived from the previous syllogisms. This is what C. Wright Mills did at the end of *The Power Elite*.

The writer is gratified that he employed "ruling categories" as a point of departure in his investigation. These categories, as Raymond Aron would say, are groups for classifying purposes, analytic categories, which are based on facts.[8] In accordance with the words of the French scholar, the minorities in question occupy positions or fulfill functions within the respective subsystems which make possible influencing those who are in government. The alternative would have been to start from the "ruling class," as preferred by Jean Meynaud.[9] This debate within the French Political Science Association culminated in February, 1965, with an ample majority in favor of Aron, or perhaps the writer so interpreted it because at that time he had already published this investigation using the "ruling categories" concept which Aron had proposed.

At the end of the Spanish version of *Los que mandan*, the conclusion was reached that there is no ruling class in Argentina, a statement which had various meanings. One of them is that there is no identification between the "ruling categories" employed and any socioeconomic class. It is still the writer's opinion that this is accurate, but perhaps a further explanation may be required. It is possible to speak of a "quasi-group," that is, a class in itself, but never a class for itself. These ruling categories appear as groups which share similar political beliefs, but without a class consciousness or organization, with latent and manifest interests which are not always well articulated. This is the reason the writer is gratified that he did not start his work on the basis of the "ruling class" concept. Even though other studies may arrive at a final identification, in this work it will have occurred only in the exceptional cases just indicated.

One last explanation: In this type of work maturity also means realizing something that the critics failed to notice. This investigation lacks a chapter or a half chapter on the public and private banking-financing sector. This is a lack which today seems very important to the writer because during a similar study he conducted in Chile it became clear that the core of the economic power of any capitalist system is the means and instruments of financing and those who administer them, even though the latter may not be the most brilliant individuals nor arouse the most interest in the press or among political commentators. Therefore *Los que mandan* is deficient in this respect. The writer has come to realize this after additional maturing, even though no intellectual sector has pointed this out in its criticism of the

275

book. This is doubtless because they were concerned with other problems of either a methodological or an abstract character or with those of a purely formal nature, and being preoccupied with these, part of reality escaped them, as it did the writer.

Notes

1. J. L. de Imaz, "Una hipotética elite política" in Instituto de Ciencia Política, Universidad del Salvador, *La revolución Argentina, análisis y perspectivas* (Buenos Aires: Ediciones Depalma, 1966) and J. L. de Imaz, *Nosotros, mañana* (Buenos Aires: Editorial Universitaria de Buenos Aires, 1968).

2. Helio Jaguaribe, in his report to the Meeting of Experts on Social Aspects of Economic Development in Latin America (Mexico City, December 12 to 21, 1960). Also see his *Desarrollo económico y desarrollo político* (Buenos Aires: Editorial Universitaria de Buenos Aires, 1964.

3. John William Freels, Jr., "Industrial Trade Associations in Argentine Politics," unpublished Ph.D. dissertation, University of California, Riverside, 1968.

4. Argentina holds third place in the world as to ratio of registered university students to population.

5. J. L. de Imaz, *Motivación electoral* (Buenos Aires: Instituto de Desarrollo Económico y Social, 1962).

6. Imaz, *Nosotros, mañana* (Buenos Aires: Eudeba, 1968).

7. Jorge Graciarena, *Poder y clases sociales en el desarrollo de América Latina* (Buenos Aires: Paidos, 1967).

8. Raymond Aron, "Catégories dirigeantes ou classe dirigeante?" in *Revue française de science politique*, Vol. 15. No. 1 (February, 1965).

9. Jean Meynaud, *Rapport sur la classe dirigeante italienne* (Lausanne: Études de science politique, 1964).

INDEX

Argentine Agrarian Federation, 109
Argentine Industrial Union, 135, 156
  as an interest articulator, 17
  leaders, 135–136, 137; 169
Argentine Meat Producers Association,
  106–107
Argentine Rural Society, 38, 92
  governing of, 94, 98
  interests represented, 100
  leaders, 95–97, 99, 117–119
  membership, 94–95, 97, 104
  political activities, 120
  social mobility, 97
  under Perón, 121
  upper class membership, 96
Armed Forces. See Military

Banking, 126, 157, 158
Bismarckianism, 265–267, 269
Buenos Aires Province, 58, 95, 99, 101,
  102, 107

Catholic Church
  bishops
    background of, 179–183, 265
    education of, 184–186
    role of, 178
  constitutional recognition of, 10, 174
  educational intervention, 176
  influence in power groups, 176
  the *Patronato*, 178, 269
  political intervention, 4, 175–176
  relations between Church and state,
    175–177
  rejuvenation of, 179–180
  role in society, 188–189
Chamber of Commerce
  leaders, 135, 136, 137
Círculo de Armas, 13, 247
Class
  entrepreneurial, 157
  upper

  cohesion, 129–131
  in the diplomatic corps, 127
  intellectuals, 128
  in the judicial branch, 126
  membership in, 129
  in the military, 62
  political power, 1, 22, 122–123,
    127, 128, 130
  social mobility, 131
  surrendering of political power, 2,
    127, 129
  urban lower, political power of, 3
Colombo, Luis, 167
Conservatives, 209, 245
  party gains, 8
Constitutions
  Constitution of 1853, 8
  under Perón, 8
Cooperatives, 109

Democracy, 272, 273

Electoral System, 260. *See also* Sáenz
  Peña Act
Elites
  developmental, 6
  entrepreneurial, 142–143, 168, 269
  labor, 270
  religious, 269–270
  ruling, 242, 245, 248, 250, 267–271
    background of, 261–263
    "circulation of elites", 124–125
    from middle sectors, 33
    from popular sectors, 34
    from traditional upper class, 16, 33
    origins, 246–247
    rebuilding of, 248, 254
  traditional
    in government, 121–122
Entrepreneurial Groups. *See also* Foreign Entrepreneurial Groups

277

279